American Prose and
Criticism, 1900-1950

AMERICAN LITERATURE, ENGLISH LITERATURE, AND WORLD LITERATURES IN ENGLISH: AN INFORMATION GUIDE SERIES

Series Editor: Theodore Grieder, Curator, Division of Special Collections, Fales Library, New York University

Associate Editor: Duane DeVries, Associate Professor, Polytechnic Institute of New York Brooklyn

Other books on American literature in this series:

AMERICAN DRAMA TO 1900—*Edited by Walter J. Meserve*

MODERN DRAMA IN AMERICA AND ENGLAND, 1950-1970—*Edited by Richard H. Harris**

AMERICAN FICTION TO 1900—*Edited by David K. Kirby*

AMERICAN FICTION, 1900-1950—*Edited by James Woodress*

CONTEMPORARY FICTION IN AMERICA AND ENGLAND, 1950-1970—*Edited by Alfred F. Rosa and Paul A. Echholz*

CONTEMPORARY POETRY IN AMERICA AND ENGLAND, 1950-1970—*Edited by Martin E. Gingerich**

AMERICAN PROSE TO 1820—*Edited by Donald Yannella and John Roch*

AMERICAN PROSE AND CRITICISM, 1820-1900—*Edited by Elinore H. Partridge**

LITERARY JOURNAL IN AMERICA TO 1900—*Edited by Edward E. Chielens*

LITERARY JOURNAL IN AMERICA, 1900-1950—*Edited by Edward E. Chielens*

AFRO-AMERICAN FICTION, 1853-1976—*Edited by Edward Margolies and David Bakish*

AFRO-AMERICAN POETRY AND DRAMA, 1760-1975—*Edited by William P. French, Michel J. Fabre, Amritjit Singh, and Genevieve Fabre*

AUTHOR NEWSLETTERS AND JOURNALS—*Edited by Margaret C. Patterson*

*in preparation

The above series is part of the

GALE INFORMATION GUIDE LIBRARY

The Library consists of a number of separate series of guides covering major areas in the social sciences, humanities, and current affairs.

General Editor: Paul Wasserman, Professor and former Dean, School of Library and Information Services, University of Maryland

Managing Editor: Denise Allard Adzigian, Gale Research Company

American Prose and Criticism, 1900-1950

A GUIDE TO INFORMATION SOURCES

*Volume 35 in the American Literature, English
Literature, and World Literatures in English
Information Guide Series*

Peter A. Brier

*Professor of English
California State University, Los Angeles*

Anthony Arthur

*Professor of English
California State University, Northridge*

Gale Research Company
Book Tower, Detroit, Michigan 48226

820283

Library of Congress Cataloging in Publication Data

Brier, Peter A.
  American prose and criticism, 1900-1950.

  (American literature, English literature, and
world literatures in English information guide
series ; v. 35) (Gale information guide library)
  Bibliography: p.
  Includes index.
  1. American prose literature—20th century—
Bibliography. 2. Criticism—United States—
Bibliography. I. Arthur, Anthony. II. Title.
III. Series.
Z1231.P8B74 [PS362] 016.81'08'0052   74-11520
ISBN 0-8103-1214-X   AACR2

For Nurith and Carolyn

VITAE

Peter A. Brier is professor of English at California State University, Los Angeles. He received his B.A. from Yale University, his M.A. from Harvard University, and his Ph.D. through the Intercollegiate Program of Graduate Studies (Occidental College and the Claremont Graduate School). In 1978-79 he was Maitre de conferences at the University of Clermont-Ferrand, France, where he taught English and American literature. He has published several articles on nineteenth-century English and contemporary American authors. He has edited secondary bibliographies on Victorian authors.

Anthony Arthur is professor of English at California State University, Northridge. He received his B.A. from Allegheny College, his M.A. from Pennsylvania State University, and his Ph.D. from State University of New York, Stony Brook. In 1980 he was senior visiting lecturer in American studies at the University of Budapest, as a Fulbright scholar. He has published several articles on English and American authors and is the editor of CRITICAL ESSAYS ON WALLACE STEGNER (Boston: G.K. Hall, 1981).

CONTENTS

Contents

Contents

GENERAL PREFACE

This information guide is divided into two independently researched and compiled parts: "American Prose, 1900-1950" (Anthony Arthur) and "American Criticism, 1900-1950" (Peter A. Brier). Before beginning, we agreed to concentrate on expository prose writers and theoretical critics who transcend the idiom and intention of purely journalistic or academic writing. This approach forced us to make difficult choices. Some fine journalistic and academic critics have been excluded or given somewhat cursory attention.

Our organization reflects the essential difference between our subjects. For example, the section entitled "Individual Bibliographical Essays: Major Critics" concentrates on figures who crystallize the theoretical trends discussed in the "Introduction: Literary Criticism." "American Prose, 1900-1950" on the other hand, is less characterized by trends or movements than it is by the variety of its writers, a fact reflected in the classifications of the noncritical prose.

We have maintained separate sections on "General Bibliographical Aids" (part 1 in each division). Although this has resulted in a few multiple citations, in each case the annotation has stressed either the aid's pertinence to literary criticism or noncritical prose. We have dispensed with any acronyms or abbreviations for periodicals, but our indexes combine the two parts of the book, including noncritical prose with literary criticism, and provide numerous opportunities for cross-references. Readers will, we suspect, discover that we have failed to mention a few important primary and secondary materials. We threw out a wide net, but undoubtedly important works escaped us. For any unforgivable omissions, we ask to be forgiven.

In recent years, many reprint houses have begun to provide facsimile versions of out-of-print books. As, in most cases, these reprint editions do not provide significant textual or scholarly changes, we have chosen to guide our readers to the original editions of all primary materials. When reprints of secondary materials are significant, we have mentioned them. Original editions are often more accessible to library researchers than the more expensive contemporary reprints.

General Preface

We have not been afraid to evaluate. Our only defense for lapses in accuracy and failures in judgment is that to presume to infallibility or authority, in a project where the ideas of so many brilliant minds jostle like stars on a June night, would be the highest vanity. We judged for the joy of it. Bear with us.

Peter A. Brier
Anthony Arthur

ACKNOWLEDGMENTS

We would like to express our appreciation to the reference staffs of the John F. Kennedy Memorial Library at California State University, Los Angeles; the Delmar T. Oviatt Library at California State University, Northridge; and the University Research Library at the University of California, Los Angeles. In the great tradition of the large urban American Library, the staff of the Literature Room at the Main Branch of the Los Angeles Public Library was most helpful.

Our thanks go also to Kraig Tevis and Josie I. Del Valle of the English department secretarial staff at California State University, Los Angeles, and to Alice Allen of the English department secretarial staff at California State University, Northridge. The advice, encouragement, and patience of our general editor, Theodore Grieder, was more than appreciated.

AMERICAN PROSE, 1900-1950

INTRODUCTION: NONCRITICAL PROSE

Because the quantity of American nonfiction prose excluding literary criticism is so large, it is necessary to explain, first, what it includes and, second, how it differs in kind from fiction and criticism.

Nonfiction prose is here understood to mean that which was written for a general audience: that is, one whose reading extends beyond the merely trivial or ephemeral, on the one hand, or the narrowly professional, on the other. It is the audience which today reads HARPER'S as well as TIME, which at least occasionally joins a bookclub, and which can perceive a stylistic difference between Kurt Vonnegut and Joan Didion.

The subjects covered by the writers included here are as varied as the interests of their general audience. I have divided the writers into three groups according to their general audience. The first group, entertainers, includes such writers as James Thurber, F.P. Adams, and Alexander Woollcott--that is, humorists, light essayists (practitioners of what used to be known as belles lettres), and commentators on the popular arts.

The second group, teachers, includes writers whose primary purpose it is to persuade or to instruct. These writers may be thought of as falling into two subcategories: thinkers and advocates, such as Henry Adams, H.L. Mencken, and Walter Lippmann, and interpreters of the past--the authors of popular histories, such as Bernard DeVoto, or of biographies and autobiographies, such as William Allen White. The third group, reporters, includes writers who see and describe conditions, events, and places. It includes political correspondents (Dorothy Thompson), travelers (Lowell Thomas), and writers on nature and science (John Muir).

The basic principle of selection has been to determine which writers during this period wrote the most work of lasting interest in terms of content and, equally important, of style. Based on my evaluation of the different writers' work, which includes an appraisal of the interest shown by the compilers of the standard bibliographies and critical histories of American literature, I have ranked writers according to three different categories of importance. For the most significant writers, those in group A under each heading, I have included a list of primary works and an annotated bibliography of secondary material. The writers included in group B are discussed in separate paragraphs which sum up their contributions and include pertinent references to secondary materials. Writers in group C receive honorable mention in two or three sentences.

The following questions were considered in selecting these writers from the hundreds commonly included in standard guides:

1. Were their major works written between 1900 and 1950? Some writers' birth and death dates indicate that they are essentially nineteenth-century figures, such as William James, but his most important books were published within this period, and he must be included; Joseph Wood Krutch, on the other hand, who was active as a professor of dramatic literature and as a critic in the 1930s and 1940s, did not write his books on the desert until after 1950; because these are the books which in my judgment will outlast all his other work, he is not listed here, though he certainly should be in any companion volume to come.

2. Are the writers (a) included in at least one of these standard reference works: TWENTIETH CENTURY AUTHORS (1943), ENCYCLOPEDIA OF AMERICAN LITERATURE (1963), OXFORD COMPANION TO AMERICAN LITERATURE (1964), LITERARY HISTORY OF THE UNITED STATES and the accompanying bibliography (1974); (b) the subject of academic, scholarly, or professional interest, as indicated by articles or books about them and their work; (c) included in prose anthologies used for high school or college writing courses?

3. Are they primarily identified as writers about subjects rather than as participants or practitioners? Although Albert Einstein wrote a few charming essays and letters, he is not included; William Beebe, although he was a thoroughly capable scientist, will be remembered best as a writer about science, and he is included. Theodore Roosevelt and Woodrow Wilson are both good writers compared to most other presidents, but their works would no longer be mentioned at all except for the political eminence of their authors, and they are not included. Neither are Bernard Berenson, the art critic; Margaret Mead, the anthropologist; Samuel Eliot Morrison, the historian; or David Riesman, the sociologist. Though all are worthy of inclusion in a comprehensive bibliography, the principles of selection used here require that they be omitted.

4. Are these writers ones whose reputations rest on nonfiction or noncritical prose, rather than writers who may have written distinguished nonfiction (Hemingway's THE GREEN HILLS OF AFRICA, Fitzgerald's THE CRACK-UP, Edmund Wilson's TO THE FINLAND STATION), but are primarily thought of as writers of fiction or criticism?

The degree to which affirmative answers to all of these questions could be made determined whether a writer would be included, and in which category of importance. There are three predictable reactions which a reasonably careful reader might have after perusing the list of writers covered here. The first would involve surprise and perhaps puzzlement that there are so many once-famous and now-unfamiliar names among them; the second would be curiosity at the comparative lack of critical comment on even the more eminent of these writers (those in category A) as compared to the number of articles written on critics of literature; and the third reaction might be a suspicion, derived from the first two, that many of these writers are inferior, by and large, to novelists and critics. Otherwise they would not have been relegated to obscurity by both the general reading public and by critics and scholars.

The most important reason for the decline in the reputations of and the loss of interest in many of these writers is that they deal with ideas or with facts that are part of our past. Though it may seem paradoxical that good work on un-changing subjects should pass from the public eye, such work is often the victim of the reading public's natural inclination to peruse what is most recently pub-lished, coupled with the publishing industry's phenomenal capacity to produce books. It seems to be true that any subject of lasting interest which is fixed in time and place--the life of Lincoln, for example--will be examined anew by each generation. Anything which is not fixed--fads, attitudes, fashions--lacks sufficient inherent interest to be written about again or to be read widely by later generations. Either way, the survival of an author's work past his own time is difficult. Who will read Constance Rourke's excellent 1936 account of the life of Audubon when a new biography, not greatly different in quality or scope, is published in 1978? Why read Brand Whitlock's account of his tenure as ambassador to Belgium during World War I when there is Barbara Tuchman's recent and definitive THE GUNS OF AUGUST? What is the point of reading Richard Halliburton on India and Lowell Thomas on Tibet when the conditions and places they described have changed so radically?

It should also be stressed that much of what is written in this category of non-critical prose was not intended to last beyond its immediate time. It was "oc-casional," prompted by something which the writer assumed his reader knew about--theater reviews, political commentary, reactions to disasters, public personalities--and it was full of allusions to books and fads, even slang that twenty years later would require an introduction and footnotes for a reader to comprehend what was written. Even when the facts are not a problem, con-ditions and attitudes may have changed significantly. George Ade, listed among the entertainers in this volume, was a popular and talented writer, known especially for his fables. These fables, which hinged upon sympathetic reader identification with the so-called revolt from the small town in the early 1900s, are no less amusing or trenchant now than when they were written, but the small town today strikes many readers whose grandparents and parents fled it long ago as a desirable alternative to today's suburbs and slums. Ade's fables therefore no longer have their emotional appeal: they are interesting for stylists and for social historians, but the reader today looking simply for entertainment will read today's Ade, Art Buchwald.

Finally, the first half of the twentieth century in the United States was a golden age for the novel--the age of Hemingway, Fitzgerald, Steinbeck, Lewis, Dreiser,

Introduction: Noncritical Prose

Cather, and many other gifted writers who established the novel as our primary popular art form. Coincidentally, it was at least a silver age for criticism, for the literature of the period attracted some of our best writers to it as critics-- writers who might otherwise have been drawn to nonfiction other than criticism. The prose writers thus suffered the fate which befalls anyone working in a medium which is not the center of attention for a given time. Much the same fate has been visited upon the novelist today, for there are many literate people who are more conversant with film or even television than they are with fiction, which has lost its primacy as our most popular art form. Many talented young people who thirty years ago would have been novelists are now directors and scriptwriters.

A proper historical perspective would suggest that for prose writers the period under discussion here represents a hiatus between periods of comparatively greater influence for the genre and its practitioners. The great flowering of the essay in the nineteenth century in England and the United States produced a number of renowned writers who fit the category of nonfiction prose: Thoreau, Emerson, and Oliver Wendell Holmes in this country, and Carlyle, Ruskin, and Arnold in England, to name only a few. Similarly, the burgeoning influence of what is sometimes called the "new journalism" in the last twenty years-- with such writers as Truman Capote, Norman Mailer, Tom Wolfe, and Joan Didion--suggests that the genre of nonfiction prose is regaining some of the vitality and popularity it had in the nineteenth century.

There are, however, several benefits to be derived from a knowledge of the noncritical prose writers included in this guide which I believe justify the attention here given to them. First, their works contain much information that is either unavailable elsewhere or not conveyed so well, even if it has been retold. There is no better or more entertaining social history of the 1920s than Frederick Lewis Allen's ONLY YESTERDAY; Will Durant's THE STORY OF PHILOSOPHY is still the clearest and most gracefully written introduction to the history of philosophy for the nonspecialist; only in John Muir will you find a poet-naturalist to describe the beauty of Yosemite nearly a century ago.

Second, the angle of vision by which a writer sees a topic conveys nuances of mood and tone which later, more fully informed writers dealing with the same topic cannot duplicate. A work provides an unconscious and therefore reliable index to the values of the time when it was written. For example, social historians should note the number of books in the 1920s and before which provide keys to the past and to ways of coping with quantities of information, such as Hendrik van Loon's THE STORY OF MANKIND, James Harvey Robinson's THE ART OF THINKING, and Henry Adams' AUTOBIOGRAPHY. When these books are set beside the recent best-selling nonfiction of what Tom Wolfe has called the "me decade," dealing with Essalen, est, mid-life crisis, "parenting," and sexual dysfunction, they provide valuable indexes to social attitudes.

A third benefit to be gained from studying these writers is that they are all professionals, dealing with problems of collecting and organizing information according to a particular purpose and for a particular kind of audience; they have done successfully what many of us are trying to teach students of writing to do now. Here is a huge library of examples of the various patterns of exposition taught in the classroom.

Finally, there is material here for scholarly study. A thorough search of the standard bibliographical and critical sources has revealed very little to me in the way of scholarship about most of these writers, excluding Mencken, James, and Adams. In 1977 there were 59 articles listed in the MLA INTERNATIONAL BIBLIOGRAPHY, the standard index of scholarly publications, on Fitzgerald, 82 on Hemingway, and 115 on Faulkner. During that same year there were a total of 33 articles on the eighty-five writers listed here, and 12 of those were on Henry Adams alone. Candidates for advanced degrees who complain that there are no interesting subjects not done to death should examine the possibilities of the American autobiography in William Allen White, Curtis Bok, and Mary Austin; the narrative technique used by Bernard DeVoto in his histories of the West; the use of metaphor in John Muir and Loren Eiseley; and the origins of ecological awareness in Aldo Leopold, to name only a few possibilities.

Anthony Arthur

Part I

GENERAL BIBLIOGRAPHICAL AIDS

A. HANDBOOKS

Curley, Dorothy Nyren, et al., eds. A LIBRARY OF LITERARY CRITICISM:
MODERN AMERICAN LITERATURE. 3 vols. 4th ed. New York: Frederick
Unger, 1969.

> These volumes contain a useful collection of excerpts from critical
> works on individual American authors of the twentieth century.

Hart, James D., ed. THE OXFORD COMPANION TO AMERICAN LITERA-
TURE. 4th ed. New York: Oxford University Press, 1965.

> Hart gives short biographies and bibliographies of American au-
> thors, with more than one thousand summaries of American literary
> works, entries on literary schools and movements, and other in-
> formation.

Herzberg, Max J., ed. THE READER'S ENCYCLOPEDIA OF AMERICAN LIT-
ERATURE. New York: Crowell, 1962.

> Perhaps the most comprehensive reference book on its subject, it
> includes entries on authors, titles, literary characters, periodicals,
> literary groups, historical figures, and other topics related to
> literature.

Johnson, Allen, et al., eds. DICTIONARY OF AMERICAN BIOGRAPHY.
22 vols. New York: Scribner's, 1928-58.

> This indispensable series includes 14,870 biographies of "Americans
> who have made memorable contributions to our national life."

Kunitz, Stanley J., and H. Haycraft, eds. TWENTIETH CENTURY AUTHORS.
New York: Wilson, 1942. FIRST SUPPLEMENT, 1955.

> With the supplement, 2,550 names are includes, along with
> critical summations and references for many; this is an indispen-
> sable first source.

Magill, Frank N., ed. MASTERPLOTS: AMERICAN FICTION SERIES. 12 vols. New York: Salem Press, 1954-76.

_____. MAGILL'S LITERARY ANNUAL. Englewood Cliffs, N.J.: Salem Press, 1977-- . Annual.

This series provides essay-reviews of two hundred selected titles.

Spiller, Robert E., et al., eds. LITERARY HISTORY OF THE UNITED STATES: HISTORY. 4th ed., rev. New York: Macmillan, 1974.

This title is to be distinguished from Spiller's BIBLIOGRAPHY. His work has resulted in an indispensable guide by fifty-five scholar-contributors.

B. BIBLIOGRAPHIES AND CHECKLISTS

ABSTRACTS OF ENGLISH STUDIES. Urbana, Ill.: National Council of Teachers of English, 1958-- . 10 per year.

Here are brief summaries of articles, including ones on American literature, appearing in scholarly journals; in 1972, AES began to cover monographs as well.

AMERICAN LITERARY REALISM. Arlington: University of Texas at Arlington, 1967-- . Quarterly.

This is indispensable because of its thorough bibliographical studies of works by and about American realists.

AMERICAN LITERATURE. Durham, N.C.: Duke University Press, 1929-- . Quarterly.

Each issue includes a listing of "Articles on American Literature Appearing in Current Periodicals." Furthermore, the book reviews published in each issue of AL are consistently reliable.

AMERICAN LITERATURE ABSTRACTS. San Jose, Calif.: San Jose State University, 1967-- . Semiannual.

Here are brief summaries of articles on American literature appearing in scholarly journals.

Blanck, Jacob, comp. BIBLIOGRAPHY OF AMERICAN LITERATURE. 6 vols. to date. New Haven, Conn.: Yale University Press, 1955-- .

This is a multivolume attempt to describe bibliographically the American literary works which have "enjoyed something resembling recognition," and is agreed to be the most detailed and authoritative

work of its kind. Its many author bibliographies are largely
definitive.

BOOK REVIEW DIGEST. New York: H.W. Wilson, 1905-- . Monthly, except February and July.

    The student of American fiction, or any other subject, is well
    advised to use this compilation of short excerpts from book reviews.

Eichelberger, Clayton L., comp. A GUIDE TO CRITICAL REVIEWS OF UNITED
STATES FICTION, 1870-1910. Metuchen, N.J.: Scarecrow, 1971.

    This book is useful for its references to many of the earlier au-
    thors covered in this volume, as well as for authors of fiction.

Gerstenberger, Donna, and George Hendrick, comps. THE AMERICAN NOVEL
1789-1959: A CHECKLIST OF TWENTIETH-CENTURY CRITICISM. Denver:
Alan Swallow, 1961.

_____. THE AMERICAN NOVEL: A CHECKLIST OF TWENTIETH CENTURY
CRITICISM ON NOVELS WRITTEN SINCE 1789. Vol. 2: CRITICISM WRIT-
TEN 1960-1968. Chicago: Swallow Press, 1970.

    Each of these two volumes is divided into two sections: (1) in-
    dividual authors (where criticism is listed under three categories:
    individual novels, general studies, and bibliographies); and (2)
    criticism of the American novel as a genre. References to such
    figures as DeVoto, included in this present guide, are included.

Leary, Lewis G., comp. ARTICLES ON AMERICAN LITERATURE, 1900-1950
(1954); ARTICLES ON AMERICAN LITERATURE, 1950-1967. [Durham, N.C.:
Duke University Press, 1970.]

    Although the bulk of each volume is devoted to articles on
    novelists and poets, there are also sections on noncritical prose
    and entries on individuals discussed in this present guide.

MLA INTERNATIONAL BIBLIOGRAPHY OF BOOKS AND ARTICLES OF THE
MODERN LANGUAGES AND LITERATURES. New York: Modern Language
Association, 1921-- . Annual.

    Selections for this essential reference source come from various
    book sources and from a master list of hundreds of periodicals in
    literature and languages. It is of particular value for its in-
    clusion both of less-known writers and references to them in
    journals which may be considered obscure.

Spiller, Robert E., et al., eds. LITERARY HISTORY OF THE UNITED STATES:
BIBLIOGRAPHY. 4th ed., rev. New York: Macmillan, 1974.

There are four main sections, all useful: a guide to bibliographical resources, bibliographies of literature and culture, bibliographies of movements and influences, and bibliographies of
207 individual authors.

Woodress, James, ed. AMERICAN LITERARY SCHOLARSHIP: AN ANNUAL.
Durham, N.C.: Duke University Press, 1963-- .

These are essays by various hands "summarizing the year's work
in some segment of American literary scholarship."

_____, comp. DISSERTATIONS IN AMERICAN LITERATURE, 1891-1966.
3rd ed. Durham, N.C.: Duke University Press, 1968.

This source includes forty-seven hundred dissertations, listed under
individual authors as well as topics and subtopics. It also includes dissertations written in other countries.

C. STUDIES AND TEXTS ON INTELLECTUAL BACKGROUNDS

Brodbeck, Max, James Gray, and Walter Metzger. AMERICAN NONFICTION
1900-1950. Chicago: Regnery, 1952.

This book contains three essential essays by the joint authors,
respectively, entitled "Philosophy in America," "The Journalist
as Literary Man," and "American Social Thought in the Twentieth
Century." Most of the writers included in this present Gale Research guide are mentioned in at least one of the three essays,
of which the second is the most directly useful.

Cargill, Oscar. INTELLECTUAL AMERICA. New York: Macmillan, 1941.

Cargill concentrates on writers in the 1920s and 1930s.

Commager, Henry Steele. THE AMERICAN MIND. New Haven: Yale University Press, 1950.

This is an examination of American thought and character since
1880 by one of our most prominent historians.

Horton, Rod W., and Herbert W. Edwards. BACKGROUNDS OF AMERICAN
LITERARY THOUGHT. 3rd ed. Englewood Cliffs, N.J.: Prentice Hall, 1974.

The authors give a clear outline of major ideas, with useful comparative charts in an appendix opposing them to each other in
outline form. The book is stronger on the pre-1950 period than
on ideas and events since 1950.

Day, Martin S. HISTORY OF AMERICAN LITERATURE: FROM 1910 TO THE
PRESENT. New York: Doubleday, 1971.

Day provides a section on "Prose of the Early Twentieth Century" with entries on a number of writers included in this present Gale guide. The book lacks a bibliography of secondary materials, but it is useful for putting prose writers in perspective relative to their contemporaries in the novel and criticism.

Fox, Daniel M. "The Achievement of the Federal Writers' Project." AMERICAN QUARTERLY, 13 (1961), 3-19.

Fox discusses the American Guide Series, part of the Federal Writers' Project, as valuable "catch-alls" for the American experience. The writing in the series was uneven, he says, but sometimes brilliant; he cites as support Conrad Aiken's description of the contrasting towns of Deerfield and Lawrence in the Massachusetts guide. This is a fascinating account of a landmark of noncritical prose, a body of work which Lewis Mumford called "the finest contribution to American patriotism that has been written in our generation," meaning the generation which experienced the Depression of the 1930s.

Hackett, Alice Payne, and James Henry Burke. 80 YEARS OF BEST SELLERS 1895-1975. New York: Bowker, 1977.

This book includes material from Hackett and Burke's earlier work on the same subject; it is essential not only for data but for explanatory and interpretive background, and it has a good bibliography of critical works on the subject of the popular book.

Hart, James D. THE POPULAR BOOK: A HISTORY OF AMERICA'S LITERARY TASTE. New York: Oxford University Press, 1950.

This pioneering book on popular culture examines the books actually read in this country, as opposed to those recommended by critics and teachers, from the days of the Puritans to World War II.

Jones, Howard Mumford. THE AGE OF ENERGY: VARIETIES OF AMERICAN EXPERIENCE, 1865-1915. New York: Viking, 1971.

An exciting, brilliant exploration of American culture during its most expansive period, this is the best available single study of many of the themes and ideas developed by such figures as William James, Henry Adams, and H.L. Mencken.

Trachtenberg, Alan, ed. CRITICS OF CULTURE: LITERATURE AND SOCIETY IN THE EARLY TWENTIETH CENTURY. New York: John Wiley and Sons, 1976.

The editor provides sections from works by Santayana, Mencken, Walter Lippmann, and other writers, with introductory notes and a very good annotated bibliography.

D. RHETORICAL STUDIES

1. Writing Style

Barzun, Jacques. SIMPLE AND DIRECT: A RHETORIC FOR WRITERS. New York: Harper and Row, 1975.

> One of our most distinguished scholar-critics offers his suggestions for better writing.

Gibson, Walter. TOUGH, SWEET AND STUFFY: AN ESSAY ON MODERN AMERICAN PROSE STYLES. Bloomington: Indiana University Press, 1966.

> Gibson revises the traditional divisions of low, middle, and high levels of diction according to contemporary usage; there is an excellent chapter on literary techniques used in modern journalism.

Newman, Edwin. STRICTLY SPEAKING. New York: Bobbs-Merrill, 1974.

_____. A CIVIL TONGUE. New York: Bobbs-Merrill, 1976.

> In these volumes the television commentator provides examples of what he sees as a variety of errors of taste and judgment and offers astringent comments on both the mistakes and their perpetrators.

Podhoretz, Norman. "The Article as Art." HARPER'S MONTHLY, 217 (1958), 74-81.

> The author argues that James Baldwin and other post-World War II writers, such as James Agee and Mary McCarthy, show a "clarity, subtlety, and vividness" in their nonfiction which is absent from their fiction. He says that discursive novelists have been preempted in a utilitarian age by writers whose imagination is "vitalized by contact with a disciplined intelligence and a restless interest in the life of the times."

Tate, Gary, ed. TEACHING COMPOSITION: TEN BIBLIOGRAPHICAL ESSAYS. Abilene: Texas Christian University Press, 1976.

> This is the best single source of information on current trends in the teaching of writing.

2. Writing Texts and Handbooks

There are many writing handbooks which include examples of good and bad writing with corrective exercises, and which use selections from many of the writers included in this Gale guide as models for imitation. Among the best are the following:

Baker, Sheridan. THE PRACTICAL STYLIST. 2nd ed. New York: Crowell, 1969.

> In this standard text Baker develops his famous "keyhole" device of organization.

Brooks, Cleanth, and Robert Penn Warren. MODERN RHETORIC. Shorter 3rd ed. New York: Harcourt Brace Jovanovich, 1972.

Crews, Frederick. THE RANDOM HOUSE HANDBOOK. 2nd ed. New York: Random House, 1977.

Gorrell, Robert M., and Charlton Laird. MODERN ENGLISH HANDBOOK. 5th ed. Englewood Cliffs, N.J.: Prentice Hall, 1972.

E. ANTHOLOGIES

Among the hundreds of anthologies used in colleges and universities for courses in writing, the following stay in print and are particularly useful for providing a sense of who our best prose writers are considered to be.

Eastman, Arthur M., et al. THE NORTON READER. 4th ed. New York: Norton, 1977.

Levin, Gerald. PROSE MODELS. 3rd ed. New York: Harcourt Brace Jovanovich, 1976.

Muscatine, Charles, and Marlene Griffith. THE BORZOI COLLEGE READER. 3rd ed. New York: Knopf, 1976.

Schorer, Mark, et al. HARBRACE COLLEGE READER. 5th ed. New York: Harcourt Brace Jovanovich, 1976.

The following literary anthologies are used not to teach writing but to teach literature, but they are the best sources of information about nonfiction prose writers beyond the standard biographical indexes noted above.

Brooks, Cleanth, R.W.B. Lewis, and Robert Penn Warren, eds. AMERICAN LITERATURE: THE MAKERS AND THE MAKING. New York: St. Martin's, 1973.

> An exhaustively thorough anthology, this book is the result of a collaboration by three major figures in American literature and criticism; the introductory essays and notes match the high expectations which the names of the editors raise.

Schorer, Mark. THE LITERATURE OF AMERICA: TWENTIETH CENTURY. New York: McGraw-Hill, 1970.

> This collection is valuable for the wide range of authors represented in it.

Thorp, Willard, Merle Curti, and Carlos Baker. AMERICAN ISSUES: THE SOCIAL RECORD. 2nd ed. New York: Lippincott, 1944.

> The emphasis in this volume is on nonfiction prose writers, including many who are omitted by most other collections but figure prominently in this present Gale guide--for example, George Ade, Thorstein Veblen, and Lincoln Steffens.

F. SERIAL STUDIES

Allen, Frederick Lewis. "One Hundred Years of HARPER'S." HARPER'S MONTHLY, 201 (1950), 23-36.

> Allen gives an account of the history of the magazine and its growth to national prominence in the context of such other publications as THE REVIEW OF REVIEWS.

Amory, Cleveland, and Frederick Bradlee, eds. "VANITY FAIR," SELECTIONS FROM AMERICA'S MOST MEMORABLE MAGAZINE: A CAVALCADE OF THE 1920S AND 1930S. New York: Viking, 1960.

> Frank Crowninshield emerges from Amory's introduction and Bradlee's profile as an exceptional editor; the collection is a comprehensive anthology of prose, fiction, poetry, and caricature from the only competitor of THE NEW YORKER for sophistication and percipience in spotting new talent. The book covers the period 1914 to 1936 and contains selections by Woollcott, Parker, Philip Wylie, and many other authors discussed in this present Gale guide.

Chielens, Edward E., ed. THE LITERARY JOURNAL IN AMERICA, 1900-1950. American Literature, English Literature, and World Literatures in English Information Guide Series, vol. 16. Detroit: Gale Research Co., 1977.

> This volume is an essential companion to this present guide to English literary journals. Chielens includes not only the relatively obscure little magazines but also those with much larger circulation, such as COLLIER'S, SATURDAY REVIEW OF LITERATURE, and THE NEW YORKER. Many of the writers discussed in this present guide, especially those connected with periodical journalism, are instructively placed in their proper context by Chielens; particularly valuable are his sections on THE NEW YORKER and on the MERCURY when it was edited by Mencken and George Jean Nathan.

Cousins, Norman. "Our Times and the MERCURY." SATURDAY REVIEW, 37 (1954), 22.

> Cousins finds the total lack of "respect for the mechanism of hope in man" responsible for the ultimate demise of the MERCURY as a respected literary journal.

Gohdes, Clarence. "The ATLANTIC Celebrates Its Hundredth Birthday." SOUTH ATLANTIC QUARTERLY, 57 (1958), 163-67.

> In a negative review of JUBILEE: ONE HUNDRED YEARS OF THE "ATLANTIC," selected and edited by Edward Weeks and Emily Flint (Boston: Little, Brown, 1957), Gohdes laments what he sees as a decline from the purer literary atmosphere which prevailed under Bliss Perry and earlier nineteenth-century editors.

Hagemann, E.R., and James E. Marsh. "Contributions of Literary Import to ESQUIRE 1933-1941: An Annotated Checklist." BULLETIN OF BIBLIOGRAPHY, 22 (1957), 33-40, 69-72.

> The authors show that during the first eight years of the magazines's existence, under the editorial guidance of Arnold Gingrich, "there was published a surprising amount" of good literature.

Hohenberg, John. THE PULITZER PRIZES: A HISTORY OF THE AWARDS IN BOOKS, DRAMA, MUSIC AND JOURNALISM, BASED ON THE FILES OVER SIX DECADES. New York: Columbia University Press, 1974.

> Containing lists, documentary notes, and a full index, this is a valuable book for appraising journalism which in some cases has literary merit.

Mott, Frank Luther. A HISTORY OF AMERICAN MAGAZINES. 5 vols. Cambridge: Harvard University Press, 1930-68.

> This standard work includes information on the history and economics of publishing generally, as well as individual profiles of magazines and editors.

Peterson, Theodore. MAGAZINES IN THE TWENTIETH CENTURY. 2nd ed. Urbana: University of Illinois Press, 1964.

> A study of the magazine field, with useful information on readership, advertising, and the economics of publishing, this book contains lengthy discussions of THE NEW YORKER and the AMERICAN MERCURY.

Part II

INDIVIDUAL AUTHORS

The principal works of the major authors (those in group A in each of the three general categories of entertainers, teachers, and reporters) are listed chronologically; works about them are listed alphabetically.

Writers of the second rank (those included in group B in the three categories) are described in brief essays, which include selected critical and biographical materials.

Writers of the third rank (those included in group C) are identified briefly in connection with their best-known works only.

Category 1

ENTERTAINERS: GROUP A

GEORGE ADE (1866-1944)

"Once upon a Time," wrote George Ade in a typical newspaper column "fable," "there was a slim Girl with a Forehead that was shining and Protuberant, like a Bartlett Pear. When asked to put Something in an Autograph album she invariably wrote the Following, in a tall, dislocated Backhand:

> 'Life is Real; Life is Earnest,
> And the Grave is not its Goal.'
> That's the kind of Girl she was."

Amiable cynicism, amusement at banal pretense, an eye for the telling detail, and an ear for current slang: these were the distinguishing characteristics of FABLES IN SLANG (1900), the volume which established Ade as a household word for a generation of Americans. More than merely popular, Ade was also respected by his fellow writers: William Allen White once said "I would rather have written FABLES IN SLANG than be President," and the hard-to-please H.L. Mencken thought Ade was a genuine literary craftsman deserving of "a respectable place in the second rank" of writers. Overvalued by some critics, such as Walter Raleigh, who in 1915 half-seriously suggested that Ade was "the greatest living American writer," the Indiana native is forgotten now by the general public that gave him his fame and a comfortable living; nor does he figure prominently in literary histories. Yet one of modern America's most perceptive and amusing humorists, Jean Shepherd, has adapted some of Ade's stories for his radio show with great success; and, as the following bibliography indicates, students of language and popular culture still find Ade's contributions to be of considerable interest.

PRINCIPAL WORKS

Ade's fables and essay collections are listed here; his plays are omitted.

DOC' HORNE, 1899
FABLES IN SLANG, 1900
MORE FABLES, 1900
FORTY MODERN FABLES, 1901

THE GIRL PROPOSITION, 1902
IN BABEL, 1903
PEOPLE YOU KNOW, 1903
BREAKING INTO SOCIETY, 1904
IN PASTURES NEW, 1906
KNOCKING THE NEIGHBORS, 1912
ADE'S FABLES, 1914
HAND-MADE FABLES, 1920
BANG! BANG!, 1928
THIRTY FABLES IN SLANG, 1930
THE PERMANENT ADE. Ed. Fred C. Kelly, 1947
THE AMERICA OF GEORGE ADE. Ed. Jean Shepherd, 1960

BIBLIOGRAPHY

Russo, Dorothy Ritter. A BIBLIOGRAPHY OF GEORGE ADE, 1866-1944.
Indianapolis: Indiana Historical Society, 1947.

BIOGRAPHY

Ade wrote nineteen magazine articles which covered his life and writing career
and which are listed in Coyle (see Critical Works, below).

Kelly, Fred C. GEORGE ADE: WARMHEARTED SATIRIST. Indianapolis:
Bobbs-Merrill, 1947.

> This is the only full-length biography of Ade, but it depends too
> heavily on interviews and autobiographical articles, and is not
> annotated.

Matson, Lowell. "Ade: Who Needed None." LIBRARY REVIEW, 5 (1961),
99-114.

> Matson gives a biographical sketch and a well-done overview of
> Ade's career.

CRITICAL WORKS

Bauerle, R.F. "A Look at the Language of George Ade." AMERICAN SPEECH,
33 (1958), 77-79.

> This is a sketchy analysis of Ade's slang.

Cargill, Oscar. INTELLECTUAL AMERICA. New York: Macmillan, 1941.

> Ade is dismissed along with his fables as part of the "revolt from
> the village" and nothing more.

Clark, John Abbott. "Ade's Fables in Slang: An Appreciation." SOUTH ATLANTIC QUARTERLY, 46 (1947), 537-44.

> Clark provides an energetic defense of Ade, whom he finds "vividly ageless in the matter of epithet and idiom."

Coyle, Lee. GEORGE ADE. New York: Twayne, 1964.

> Ade is in the literary mainstream, Coyle says, as "the wry philosopher enthroned for his hour upon Poor Richard's cracker barrel," though now relegated to the "limbo of vernacular raconteurs" despite much in his work that is "vivid and meaningful." Coyle contains a good bibliography.

Dickinson, T.H. PLAYWRIGHTS OF THE NEW AMERICAN THEATRE. New York: Macmillan, 1925.

> The author praises Ade's plays, which no longer seem to merit praise, and lauds the fables for their "insight into character and pungency of expression."

Duffey, Bernard. THE CHICAGO RENAISSANCE IN AMERICAN LETTERS. East Lansing: Michigan State College Press, 1954.

> Duffey dismisses the fables and their language as superficial.

Evans, Bergen. "George Ade, Rustic Humorist." AMERICAN MERCURY, 70 (1950), 321-29.

> This is a good analysis by a popular critic of the fables as travesties of McGuffey's Readers.

Howells, William Dean. "Certain of the Chicago School of Fiction." NORTH AMERICAN REVIEW, 136 (1903), 734-46.

> America's leading critic of the period considers Ade the embodiment of the American spirit--"Living one slang, living one life, meaning one thing."

_____. "Editor's Easy Chair." HARPER'S MONTHLY, 134 (1917), 442-45.

> In this appreciation of IN BABEL, Howells places Ade in the tradition of American humor which includes Mark Twain.

Masson, Thomas. OUR AMERICAN HUMORISTS. New York: Moffat, Yard, 1922.

> Masson describes the fables as "concentrated food, to be taken as a tonic, say one or two after a meal."

Mencken, H.L. PREJUDICES: FIRST SERIES. New York: Knopf, 1919.

> In one of the best essays on Ade's work, Mencken praises the humorist for his contributions to the American idiom.

Pattee, Fred Lewis. THE NEW AMERICAN LITERATURE. New York: Century, 1930.

> The respected literary historian finds that there is "an element that is more than mere buffoonery" in Ade's work.

Van Doren, Carl. "Old Wisdom in a New Tongue." CENTURY, 105 (1923), 473-80.

> Ade is praised as "a satirist of genius," belonging "so unquestionably to his folk that he has a license to ridicule it."

JAMES GROVER THURBER (1894-1961)

James Thurber's long-time friend and colleague, E.B. White, has noted that there were "at least two, probably six Thurbers. His thoughts were always a tangle of baseball scores, Civil War tactical problems, Henry James, personal maladjustments, terrier puppies, literary rip tides, ancient myths and modern apprehensions." Unclassifiable as a man, somewhat like Walter Mitty, his most famous character, Thurber produced a unique body of work, consisting of short stories, fables, drama, essays, fantasies, short biographies, cartoons, and drawings, all touched with wit and humor.

Thurber's appeal as a writer extends well beyond the sophisticated confines of THE NEW YORKER, where most of his work appeared, but he was always an elegant stylist who resisted the simpler forms of burlesque comedy. Thurber is widely admired by other writers for his masterful sense of rhythm, tone, and diction, reflected in a style as limber as a whip and, when necessary, as biting. Like Jonathan Swift, Thurber had a keen eye for intellectual pretension and hypocrisy, which he deflated with crisp satire; and like George Orwell, he objected vehemently to both the trivialization of language and to its increasing political corruption. He was dismissed after his death by John Updike as an inconsequential writer, but Thurber's best work, though small in terms of bulk and limited in range, is sure to survive.

PRINCIPAL WORKS

THE OWL IN THE ATTIC AND OTHER REFLECTIONS, 1931
THE SEAL IN THE BEDROOM AND OTHER PREDICAMENTS, 1932
MY LIFE AND HARD TIMES, 1933
THE MIDDLE-AGED MAN ON THE FLYING TRAPEZE, 1935
LET YOUR MIND ALONE! AND OTHER MORE OR LESS INSPIRATIONAL
    PIECES, 1937
THE LAST FLOWER, A PARABLE IN PICTURES, 1939
FABLES FOR OUR TIME AND FAMOUS POEMS ILLUSTRATED, 1940
MY WORLD--AND WELCOME TO IT, 1942
MANY MOONS, 1943 Play
MEN, WOMEN AND DOGS, A BOOK OF DRAWINGS, 1943

THE GREAT QUILLOW, 1944
THE THURBER CARNIVAL, 1945
THE WHITE DEER, 1945
THE BEAST IN ME AND OTHER ANIMALS, A NEW COLLECTION OF PIECES
    AND DRAWINGS ABOUT HUMAN BEINGS AND LESS ALARMING CREA-
    TURES, 1948
THE 13 CLOCKS, 1950
THE THURBER ALBUM, A NEW COLLECTION OF PIECES ABOUT PEOPLE, 1952
THURBER COUNTRY, A NEW COLLECTION OF PIECES ABOUT MALES AND
    FEMALES, MAINLY OF OUR OWN SPECIES, 1953
THURBER'S DOGS, A COLLECTION OF THE MASTER'S DOGS, WRITTEN AND
    DRAWN, REAL AND IMAGINARY, LIVING AND LONG AGO, 1955
A THURBER GARLAND, 1955
FURTHER FABLES FOR OUR TIME, 1956
ALARMS AND DIVERSIONS, 1957
THE WONDERFUL O, 1957
THE YEARS WITH ROSS, 1959 (biography of Harold Ross, editor of THE NEW
    YORKER).
LANTERNS AND LANCES, 1961
CREDOS AND CURIOS, 1962
A THURBER CARNIVAL, 1962

COAUTHORED WORKS

MANY MOONS. A MUSICAL COMEDY IN TWO ACTS, 1922 (with W.W.
    Hevens, William Heid, and R.E. Fidler).
IS SEX NECESSARY: OR WHY YOU FEEL THE WAY YOU DO, 1929 (with
    E.B. White).
THE MALE ANIMAL, 1940 (with Elliot Nugent).

BOOKS ILLUSTRATED OR INTRODUCED

Hawes, Elizabeth. MEN CAN TAKE IT. James Thurber, illus. New York:
Random House, 1939.

Kinney, James R., and Ann Honeycutt. HOW TO RAISE A DOG: IN THE
CITY . . . IN THE SUBURBS. James Thurber, illus. New York: Simon and
Schuster, 1953.

Marquis, Don. HER FOOT IS ON THE BRASS RAIL. James Thurber, illus.
[New York]: Pvt. Ptd., 1935.

Mian, Mary. MY COUNTRY-IN-LAW. Intro. by James Thurber. Boston:
Houghton Mifflin, 1946.

Mostes, Alice Leone. NO NICE GIRL SWEARS. James Thurber, illus. New York: Knopf, 1933.

Samuels, Margaret. IN A WORD. James Thurber, illus. New York: Knopf, 1939.

Sayre, Joel. PERSIAN GULF COMMAND. Intro. by James Thurber. New York: Random House, 1945.

BIBLIOGRAPHY

Bowden, Edwin T. JAMES THURBER: A BIBLIOGRAPHY. Columbus: Ohio State University Press, 1969.

BIOGRAPHY

Bernstein, Burton. THURBER: A BIOGRAPHY. New York: Dodd Mead, 1975.

> This is the "authorized, if not approved" biography of Thurber (his widow felt it was ultimately too negative a portrait); it was well received by reviewers as an overdue exploration of the life and times of a major American humorist. Bernstein uses previously unpublished Thurber letters in addition to a number of the famous drawings to document the despair which was a part of Thurber's life (he was blind in his later years) and the brightness of wit and humor that alleviated his distress.

CRITICAL STUDIES

Blair, Walter. HORSE SENSE IN AMERICAN HUMOR. Chicago: University of Chicago Press, 1942.

> Blair's major emphasis is on the racy tradition of American humor in the nineteenth century, but he comments on Benchley, Thurber, and others.

Bohn, William E. I REMEMBER AMERICA. New York: Macmillan, 1962.

> The author praises Thurber as an unreconstructed individualist.

Churchill, Allen. "Harold Ross, Editor of THE NEW YORKER." COSMOPOLITAN, May 1948, pp. 46-47, 174-78.

> This article includes comments on the friendship between Thurber and E.B. White.

Coates, Robert M. "Thurber, Inc." SATURDAY REVIEW OF LITERATURE, 21 (2 December 1939), 10–11.

> This is a survey of Thurber's work to that date by a friend whose avant-garde work the humorist admired.

Colby, Frank M. "Humour." CIVILIZATION IN THE UNITED STATES. Ed. Harold Stearns. New York: Harcourt, Brace, 1922.

> The British spelling of "humor" reflects the supercilious and glumly skeptical tone of this essay, whose author doubts that there is such a thing as American humor.

Cowley, Malcolm. "James Thurber's Dream Book." NEW REPUBLIC, 62 (1945), 362–63.

> This is a review of THE THURBER CARNIVAL.

_____. "Lions and Lemmings, Toads and Tigers." REPORTER, 25 (13 December 1956), 42–44.

> In this review of FURTHER FABLES FOR OUR TIME, Cowley offers some observations on Thurber's Joycean use of language.

DeVries, Peter. "James Thurber: The Comic Prufrock." POETRY, 63 (1943), 150–59.

> A fellow humorist whose work is similar in style and subject to Thurber's provides perceptive criticism of his work.

Drennan, Robert, ed. THE ALGONQUIN WITS. New York: Citadel, 1968.

> This is a collection of witticisms of the famous Round Table at the Algonquin Hotel in Manhattan. The wits included Alexander Woollcott, Dorothy Parker, and others besides Thurber. The account is tiresome at a stretch, but instructive.

Elias, Robert M. "James Thurber: The Primitive, the Innocent, and the Individual." AMERICAN SCHOLAR, 27 (1958), 355–63.

> A Dreiser scholar, Elias finds merit in Thurber as a close observer and critic of society.

Enck, John, et al., eds. THE COMIC IN THEORY AND PRACTICE. New York: Appleton-Century-Crofts, 1960.

> This is an excellent sourcebook which contains many classic statements on humor, including Bergson's theory of rigidity, which is useful in appraising Thurber's work.

Friedrich, Otto. "James Thurber: A Critical Study." DISCOVERY, 5 (1955), 158-92.

> The author examines the influence of Henry James on Thurber's criticism.

Grant, Jane. ROSS, THE NEW YORKER, AND ME. New York: Reynal, with Morrow, 1969.

> This is an account of the literary and social lives from 1919-51 of Harold Ross, the founder of the magazine, and his first wife.

Hackett, Francis. ON JUDGING BOOKS IN GENERAL AND PARTICULAR. New York: John Day, 1947.

> Hackett includes here a good essay on Thurber's Romantic non-conformity.

Holmes, Charles S. THURBER: A COLLECTION OF CRITICAL ESSAYS. Englewood Cliffs, N.J.: Prentice-Hall, 1974.

> The introduction places Thurber in the tradition of Mark Twain, both as humorist and as stylist and notes the comparative sparsity of critical commentary about his work.

Kramer, Dale. ROSS AND THE NEW YORKER. New York: Doubleday, 1951.

> Kramer was considered an outsider by the regular writers for the magazine, and his account was resented by some of them; but it is replete with interesting anecdotes.

Morsberger, Robert E. "The World of Walter Mitty." UTAH ACADEMY PROCEEDINGS, 37 (1960), 37-43.

> The author analyzes the themes of frustration and the elements of fantasy in the fiction.

"Salute to Thurber." SATURDAY REVIEW, 44 (25 November 1961), 14-18.

> Here are reminiscences and comments by E.B. White, Malcolm Cowley, Peter DeVries, and others.

Schlamm, William S. "The Secret Lives of James Thurber." FREEMAN, 2 (1952), 736-38.

> Thurber is attacked for his satirical criticism of Senator Joseph McCarthy.

Taylor, Wilfred. "James Thurber." ROTHMILL QUARTERLY (1958), pp. 92-101.

> This essay provides a British perspective.

"Thurber and His Humor--Up with the Chuckle, Down with the Yuk." NEWS-WEEK, 4 February 1957, pp. 52-56.

> Some of the subtleties of Thurber's satire are examined here.

Updike, John. "Indignations of a Senior Citizen." NEW YORK TIMES BOOK REVIEW, 25 November 1962, p. 5.

> The novelist dismisses most of Thurber's work as insignificant and unconvincing.

Van Doren, Mark. THE AUTOBIOGRAPHY OF MARK VAN DOREN. New York: Harcourt, Brace, 1958.

> Van Doren, a noted scholar, was also Thurber's friend and neighbor; here he discusses the writer's blindness and his pessimism.

Weales, Gerald. "The World in Thurber's Fables." COMMONWEAL, 55 (1957), 409-11.

> The writer connects Thurber's increased pessimism with his growing political disenchantment, as seen in the fables.

White, E.B. "James Thurber." THE NEW YORKER, 37 (1961), 247.

> THE NEW YORKER's obituary was written by Thurber's old friend and associate.

E[LWYN] B[ROOKS] WHITE (1899-)

If there is one children's book written by an American in the last thirty years
that has been awarded both love and respect, it is CHARLOTTE'S WEB; if there
is one book on the elements of good writing that has achieved almost the status
of a household word, it is ELEMENTS OF STYLE; and if there is one magazine
that is widely considered as a touchstone for sophisticated prose style, it is THE
NEW YORKER, for which White wrote the "Notes and Comments" section. It
is surprising that one man could achieve not merely excellence but mastery in
three related but disparate areas; it is little short of astonishing that he should
have achieved so much and written, in terms of volume, comparatively little,
and nothing at all in the major prose form of our time, the novel. The source
of White's appeal and of his excellence lies in his punctilious devotion to the
search for the right word--as an undergraduate at Cornell he chided the typical
student in this way: "Little delicacies of expression are entirely beyond his
reach. He is unable to express the shades of meaning which are in his mind."
As any reader of White's famous "Once More to the Lake" and other essays will
agree, he accomplishes those "little delicacies" of expression, and through them
conveys an often haunting awareness of the transcience of life.

The essence of White's appeal becomes clear upon a careful reading of his work:
he conveys the insights of a skeptical moralist and sturdy individualist with
grace, wit, and compassion, as in "The Morning of the Day They Did It" ("It"
being the accidental atomic destruction of the world). The inclusion of White's
work in so many high school and college anthologies seems amply justified.

PRINCIPAL WORKS

HO-HUM: NEWSBREAKS FROM THE NEW YORKER, 1931
ANOTHER HO-HUM, 1932
EVERY DAY IS SATURDAY, 1934
FAREWELL TO MODEL T, 1936
QUO VADIMUS: OR THE CASE FOR THE BICYCLE, 1939
ONE MAN'S MEAT, 1942
STUART LITTLE, 1945 (children's novel)
THE SECOND TREE FROM THE CORNER, 1954

AN E.B. WHITE READER. Ed. William W. Watt and Robert W. Bradford, 1966
THE TRUMPET OF THE SWAN, 1970 (children's novel)
ESSAYS OF E.B. WHITE, 1977

COAUTHORED WORKS AND INTRODUCTIONS

Jones, Roy E., and E.B. White. A BASIC CHICKEN GUIDE FOR THE SMALL FLOCK OWNER. Intro. by E.B. White. New York: William Morrow, 1944.

Marquis, Don. THE LIVES AND TIMES OF ARCHY AND MEHITABEL. Intro. by E.B. White. New York: Doubleday, 1950.

Strunck, William, Jr., and E.B. White. THE ELEMENTS OF STYLE. New York: Macmillan, 1959.

Thurber, James. THE OWL IN THE ATTIC. Intro. by E.B. White. New York: Grosset and Dunlap, 1931.

White, E.B., and Katherine S. White, eds. A SUBTREASURY OF AMERICAN HUMOR. New York: Coward-McCann, 1941 (Letters).

White, E.B. LETTERS OF E.B. WHITE. Ed. Dorothy Lobrans Guth. New York: Harper and Row, 1976.

CRITICAL WORKS

Bacon, Leonard. "Humors and Careers." SATURDAY REVIEW OF LITERATURE, 20 (29 April 1939), 3-4, 22.

> Bacon argues for the permanence of White and Thurber as compared to other humorists.

_____. "How to Break a Rib." SATURDAY REVIEW OF LITERATURE, 24 (22 November 1941), 7-8.

> This brief comment praises White's unpretentious skill.

Beck, Warren. "E.B. White." COLLEGE ENGLISH, 7 (1946), 367-73.

> This is an instructive appraisal of White's prose style.

Elledge, Scott. Untitled review of ONE MAN'S MEAT. CARLETON MISCELLANY, 4 (1964), 83-87.

> The writer discusses White's gentle irony.

Frank, Susan. "Interview with E.B. White." CORNELL DAILY SUN, 9 October 1964, pp. 82, 88.

> This interview by a student journalist contains interesting information about White's college days at Cornell.

"Go Climb a More Meaningful Tree." COMMONWEAL, 51 (1950), 573.

> A rare example of negative criticism of White is found here.

Gold, Herbert. Untitled review of THE POINTS OF MY COMPASS. SATURDAY REVIEW, 45 (24 November 1962), 30.

> Gold comments positively on White's admiration for Thoreau, but disapproves mildly of his cool restraint.

Krutch, Joseph Wood. "The Profession of a New Yorker." SATURDAY REVIEW OF LITERATURE, 38 (30 January 1954), 15-16.

> Krutch reviews THE SECOND TREE FROM THE CORNER and comments on White's relationship with THE NEW YORKER.

Maloney, Russell. "Tilley the Toiler." SATURDAY REVIEW OF LITERATURE, 30 (30 August 1947), 7-10, 29, 32.

> Maloney discusses White's important role as writer for the "Notes and Comment" section of THE NEW YORKER.

Nordell, Roderick. "The Writer as a Private Man." CHRISTIAN SCIENCE MONITOR, 31 October 1962, p. 9.

> This is an interesting interview with White about his seldom-discussed private life.

Nordstrom, Ursula. "Stuart, Wilbur, Charlotte: A Tale of Tales." NEW YORK TIMES BOOK REVIEW, 12 May 1974, pp. 8, 10.

> Nordstrom, a writer of children's books herself, provides a good explanation of the appeal of White's books for children.

Sampson, Edward. E.B. WHITE. New York: Twayne, 1974.

> This is the only full-length published study of White. It is well written, balanced, and has a good bibliography. Sampson presents White as "both a commentator on the American scene and as a literary artist."

Schott, Webster. "E.B. White Forever." NEW REPUBLIC, 147 (24 November 1962), 23-24.

> This negative review of THE POINTS OF MY COMPASS attacks

White's urbane, restrained preoccupation with what the reviewer regards as trivial matters.

Steinhoff, William R. "'The Door,' 'The Professor,' 'My Friend the Poet (Deceased),' 'The Washable House,' and 'The Man out in Jersey.'" COLLEGE ENGLISH, 23 (1961), 229-32.

The author examines the titles he treats as examples of fiction, not simply as nicely wrought prose.

Thurber, James. "E.B. White." SATURDAY REVIEW OF LITERATURE, 18 (15 October 1938), 8-9.

White's most notable colleague provides a witty appreciation of him as a person and in connection with THE NEW YORKER.

Van Gelder, Robert. WRITERS AND WRITING. New York: Scribner's, 1946.

This volume contains one of the rare interviews with White.

Walker, Stanley. "Books." NEW YORK HERALD TRIBUNE, 21 October 1962, p. 5.

In this essay White's restraint in an age of increasing excess is praised.

Weatherby, W.J. "A Modern Man of Walden." MANCHESTER GUARDIAN WEEKLY, 14 February 1963, p. 14.

This interview focuses on White's relationship to the writings and the character of Thoreau.

Category 1

ENTERTAINERS: GROUP B

F[RANKLIN] P[IERCE] ADAMS (1881-1960)

Adams was "the godfather," according to one account, of the newspaper humorous essay, and his column "The Conning Tower" was a staple of American journalism at its literate best. The column traveled with "FPA," as its author was known, from newspapers in Chicago to New York, and also served as a forum for a member of fellow writers--among them Ring Lardner, Sinclair Lewis, Edna Ferber, Dorothy Parker, and George Kaufman. Among Adams' more interesting volumes of collected essays are NODS AND BECKS (1944) and THE DIARY OF OUR OWN SAMUEL PEPYS (2 vols., 1935), an ongoing experiment in autobiographical form. Surprisingly, except for entries in the standard biographical indexes and brief passages in memoirs and studies of other writers, Adams has received no critical attention.

ROBERT BENCHLEY (1889-1960)

A more equable but less prolific humorist than his friend and THE NEW YORKER associate James Thurber, Robert Benchley began a family tradition of writing that extends to his grandson, Peter, author of the bestseller, JAWS. Benchley's self-caricature as a bumbler--beset by technology, mass man, and mass media-- was conveyed through the familiar essay, rooted in tradition but attuned to his times. See for example his "how" pieces: instructions on how not to accomplish the end in question (i.e., "How to Avoid Colds," "How to Understand Music"). These are the lineal descendents of Ben Franklin's "Rules by Which a Great Empire May Be Reduced to a Small One." They are, at the same time, part of a fairly common subgenre of humor, the antiinstructional parody, as seen in Donald Ogden Stewart's PERFECT BEHAVIOR (1921), a parody of Emily Post; Fred C. Kelly's HOW TO LOSE YOUR MONEY PRUDENTLY (1933); and the prolific Will Cuppy's HOW TO BECOME EXTINCT (1933), among other works. Benchley's most familiar titles include THE EARLY WORM (1927); FROM BED TO WORSE: OR, COMFORTING THOUGHTS ABOUT THE BISON (1927); and MY TEN YEARS IN A QUANDARY, AND HOW THEY GREW (1936). For a readable and representative collection, see his son Nathaniel's THE BENCHLEY ROUNDUP (New York: Harper and Brothers, 1954). Nathaniel Benchley's ROBERT BENCHLEY, A BIOGRAPHY, was published in 1955 (New York: McGraw-Hill). Norris Yates's ROBERT BENCHLEY (New York: Twayne, 1968) is the only critical study, fortunately a good one.

CLARENCE [SHEPHARD] DAY, JR. (1874-1935)

Day memorialized his father in LIFE WITH FATHER (1935) as an ebullient, humorous, irascible domestic tyrant, an account which was turned into an appealing stage play in 1939, after Day's death, and which has since been made into at least two movies. Despite the popular appeal of LIFE WITH FATHER, however, Day's humor was sophisticated and unorthodox--often, as in THIS SIMIAN WORLD (1920), more serious than it appeared to be. Admired as a stylist by writers as different as Alexander Woollcott and Oliver Wendell Holmes, Jr., Day is often referred to as a "writer's writer." His other books include THE CROW'S NEST (1921), THOUGHTS WITHOUT WORDS (1923), GOD AND MY FATHER (1932), IN THE GREEN MOUNTAIN COUNTRY (1934), and the posthumously published LIFE WITH MOTHER (1936).

FINLEY PETER DUNNE (1867-1936)

A Chicago journalist, Dunne created Mr. Dooley, an Irish saloon keeper, as a vehicle for amusing social observation. Current events, politicians, and manners and attitudes were captured in a series of collections, beginning with MR. DOOLEY IN PEACE AND WAR (1898) and concluding with MR. DOOLEY ON MAKING A WILL (1919). Dunne's (or Mr. Dooley's) observations still have pungency: "'The American nation in the Sixth Ward is a fine people,' he says. 'They love th' eagle,' he says, 'on the back iv a dollar.'" However, dialect humor contains built-in limitations of time and place, and Dunne is remembered now primarily by scholars.

MAX EASTMAN (1883-1969)

Eastman was the son of clergyman and the author of two valuable and popular books, THE ENJOYMENT OF POETRY (1913) and THE ENJOYMENT OF LAUGHTER (1936). He was also a Marxist who helped to found and edit THE MASSES in 1911 and THE LIBERATOR in 1917, both important radical magazines. In 1917 he was tried for sedition in connection with antiwar statements made in THE LIBERATOR, but he continued to lead a full and active life as a poet, writer, and editor. Evidence of continued interest in Eastman is indicated by the recent biography, William L. O'Neill's THE LAST ROMANTIC: A LIFE OF MAX EASTMAN (New York: Oxford University Press, 1978).

DON[ALD ROBERT PERRY] MARQUIS (1878-1937)

Don Marquis established a firm and lasting hold on the newspaper-reading American public with his literary cockroach, archy, who wrote free verse and eschewed formalities of punctuation and capitalization because he was unable to operate the typewriter shift key. Through archy and his insouciant friend, mehitabel the cat ("oh i should worry and fret/ death and i will coquette/ there is a dance in the old dame yet/ toujours gai toujours gai"), Marquis offered com-

fortably cynical observations on sex ("the females of all species are most dan-
gerous when they appear to retreat"), happiness ("an optimist is a guy that has
never had much experience"), and sundry topics. In ARCHY AND MEHITABEL
(1927) and its sequels, as well as in other humorous works such as HERMIONE
AND HER LITTLE GROUP OF SERIOUS THINKERS (1916) and THE OLD SOAK'S
HISTORY OF THE WORLD (1924), Marquis was consistently a popular success.
A recent interesting treatment of his humor on a scholarly level is Edward A.
Martin, "A Puritan's Satanic Flight: Don Marquis, Archy, and Anarchy,"
SEWANEE REVIEW, 83 (1975), 635-42.

CHRISTOPHER [DARLINGTON] MORLEY (1890-1957)

That Christopher Morley is best rememberd for his novel, KITTY FOYLE (1939),
is an indication of how the essay as a literary form has declined in terms of
popular taste. For it is in Morley's essays that his true merit shines best; like
Charles Lamb, Morley had a natural curiosity and largely amiable interest in
everything that showed the interconnections of life and literature; and he became that relatively rare thing in modern America, a "man of letters." Greatly
generous in promoting the literary reputations of fellow writers as different as
Don Marquis and Walt Whitman, Morley achieved national influence as a
columnist for the SATURDAY REVIEW OF LITERATURE and as a director of the
Book-of-the-Month Club. His essays ranged from travel pieces about England,
always keyed to historical events with literary associations, to considerations of
Yeats, Bacon, and Mark Twain.

Always easy and unpretentious, Morley has received less than his share of recognition by modern readers for whom pleasure is not enough, and who fail to
see how pertinent some of his central ideas remain. Note for example his
comment of fifty years ago on "the sense of place," or "roots," so popular recently: "To be deeply rooted in a place that has meaning is perhaps the best
life a child can have." On the other hand, it is interesting to note that
Morley, so involved with the literary and personal past, was intrigued as well
by the technological future: his 1937 collection of essays, THE TROJAN HORSE,
is dedicated to "Buckminster Fuller, scientific idealist."

In addition to KITTY FOYLE, Morley's other familiar titles are PARNASSUS
ON WHEELS (1917), SWISS FAMILY MANHATTAN (1933), and THE MAN WHO
MADE FRIENDS WITH HIMSELF (1949). The only thorough account of his
writing career is Mark I. Wallach and Jon Bracker, CHRISTOPHER MORLEY
(New York: Twayne, 1976). Guy R. Lyle and H. Tatnall Brown, Jr., com-
piled A BIBLIOGRAPHY OF CHRISTOPHER MORLEY (Washington, D.C.: Scare-
crow Press, 1952). "In Memoriam: Christopher Morley" (New York: Book-of-the-
Month Club, 1957) is a ten-page pamphlet sent to club members after Morley's
death, containing appreciations by Clifton Fadiman, John P. Marquand, Norman
Cousins, Harrison Smith, and J. Donald Adams.

DOROTHY [ROTHSCHILD] PARKER (1893-1967)

Parker is remembered best for her satirical verse in such collections as NOT SO DEEP AS A WELL (1936) and AFTER SUCH PLEASURES (1933), but before turning to these works she had achieved a fearsome reputation as an acidulous critic of the theater for VANITY FAIR and THE NEW YORKER. Caustic, cynical, and clever, her appeal is engagingly yet mordantly summed up in a bit of dog-gerel called "Resume": "Guns aren't lawful/Nooses give;/ Gas smells awful; I might as well live." Not surprisingly, feminist critics today find Parker's career of interest, as indicated by Emily Toth's article, "Dorothy Parker, Erica Jong, and New Feminist Humor," REGIONALISM AND THE FEMALE IMAGI-NATION, 3, Nos. 2-3 (1977-78), 70-85. Arthur F. Kinney, DOROTHY PARKER (Boston: Twayne, 1978), uses new information and manuscript letters in an effort to place Parker in the context of modern American literature.

GILBERT [VIVIAN] SELDES (1893-1970)

Gilbert Seldes led an unusually active and varied life as a writer; he was, at different times, music critic for the PHILADELPHIA EVENING LEDGER, foreign correspondent during World War I, managing editor of the DIAL, and a director of television programming for the Columbia Broadcasting System. Interested in all aspects of culture, but especially the modern forms, he wrote the bestselling THE SEVEN LIVELY ARTS in 1928. Several novels, numerous scripts for radio and television, and a dozen other works on movies, prohibition, television, and audience reactions and expectations were not enough to fill Seldes' days-- he also wrote two detective novels under the name of Foster Johns. Edmund Wilson--"Gilbert Seldes and the Popular Arts," in A LITERARY CHRONICLE: 1920-1950 (New York: Doubleday, 1952), 49-65--gives a good appraisal of Seldes' early and later career.

FRANK SULLIVAN (1892-1978)

Sullivan is known to all readers of freshman English anthologies as the author of "The Cliche-Expert," a humorous parody which accurately reflects Sullivan's long-time fascination with ideas and words. Among his other memorable paro-dies are those of the grumpy critic Van Wyck Brooks. A columnist for the NEW YORK WORLD, THE NEW YORKER, and other periodicals, Sullivan collected his pieces under a number of titles, including THE ADVENTURES OF AN OAF (1926), A PEARL IN EVERY OYSTER (1938), and A ROCK IN EVERY SNOW-BALL (1946). See also George Oppenheimer's WELL, THERE'S NO HARM IN LAUGHING: THE COLLECTED PIECES AND LETTERS OF FRANK SULLIVAN (Garden City, N.Y.: Doubleday, 1972). Sullivan's annual Christmas letter in THE NEW YORKER was one of the magazine's best-loved traditions.

ALEXANDER WOOLLCOTT (1887-1943)

"At the hour of his death," according to his best biographer, Edwin Hoyt, Alexander Woollcott was "the most powerful literary figure in the English-speaking world." But because his personality was so abrasive the words that recur in accounts of his life are harsh indeed--"malevolence," "rancor," "cruelty," and "humiliation" among them. A gifted stylist, Woollcott's reputation as a writer has been obscured both by his troubled personality and by the fact that he devoted his career to theatrical criticism; though he raised it to a new level of art, Woollcott was dealing primarily with ephemera, and most of his writing is dated. An associate of Thurber and other members of the so-called Algonquin Club, Woollcott knew and was known by everyone in the literary and theatrical fields.

Though there has been no scholarly work done to suggest that Hoyt's assertion of Woollcott's power is more than hyperbole, there have been, astonishingly, given Woollcott's relatively slender body of work, three full-scale biographies in the thirty-five years since his death. The first, by Samuel Francis Adams, ALEXANDER WOOLLCOTT, HIS LIFE AND HIS WORLD (New York: Reynal and Hitchcock, 1945), is marred by an inconsistency of tone indicating that the author actively disliked his subject. Howard Teichman, SMART ALECK: THE WIT, WORLD, AND LIFE OF ALEXANDER WOOLLCOTT (New York: Morrow, 1975), appraises Woollcott from a theatrical perspective more as a performer than as a writer. It is a thin treatment compared to the earlier excellent study by Edwin Hoyt, ALEXANDER WOOLLCOTT, THE MAN WHO CAME TO DINNER (New York: Abelard-Schuman, 1968).

STARK YOUNG (1881-1962)

Stark Young was a novelist and poet of some stature, especially in connection with the South, and his essay ("Not in Memoriam, But in Defense") in the famous collection by southern writers called I'LL TAKE MY STAND (1930) is a model of concerned and balanced prose. He was also an influential and valuable critic of the modern theater; as drama editor for the NEW REPUBLIC and as contributor to the NEW YORK TIMES and THEATRE ARTS MONTHLY, Young brought to bear his wide scholarship and his own considerable experience as a playwright and director. His longer pieces on drama are collected in THE FLOWER IN DRAMA (1923). His letters were collected and edited by John Pilkington, STARK YOUNG: A LIFE IN THE ARTS (2 vols., Baton Rouge: Louisiana State University Press, 1975).

Category 1

ENTERTAINERS: GROUP C

Category 1

ENTERTAINERS: GROUP C

Following are some of the other writers who were popular and respected entertainers during the period from 1900 to 1950.

GELETT BURGESS (1866-1951) wrote the famous verse, "I've never seen a
purple cow . . ." in 1895, and was a widely quoted word-coiner and epi-
grammatist for the rest of his long life. He invented the word "blurb," and
also a race of horrible and funny children in GOOPS AND HOW TO BE THEM
(1900).

IRWIN S. COBB (1876-1941) wrote a number of amusing books, including OLD
JUDGE PRIEST (1916) about a bibulous, kindly old Confederate War veteran
in Kentucky. His EXIT LAUGHING (1941) is one of the better autobiographies
of this period.

WILL CUPPY (1884-1949) achieved posthumous best-sellerdom with his unconventional history, THE DECLINE AND FALL OF PRACTICALLY EVERYBODY
(1950). Previously his cheerful parodies of "how to" books--HOW TO BE A
HERMIT (1929) and HOW TO BECOME EXTINCT (1941) among them--had won
him the amused praise of such fellow writers as Charles Poore, who said Cuppy
always struck "while the irony was hot."

S[IDNEY] J[OSEPH] PERELMAN (1904-1979), a contributor to THE NEW YORKER,
of humorous sketches beginning in 1934, lampooned popular culture with punning
wit reminiscent of James Joyce; a typical example is a collection called THE
ROAD TO MILTOWN: OR, UNDER THE SPREADING ATROPHY (1957). An
engaging personal profile of Perelman as "anarchist and archwit" is that by
Alan Brien, "The Man in the Ironic Mask," QUEST, 3 (November 1978), 49-
52, 94-95.

WILL ROGERS (1879-1935) is usually remembered as a performer, not a writer,
but many of his famous quips about politics and American life were written as

newspaper columns before they were "performed." His writings have been collected and edited by Donald Day as THE AUTOBIOGRAPHY OF WILL ROGERS
(1949); a later collection edited by Day, SANITY IS WHERE YOU FIND IT,
appeared in 1955. Richard M. Ketchum, WILL ROGERS: HIS LIFE AND
TIMES (New York: American Heritage, 1973), traces the humorist's rise to
national celebrity.

H[ARRY] ALLEN SMITH (1907-1976)) was "the screwball's screwball," according to Fred Allen. PEOPLE CALLED SMITH (1950) and a dozen other books
have attracted a wide range of readers, including Bergan Evans, who edited
an anthology of Smith's work entitled THE WORLD, THE FLESH, AND H. ALLEN
SMITH (1954).

DONALD OGDEN STEWART (1894-1980) was born nine days before James
Thurber in the same city, Columbus, Ohio. His PARODY OUTLINE OF HIS-
TORY (1923) and AUNT POLLY'S STORY OF MANKIND (1923) were broadly
amusing commercial successes before Thurber hit his stride, but Stewart wrote
little after going to Hollywood in the 1930s. See Matthew Bruccoli's interview, "Donald Ogden Stewart," in Bruccoli et al., eds., CONVERSATIONS
WITH WRITERS I (Detroit: Gale Research Co., 1977).

Category 2

TEACHERS: GROUP A

HENRY ADAMS (1838-1918)

His dates and his distinguished heritage from America's most famous family would seem to place Henry Adams securely in the nineteenth century, but two of his major works were published after 1900, and they also happen to be two of the most significant works of prose since that date--hence his necessary inclusion in this volume. MONT-SAINT-MICHEL AND CHARTRES, privately printed in 1904 and published in a trade edition in 1913, fused medieval theology, philosophy, mysticism, sociology, economics, art, literature, and romance into a beautiful prose poem which celebrated the unity of an orderly world radically different from the chaos of the modern age. In THE EDUCATION OF HENRY ADAMS, privately printed in 1907 and published commercially after Adams' death in 1918, we have perhaps the most famous autobiography in American literature, after that of Benjamin Franklin. Here Adams pursued the attempt to establish a continuity between the medieval period and modern America; subtitled "A Study of Twentieth-Century Multiplicity," the book foreshadows some of the more ambitious efforts in later American fiction to use science as metaphor.

Indeed, as summarized rather clumsily by one literary guide--Bartholow V. Crawford et al., AMERICAN LITERATURE (New York: Barnes and Noble, 1945)--Adams' EDUCATION could easily be mistaken for a review of the modernist Thomas Pynchon's GRAVITY'S RAINBOW: "Arterializing its vigorous skepticism and alert humor, its absorptive knowledge, rich expressiveness, and extraordinary substance are veins of desperate pessimism, of disintegrative pathos, and of philosophic anarchism." It is little wonder that Adams has been the subject of a number of literary and critical studies, especially in recent years as his turn-of-the-century prophecy has come to seem increasingly plausible. "I firmly believe," Adams said, "that before many centuries more, science will be the one master of man. The engines he will have invented will be beyond his strength to control. Some day science may have the existence of mankind in its power, and the human race commit suicide by blowing up the world."

PRINCIPAL WORKS

LIFE OF ALBERT GALLATIN, 1879

Henry Adams

DEMOCRACY, AN AMERICAN NOVEL, 1880
ESTHER, A NOVEL, 1884
HISTORY OF THE UNITED STATES DURING THE ADMINISTRATIONS OF
   JEFFERSON AND MADISON, 1889-1891
MONT-SAINT-MICHEL AND CHARTRES, 1904, 1913
THE PRAYER TO THE VIRGIN OF CHARTRES, 1904 (Poem)
THE EDUCATION OF HENRY ADAMS, 1907, 1918 (Autobiography)

LETTERS

LETTERS OF HENRY ADAMS. Ed. Worthington Chauncey Ford. 2 vols. 1858-
91, 1892-1918. Boston: Houghton Mifflin, 1930, 1938.

LETTERS TO A NIECE AND PRAYER TO THE VIRGIN OF CHARTRES. Ed.
Worthington Chauncey Ford. 2 vols. in 1. Boston: Houghton Mifflin, 1920.

HENRY ADAMS AND HIS FRIENDS. Ed. H.E. Cater. Boston: Houghton
Mifflin, 1947.

BIOGRAPHY

Levenson, J.C. THE MIND AND ART OF HENRY ADAMS. Boston: Houghton
Mifflin, 1957.

> This is a readable shorter account of Adams' life and its relation
> to his works.

Samuels, Ernest. THE YOUNG HENRY ADAMS. Cambridge: Harvard University Press, 1942.

_____. HENRY ADAMS: THE MIDDLE YEARS. Cambridge: Harvard Uni-
versity Press, 1948.

_____. HENRY ADAMS: THE MAJOR PHASE. Cambridge: Harvard Uni-
versity Press, 1964.

> These three volumes comprise the essential study of Adams, and
> contain the best available bibliography.

CRITICAL WORKS

Blackmur, R.P. "The Expense of Greatness: Three Emphases on Henry Adams."
VIRGINIA QUARTERLY REVIEW, 12 (1936), 396-415.

> Blackmur argues that Adams maintained "unity of conception" and
> "definiteness of form" in diverse genres.

_____. "Harmony of True Liberalism: Henry Adams's MONT-SAINT-MICHEL AND CHARTRES." SEWANEE REVIEW, 60 (1952), 1-27.

> Adams is defended against charges of factual inaccuracy and historical misrepresentation.

_____. "The Virgin and the Dynamo." MAGAZINE OF ART, 45 (1952), 147-53.

> Adams' concept of symbols as forces is explained.

_____. "Adams Goes to School: I. The Problem Laid Out." KENYON REVIEW, 46 (1955), 597-623.

> Adams used Quincy, his home, as a symbol of imagination and Boston as a symbol of reason.

Conder, J.J. A FORMULA OF HIS OWN. Chicago: University of Chicago Press, 1970.

> This excellent study of Adams' two major literary works, the EDUCATION and CHARTRES, illustrates their author's concern with free will and determinism.

Donoghue, Denis. "The American Style of Failure." SEWANEE REVIEW, 82 (1971), 407-32.

> Adams is represented as having taken pleasure is failure, "cultivating it for all the moral superiority he got from it."

French, Warren. "Henry Adams and the 'Romantic Historians.'" In AMERICAN LITERARY SCHOLARSHIP 1974. Ed. James Woodress. Durham, N.C.: Duke University Press, 1976, pp. 205-09.

> This is a good survey of work done in the five previous years on Adams, "a star that is looming constantly larger among American literary constellations."

Harbert, Earl N. "THE EDUCATION OF HENRY ADAMS: The Confessional Mode as Heuristic Experiment." JOURNAL OF NARRATIVE TECHNIQUE, 4 (1974), 3-18.

> The emphasis on failure in Adams is found to be a technique for advancing general ideas on art and success.

Hochfield, George. HENRY ADAMS: AN INTRODUCTION AND INTERPRETATION. New York: Barnes and Noble, 1962.

> This survey describes a pattern in Adams of a search for an ideal which later is seen by him to be inadequate.

Monteiro, George. "The Education of Ernest Hemingway." JOURNAL OF AMERICAN STUDIES, 8 (1974), 91-99.

> Parallel ideas of disillusionment, without any suggestion of indebtedness to Adams, are traced in Hemingway's novels and short fiction.

Murray, James G. HENRY ADAMS. New York: Twayne, 1974.

> The first chapter on "The Metaphor of Failure" is excellent, but otherwise this study is of more interest to philosophy students than to those in literature.

Stark, Cruce. "The Historical Irrelevance of Heroes: Henry Adams's Andrew Jackson." AMERICAN LITERATURE, 47 (1974), 170-81.

> Stark explains Adams' thesis that the nature of democracy precludes heroes and that historians must lead the way with the scholar's pen toward tracing the confusion created by the hero's sword.

White, Lynn, Jr. "Dynamo and Virgin Reconsidered." AMERICAN SCHOLAR, 27 (1958), 183-94.

> Significant questions are raised here about the validity of Adams' procedures in writing history.

Winters, Yvor. "Henry Adams; or, the Creation of Confusion." In THE ANATOMY OF NONSENSE. Norfolk, Conn.: New Directions, 1943, pp. 23-87; rpt. IN DEFENSE OF REASON. New York: Morrow, 1947.

> The so-called unity of MONT-SAINT-MICHEL AND CHARTRES is attacked as an illusion without historical foundation.

WILLIAM JAMES (1842-1910)

As the father of modern psychology and as the foremost exponent of that quintessentially American philosophy, pragmatism, William James is without question one of the most influential thinkers and writers in our history. Arguing persuasively that truth must be judged by actions and not by abstract concepts, James influenced both critical theory and practice to the degree that he was an essential catalyst in the movement away from idealism toward literary naturalism. At the same time, James resisted the pessimistic determinism of the literary naturalists, arguing that mankind gives considerable evidence of adaptability to a world which "was not made for it, but in which it grew." Such adjustments as the race makes will never be permanent, for the world is constantly changing, but change is to be viewed as an opportunity for further development rather than a threat. It is not being or existing which is important but becoming or persisting; pragmatism must be understood as the philosophy of "making good."

For all the weight and influence of his ideas, James was also a direct, vivid, colloquial, and often humorous writer whose prose, even in his scientific works, offers a wealth of illustrative examples and anecdotes. So accessible was his writing, in contrast to the later novels of his brother Henry, noted for their complex ironic characterizations, that some readers felt both writers had missed their true callings: William was a psychologist who wrote like a novelist, Henry a novelist who wrote like a psychologist.

PRINCIPAL WORKS

THE PRINCIPLES OF PSYCHOLOGY, 2 vols., 1890
PSYCHOLOGY, BRIEFER COURSE, 1892
THE WILL TO BELIEVE AND OTHER ESSAYS IN POPULAR PHILOSOPHY, 1897
HUMAN IMMORTALITY: TWO SUPPOSED OBJECTIONS TO THE DOCTRINE,
1899
TALKS TO TEACHERS ON PSYCHOLOGY, AND TO STUDENTS ON SOME
OF LIFE'S IDEALS, 1899
THE VARIETIES OF RELIGIOUS EXPERIENCE: A STUDY IN HUMAN NATURE,
1903

PRAGMATISM, A NEW NAME FOR SOME OLD WAYS OF THINKING, 1907
A PLURALISTIC UNIVERSE: HIBBERT LECTURES ON THE PRESENT SITUATION
    IN PHILOSOPHY, 1909
THE MORAL EQUIVALENT OF WAR, 1910
ESSAYS IN RADICAL EMPIRICISM, 1912
COLLECTED ESSAYS AND REVIEWS. Ed. R.B. Perry, 1920
WILLIAM JAMES ON PSYCHICAL RESEARCH. Ed. and comp. by Gardner
    Murphy and Robert O. Bellou, 1969

LETTERS

THE LETTERS OF WILLIAM JAMES. 2 vols. Ed. by his son Henry James.
Boston: Atlantic Monthly Press, 1920.

THE THOUGHT AND CHARACTER OF WILLIAM JAMES AS REVEALED IN UN-
PUBLISHED CORRESPONDENCE AND NOTES, TOGETHER WITH HIS PUBLISHED
WRITINGS. Ed. Ralph Barton Perry. 2 vols. Boston: Little, Brown, 1935.

> These volumes contain much otherwise unavailable primary material.

BIBLIOGRAPHY

McDermott, John. ANNOTATED BIBLIOGRAPHY OF THE WRITINGS OF
WILLIAM JAMES. New York: Longmans, Green, 1920; Dubuque, Iowa: W.C.
Brown Reprint Library, 1964.

_____. THE WRITINGS OF WILLIAM JAMES. New York: Random House,
1967.

> This large volume of selected readings contains an updated bib-
> liography.

Skrupskelis, Ignas. WILLIAM JAMES: A REFERENCE GUIDE. Boston: G.K.
Hall, 1977.

> The subtitle is too modest; this is the best single reference source
> for James, including as it does, in addition to regular citations,
> a list of "spirit writings" supposedly communicated by James after
> his death and, more usefully, dissertations on his work.

BIOGRAPHY

Allen, Gay Wilson. WILLIAM JAMES, A BIOGRAPHY. New York: Viking,
1967.

> This is the standard biography.

Matthiessen, F.O. THE JAMES FAMILY: A GROUP BIOGRAPHY TOGETHER
WITH SELECTIONS FROM THE WRITINGS OF HENRY JAMES SENIOR, WILLIAM,
HENRY, AND ALICE JAMES. New York: Knopf, 1948.

> Matthiessen's correlation of the various family members' writings
> offers much that is essential and fascinating.

CRITICAL WORKS

Allen, Gay Wilson. "James's VARIETIES OF RELIGIOUS EXPERIENCE as Introduction to American Transcendentalism." EMERSON SOCIETY QUARTERLY,
39 (1965), 81–85.

> Allen explains James's idealism in the context of Emerson's
> thought.

Bailey, N.I. "Pragmatism in THE AMBASSADORS." DALHOUSIE REVIEW,
53 (1973), 143–48.

> William James's pragmatic theory of knowledge is discussed in
> the context of his brother's novel.

Bixler, Julius Seelye. RELIGION IN THE PHILOSOPHY OF WILLIAM JAMES.
Boston: Marshall Jones, 1926.

> This is still one of the best studies of this subject.

Brennan, Bernard P. THE ETHICS OF WILLIAM JAMES. New York: Bookman
Associates, 1961.

> This is a systematic formulation of James's moral philosophy.

Brinnin, John Malcolm. THE THIRD ROSE: GERTRUDE STEIN AND HER WORLD.
Boston: Little, Brown, 1959.

> Stein's medical studies under James are described.

Brown, William R. "William James and the Language of Personal Literature."
STYLE, 5 (1971), 151–63.

> The author uses James to illustrate his argument for developing a
> "more precise genre designation" for writing, emphasizing style.

Chapman, John Jay. MEMORIES AND MILESTONES. New York: Moffat,
1915.

> An important contemporary provides a valuable and highly per-
> sonal reminiscence of James.

Childs, K.W. "Reality in Some of the Writings of Robert Frost and William James." PROCEEDINGS OF THE UTAH ACADEMY OF SCIENCE, ARTS AND LETTERS, 44 (1967), 150-58.

> James and Frost are shown to "share a theory of knowledge that illustrates a duality in empiricism."

Edel, Leon. HENRY JAMES: THE UNTRIED YEARS (1843-1870). Philadelphia: J.B. Lippincott, 1953.

_____. HENRY JAMES: THE CONQUEST OF LONDON (1870-1881). Philadelphia: J.B. Lippincott, 1962.

_____. HENRY JAMES: THE MIDDLE YEARS (1882-1895). Philadelphia: J.B. Lippincott, 1962.

_____. HENRY JAMES: THE MASTER (1895-1916). Philadelphia: J.B. Lippincott, 1972.

> The fullest possible exploration of a major writer's life and times is provided in these volumes, in which William James figures prominently as an intellectual and artistic confidante of the novelist.

Hocks, Richard A. HENRY JAMES AND PRAGMATISTIC THOUGHT: A STUDY IN THE RELATIONSHIP BETWEEN THE PHILOSOPHY OF WILLIAM JAMES AND THE LITERARY ART OF HENRY JAMES. Chapel Hill: University of North Carolina Press, 1974.

> The title is somewhat misleading because this study is primarily devoted to understanding Henry James, not William.

Hoffman, F.J. "William James and the Modern Literary Consciousness." CRITICISM, 4 (1962), 1-13.

> The evidence of James's influence on literature is seen in the familiarity of the idea that the self is defined in terms of process, not substance.

Hull, Byron D. "HENDERSON THE RAIN KING and William James." CRITICISM, 13 (1971), 402-14.

> Dahfu, the African king in Saul Bellow's novel, is seen acting as a psychotherapist whose effectiveness depends on William James's ideas.

Johnson, Ellwood. "William James and the Art of Fiction." JOURNAL OF AESTHETICS AND ART CRITICISM, 30 (1972), 285-96.

> THE PRINCIPLES OF PSYCHOLOGY represented a turning point

in American literature for the ways it added "a new dimension in the art of characterization."

Pendleton, James D. "The James Brothers and 'The Real Thing': A Study in Pragmatic Reality." SOUTH ATLANTIC BULLETIN, 38 (1973), 3-10.

Henry James's story "The Real Thing" (1893) is discussed in terms of the pragmatic principle, or one which "stimulates the creative imagination and which works efficiently when put to use."

Royce, Josiah. WILLIAM JAMES AND OTHER ESSAYS ON THE PHILOSOPHY OF LIFE. New York: Macmillan, 1911.

Royce was James's opposite number in philosophy, and here explains his position.

San Juan, E. "William James as Prose Writer." CENTENNIAL REVIEW OF ARTS AND SCIENCE, 8 (1964), 323-36.

James's prose is examined as an "expressive medium of experience."

Santayana, George. CHARACTER AND OPINION IN THE UNITED STATES. New York: George Braziller, 1955.

Though they were friends and contemporaries at Harvard, this appraisal by the eminent thinker of James is oddly unsympathetic.

Slack, Robert C. "Willie Stark and William James." IN HONOR OF AUSTIN WRIGHT. Ed. Joseph Bain. Pittsburgh: Carnegie-Mellon University, 1972

The author pursues Robert Penn Warren's suggestion that Willie Stark, the demagogue in ALL THE KING'S MEN, is modeled after some of James's ideas on pragmatism, carried to an extreme.

Stafford, William T. "William James as Critic of His Brother Henry." PERSONALIST, 40 (1960), 341-53.

William's role as his brother's critic for forty years was of great importance in terms of ideas, style, and technique.

Stevick, Robert D. "Robinson and William James." UNIVERSITY OF KANSAS CITY REVIEW, 25 (1959), 293-301.

Parallels between Robinson's poem, "The Man Against the Sky," and James's work are examined.

Strout, Cushing. "ALL THE KING'S MEN and the Shadow of William James." SOUTHERN REVIEW, 6 (1970), 920-34.

The author examines the potential for political demagoguery when pragmatism is "abstracted from the moral sense and metaphysics that James notably had."

WALTER LIPPMANN (1889-1974)

In the course of his long and brilliant career, Walter Lippmann was a journalist, a practical political scientist, a political philosopher, a moral philosopher, a political economist, and an expert on foreign policy. He wrote scholarly books and a popular newspaper column, edited a big-city newspaper and a book of poetry, composed personality profiles of his contemporaries, and addressed university audiences. He knew Churchill, John F. Kennedy, and Khrushchev; his career spanned those of Woodrow Wilson and Richard Nixon, and he was, as one critic has noted, "beyond question the most widely-read American social thinker of the twentieth century, and one of the most respected."

Though he never claimed to be an original thinker in the sense that his admired Socrates was, Lippmann's work provides a synthesis of modern liberal thought in the United States. He argued that the natural tendency of humanity is toward authoritarian thought, because it rationalizes our primitive impulses to take command and to seek protection. Liberal thought was more difficult, comparable to a space cleared for a garden in the jungle--that is, always under attack by a hostile environment. His work is best read in this light, as an attempt to explain, defend, and extend that tenuous clearing of enlightened humanism in the jungle of our baser instincts.

PRINCIPAL WORKS

A PREFACE TO POLITICS, 1913
DRIFT AND MASTERY, 1914
THE STAKES OF DIPLOMACY, 1917
THE POLITICAL SCENE, 1919
LIBERTY AND THE NEWS, 1920
PUBLIC OPINION, 1922
THE PHANTOM PUBLIC, 1925
MEN OF DESTINY, 1927
A PREFACE TO MORALS, 1929
THE METHOD OF FREEDOM, 1934
THE GOOD SOCIETY, 1937
UNITED STATES FOREIGN POLICY: SHIELD OF THE REPUBLIC, 1943

Walter Lippmann

UNITED STATES WAR AIMS, 1944
THE COLD WAR, A STUDY IN U.S. FOREIGN POLICY, 1947
ESSAYS IN THE PUBLIC PHILOSOPHY, 1955
THE COMMUNIST WORLD AND OURS, 1959
THE COMING TESTS WITH RUSSIA, 1961
THE ESSENTIAL LIPPMANN. Ed. James Lare and Clinton Rossiter, 1963
EARLY WRITINGS. Ed. Arthur M. Schlesinger, Jr., 1970

CRITICAL WORKS

Adams, Larry L. WALTER LIPPMANN. Boston: Twayne, 1977.

> There is an "underlying unity" in Lippmann's work as a political
> and social commentator during a chaotic half century.

Childs, Marquis, and James Reston, eds. WALTER LIPPMANN AND HIS TIMES.
New York: Harcourt, Brace and World, 1959; published also as a part of the
Essay Index Reprint Series. Freeport, N.Y.: Books for Libraries Press, 1968.

> This is by far the best single source of criticism, though perhaps
> too laudatory (the volume was presented to Lippmann on the oc-
> casion of his seventieth birthday). The eminence of the eleven
> contributors, including the statesman and diplomat George F.
> Kennan, the historians Allen Nevins and Arthur M. Schlesinger,
> Jr., and NEW YORK TIMES editors and columnists James Reston
> and Arthur Krock, is testimony to Lippmann's importance. The
> best essay is Schlesinger's "Walter Lippmann: The Intellectual
> vs. Politics," pp. 189-225; Schlesinger begins with the recollec-
> tion that in the Depression it was once said that "many Americans
> would be glad to settle for Walter Lippmann as king," and pro-
> ceeds to give a valuable analysis of his place in our history as
> a public philosopher.

Dam, Hari. THE INTELLECTUAL ODYSSEY OF WALTER LIPPMANN. New
York: Gordon Press, 1973.

> This acceptable overview examines Lippmann's career as a self-
> styled publicist in "the sense of a person who is an expert on
> public affairs."

Eslau, Heinz. "Mover and Shaker: Walter Lippmann as a Young Man." AN-
TIOCH REVIEW, 11 (1951), 291-312.

> Lippmann is seen as changing from a youthful advocate of so-
> cialism to a "staid conservative . . . worried about wars, revo-
> lutions, and the confusions of human affairs" by 1940.

_____ . "Wilsonian Idealist: Walter Lippmann Goes to War." ANTIOCH REVIEW, 14 (1954), 87-108.

Eslau here examines the consequences of Lippmann's resignation from the NEW REPUBLIC in order to take on the role of intellectual propagandist in President Wilson's War Department during World War I, American participation in which he had once vigorously opposed.

Forcey, Charles. THE CROSSROADS OF LIBERALISM: CROLY, WEYL, LIPPMANN AND THE PROGRESSIVE ERA, 1900-25. London: Oxford University Press, 1961.

Though Croly is emphasized in this study, it is still a valuable work on Lippmann's early career.

Jones, Ernest. "Review of Walter Lippmann's A PREFACE TO POLITICS." IMAGO 2, No. 4 (1913), 30-35.

Jones approves and extends Lippmann's assertion, which owes much to Freud, that "much the same energies produce crime and civilization, art, vice, insanity, love, lust, and religion."

Schapsmeier, Edward, and Frederick Schapsmeier. WALTER LIPPMANN: PHILOSOPHER-JOURNALIST. Washington, D.C.: Public Affairs Press, 1969.

The last third of this study is the most valuable, dealing with Lippmann during the Kennedy-Johnson presidencies and his opposition to American involvement in Vietnam.

Weingast, David Elliott. WALTER LIPPMANN: A STUDY IN PERSONAL JOURNALISM. New Brunswick: Rutgers University Press, 1949.

This is a well-documented study of the newspaper columns, concentrating on those written between 1931-40, with a good bibliography of critical materials and sources.

Wellborn, Charles. TWENTIETH CENTURY PILGRIMAGE: WALTER LIPPMANN AND THE PUBLIC PHILOSOPHY. Baton Rouge: Louisiana State University Press, 1969.

Lippmann is discussed in the context of four major areas: "the nature of man, the malady of democracy, the meaning and function of law, and the relevance of religion."

Wright, Benjamin F. FIVE PUBLIC PHILOSOPHIES OF WALTER LIPPMANN. Austin: University of Texas Press, 1973.

Lippmann is seen as going from optimistic progressivism in his younger days to "serious and searching doubts about the nature and role of public opinion."

H[ENRY] L[OUIS] MENCKEN (1880-1956)

Although Mencken's reputation has declined somewhat since his death, he occupied a unique position of eminence at his peak, as comments by two notably independent thinkers who were his contemporaries will attest. For Edmund Wilson, Mencken was "without question . . . our greatest practicing literary journalist," and Walter Lippmann, writing in 1925, thought he was simply "the most powerful personal influence on this whole generation of educated people." Hard-nosed, hard-headed, and hard-working, Mencken was the national inconoclast who achieved fame and retains our interest today by virtue of his style. His humor was boisterous and aggressive, closer to that of Mark Twain than to the urbane sophistication of James Thurber and other contemporaries, and resting on an impressive command of the American vernacular. Always straightforward, his clear, simple, often eloquent essays survive better today than do many of the people, books, or attitudes that were his subjects.

His virulent attacks on the sentimental literature of the genteel tradition, on mindless middle-class morality, on southern Fundamentalism, and on what he considered to be weak-minded notions about the inherent goodness of the human race were balanced by his vigorous support of such writers as Theodore Dreiser, F. Scott Fitzgerald, Sinclair Lewis, Willa Cather, and Ring Lardner. Admittedly, his judgments were more often based on intuitive common sense than on formal aesthetic grounds, and his early celebration as a critic has faded with the increased recognition of the modernist writers whom he scorned or ignored, including James Joyce and T.S. Eliot. Of more value was Mencken's role as intermediary between the writers he admired and the public he sometimes mocked as the "booboisie," but who also turned to him for guidance in matters of politics, literature, and common sense; regardless of the subject, his essays were informed with a staunch sense of moral purpose and a conviction that a free people had to be pushed or prodded into thinking, or risk losing their freedom.

PRINCIPAL WORKS

GEORGE BERNARD SHAW: HIS PLAYS, 1905
THE PHILOSOPHY OF FRIEDRICH NIETZSCHE, 1908

H[enry] L[ouis] Mencken

A BOOK OF PREFACES, 1917
IN DEFENSE OF WOMEN, 1918
PREJUDICES: FIRST SERIES, 1919 (Subsequent titles in this series appeared in
1920, 1922, 1924, 1926, 1927)
THE AMERICAN LANGUAGE: A PRELIMINARY INQUIRY INTO THE DE-
VELOPMENT OF ENGLISH IN THE UNITED STATES, 1919 (Rev. eds. 1921,
1923, 1936. SUPPLEMENT 1, 1945; SUPPLEMENT 2, 1948)
NOTES ON DEMOCRACY, 1926
JAMES BRANCH CABELL, 1927
TREATISE ON THE GODS, 1927
TREATISE ON RIGHT AND WRONG, 1934
HAPPY DAYS 1880-1892, 1940
NEWSPAPER DAYS 1899-1906, 1941
HEATHEN DAYS 1890-1936, 1943

COLLECTED WORKS

A MENCKEN CHRESTOMATHY. Ed. H.L. Mencken, 1949
THE VINTAGE MENCKEN. Ed. Alistair Cooke, 1955
PREJUDICES: A SELECTION. Ed. James T. Farrell, 1958
THE BATHTUB HOAX AND OTHER BLASTS AND BRAVOS FROM THE CHICAGO
TRIBUNE. Ed. Robert McHugh, 1958
H.L. MENCKEN ON MUSIC, A SELECTION. Ed. Louis Cheslock, 1961
H.L. MENCKEN ON POLITICS, A CARNIVAL OF BUNCOMBE. Ed. Malcom
Moos, 1961
H.L. MENCKEN, THE AMERICAN SCENE: A READER. Ed. Huntington
Cairns, 1965
D-DAY AT DAYTON: REFLECTIONS ON THE SCOPES TRIAL. Ed. Jerry B.
Tompkins, 1965
H.L. MENCKEN'S "SMART SET" CRITICISM. Ed. William Nolte, 1968
THE YOUNG MENCKEN: THE BEST OF HIS WORKS. Ed. Carl Bode, 1973
A GANG OF PECKSNIFFS, AND OTHER COMMENTS ON NEWSPAPER PUB-
LISHERS, EDITORS AND REPORTERS. Ed. Theo Lippmann, Jr., 1975
MENCKEN'S LAST CAMPAIGN: H.L. MENCKEN ON THE 1948 ELECTION.
Ed. Joseph C. Goulden, 1976
MENCKEN VERSUS THE MIDDLE CLASS: A COLLECTION OF MENCKEN'S
"AMERICANA." Ed. H. Alan Wycherley, 1977

COAUTHORED WORKS AND INTRODUCTIONS

Ibsen, Hendrick. A DOLL'S HOUSE AND LITTLE EYOLF. Intro. by H.L.
Mencken. Boston: Luce, 1909.

Muir, Edwin. WE MODERNS: ENIGMAS AND GUESSES. Intro. by H.L.
Mencken. New York: Knopf, 1920

Nathan, George Jean, and H.L. Mencken. THE AMERICAN CREDO: A
CONTRIBUTION TOWARD THE INTERPRETATION OF THE NATIONAL MIND.
Preface by H.L. Mencken. New York: Knopf, 1920.

LETTERS

THE LETTERS OF H.L. MENCKEN. Ed. Guy J. Forgue. New York: Knopf, 1961.

THE NEW MENCKEN LETTERS. Ed. Carl Bode. New York: Dial, 1977.

BIOGRAPHY

Bode, Carl. MENCKEN. Carbondale: Southern Illinois University Press, 1969.

> Bode concentrates on Mencken's personal life, particularly its domestic and conservative aspects.

Kemler, Edgar. THE IRREVERENT MR. MENCKEN. Boston: Little, Brown, 1950.

> Mencken is attacked as a demagogue.

Manchester, William R. DISTURBER OF THE PEACE: THE LIFE OF H.L. MENCKEN. New York: Harper, 1950.

> An interesting study, this is the first book by the later biographer of President Kennedy and General MacArthur.

MEMOIRS

Angoff, Charles. H.L. MENCKEN, A PORTRAIT FROM MEMORY. New York: Yoseloff, 1956.

> These accounts of conversations "from memory" show Mencken's teasing, vulgar side.

Cooke, Alistair. SIX MEN. New York: Knopf, 1977.

> The prominent English journalist recalls his friendship with Mencken, among others.

Mayfield, Sara. THE CONSTANT CIRCLE: H.L. MENCKEN AND HIS FRIENDS. New York: Delacorte, 1968.

> An admiring friend paints a generous picture of Mencken and his wife.

BIBLIOGRAPHY

A DESCRIPTIVE LIST OF H.L. MENCKEN COLLECTIONS IN THE U.S. Comp. by Betty Adler. Baltimore: Enoch Pratt Free Library, 1967.

H.L. MENCKEN: THE MENCKEN BIBLIOGRAPHY. Comp. by Betty Adler with Jane Wilhelm. Baltimore: Johns Hopkins Press, 1961.

MENCKENIANA: A QUARTERLY REVIEW. Baltimore: Enoch Pratt Free Library, No. 1, Sp. 1972-- .

CRITICAL WORKS

Boyd, Ernest. H.L. MENCKEN. New York: McBride, 1925.

> This first book on Mencken, by an Irish critic, is of mainly historical interest.

Brooks, Van Wyck. THE CONFIDENT YEARS: 1885-1915. New York: Dutton, 1952.

> Contains a summation of Mencken's contributions to American letters by a major critic and contemporary.

Dolmetsch, Carl. THE "SMART SET": A HISTORY AND ANTHOLOGY. New York: Dial, 1966.

> Mencken's association with George Jean Nathan is described in detail.

Fecher, Charles A. MENCKEN: A STUDY OF HIS THOUGHT. New York: Knopf, 1978.

> This entertaining account is a demonstration of Mencken's continuing appeal, but primarily as a satirist rather than as a thinker.

Forgue, Guy Jean. H.L. MENCKEN, L'HOMME, L'OUVRE, L'INFLUENCE. Monaco: Pvt. ptd., 1967.

> This is the published Ph.D. dissertation (Univ. of Paris, 1963) by the editor of the Mencken letters.

Hobson, Fred C., Jr. SERPENT IN EDEN: H.L. MENCKEN AND THE SOUTH. Chapel Hill: University of North Carolina Press, 1974.

> This book describes Mencken's famous war with southern mores and his less-familiar encouragement of southern writers, which the author says was instrumental in bringing about the southern literary renaissance.

Kazin, Alfred. ON NATIVE GROUND, AN INTERPRETATION OF MODERN AMERICAN PROSE LITERATURE. New York: Reynal, 1942.

> Kazin offers one of the best critical perspectives written on Mencken during the 1940s.

Lippmann, Walter. "H.L. Mencken." SATURDAY REVIEW OF LITERATURE, 1 (1926), 413-14.

> Mencken's great and salutary influence as a critic of culture is praised: "he calls you a swine and an imbecile, and he increases your will to live."

Nolte, William. H.L. MENCKEN, LITERARY CRITIC. Middletown, Conn.: Wesleyan University, 1964.

> This enthusiastic endorsement of Mencken's criticism of literature shares some of its subject's deficiencies as well as his strengths.

Riggenbach, Jeff. "H.L. Mencken: Write Loudly and Carry a Big Prod." LOS ANGELES TIMES SUNDAY BOOK REVIEW, 11 June 1978, p. 3.

> This account of the great curmudgeon's 1926 visit to Los Angeles conveys a sense of his public personality.

Rubin, Louis D. "H.L. Mencken and the National Letters." SEWANEE RE-VIEW, 74 (1966), 723-28.

Ruland, Richard. THE REDISCOVERY OF AMERICAN LITERATURE. PREMISES OF CRITICAL TASTE, 1900-1940. Cambridge: Harvard University Press, 1967.

> This is an essential work for understanding the critic, particularly concerning his debates with the conservative Stuart Sherman.

Singleton, M.K. H.L. MENCKEN AND THE AMERICAN MERCURY ADVEN-TURE. Durham, N.C.: Duke University Press, 1962.

> Mencken's role as editor of the magazine when it was a powerful influence on American intellectuals is examined.

Stenerson, Douglas C. "The 'Forgotten Man' of H.L. Mencken." AMERICAN QUARTERLY, 18 (1966), 686-96.

> The role and concept of the ideal citizen are examined.

_____. H.L. MENCKEN: ICONOCLAST FROM BALTIMORE. Chicago: University of Chicago Press, 1971.

> This study covers Mencken's ideas up to 1920.

Wagner, Philip. "H.L. Mencken." In MAKERS OF AMERICAN THOUGHT, AN INTRODUCTION TO SEVEN AMERICAN WRITERS. Ed. Ralph Ross. Minneapolis: University of Minnesota Press, 1974, pp. 85-119.

> This introduction by a friend and colleague is a reprint of the Minnesota Pamphlet on American Writers, No. 62, 1966.

Williams, W.H.A. H.L. MENCKEN. New York: Twayne, 1977.

> This excellent intellectual biography demonstrates Mencken's continuing importance to students of American life and letters.

Wilson, Edmund. "The All-Star Literary Vaudeville." NEW REPUBLIC, 47 (1926), 159-60.

_____. "Mencken's Democratic Man." NEW REPUBLIC, 49 (1926), 110-11.

> Both essays are included in the author's SHORES OF LIGHT, A LITERARY CHRONICLE OF THE TWENTIES AND THIRTIES (New York: Farrar, 1952). Mencken is seen by his most important literary contemporary as more impressive for his own prose artistry than for his literary or social criticism.

Yates, Norris W. THE AMERICAN HUMORIST: CONSCIENCE OF THE TWENTIETH CENTURY. New York: Citadel, 1965.

> The personae in Mencken's satire are examined.

Category 2

TEACHERS: GROUP B

BERNARD DeVOTO (1897-1955)

Although he failed in his longing to become a successful novelist, Bernard
DeVoto's reputation today rests on his unique application of a novelist's sense
of plot, theme, setting, and characterization to a series of nonfiction works
about the American West. Opinionated and contentious, with a gift for invective like that of H.L. Mencken, his admiring contemporary, DeVoto especially scorned the opportunists who exploited the land for fame or money,
though his reading of the American experience was essentially a positive one.
His main achievement lay in reconciling the requirements of academic responsibility with the demands of the nonspecialist, middle-class reader.

Interweaving fact and theory, diary entries and poetry, travel narrative and
government correspondence, DeVoto reveals the pathos, the heroism, and above
all the varieties of personalities involved in the settling of the American West.
THE YEAR OF DECISION: 1846 appeared in 1943 and dealt with the movement
westward to California, the Mexican-American War, and the Mormon migration
to Utah. ACROSS THE WIDE MISSOURI (1947) is a history of the Rocky
Mountain fur trade, and THE COURSE OF EMPIRE (1952) is a history of America
up to the time of the Lewis and Clark expedition. DeVoto's other important
books are MARK TWAIN'S AMERICA (1932)--a combination of social history,
literary theory, and criticism--and MARK TWAIN AT WORK (1942), three
essays on Twain. DeVoto's running war with literary critics, particularly Van
Wyck Brooks for his limited (i.e., Eastern establishment) view of Twain, whom
DeVoto saw as essentially a Western writer, reached its apogee in THE LITERARY
FALLACY (1944); the ensuing battle was vigorous but inconclusive. DeVoto's
essays for HARPER'S were collected in THE EASY CHAIR (1953).

Julius Barclay, FOUR PORTRAITS AND ONE SUBJECT: BERNARD DeVOTO
(Boston: Houghton Mifflin, 1960), contains the fullest available bibliography,
as well as reminiscences by such personal friends of DeVoto as Catherine Drinker
Bowen, Edith R. Merrilees, Arthur M. Schlesinger, Jr., and Wallace Stegner.
Stegner has also edited THE LETTERS OF BERNARD DeVOTO (Garden City,
N.Y.: Doubleday, 1975) and written the life, THE UNEASY CHAIR: A BIOG-
RAPHY OF BERNARD DeVOTO (Garden City, N.Y.: Doubleday, 1974), an
affectionate detailed study written with all of Stegner's skill as a novelist and
his acuity as a historian of the West. The other major study is Orlan Sawey,

BERNARD DeVOTO (New York: Twayne, 1960), which traces DeVoto's love for the American West and his interest in the influence of the idea of the frontier on American institutions and literature. Leland Frazer, "Bernard DeVoto and the Mormon Tradition," DIALOGUE, 6 (1971), 23-38, is a discussion of DeVoto's changing attitudes toward Mormonism. Anthony Arthur, "The Case of the Diminished Hero," SAN JOSE STUDIES, 3 (1977), 97-106, examines DeVoto's novelistic use of John C. Fremont as a villain to counterpoint the heroism of the pioneers in THE YEAR OF DECISION: 1846.

JOHN DEWEY (1859-1952)

John Dewey's significance as a thinker is so great and he wrote so much over a period of seventy years that he must be included in any bibliographical survey despite the obfuscative quality of his prose style. In his most important book, THE SCHOOL AND SOCIETY (1899), Dewey argued that what had passed for education up to that time was merely a mechanical rather than a creative indoctrination in traditional beliefs. A true education, he said, should encourage the liberation and development of the individual intelligence. His studies in religion, ethics, art, science, and political philosophy made Dewey a major intellectual force, with an incalculable effect on American education and, if only indirectly, on American literature and prose style as well. Compared to other twentieth-century thinkers--for example, William James--Dewey's work has up to now provoked surprisingly little examination for its relevance to American letters.

JoAnn Boydston, director of the Center for Dewey Studies, University of Southern Illinois (Carbondale), has edited THE EARLY WORKS OF JOHN DEWEY, 1882-1898, vols. 1-5 (1965-72) and THE MIDDLE WORKS, 1899-1924, vols. 1-6 (1976-78). Volumes 11 and 12 of the projected fifteen-volume MIDDLE WORKS will be published in 1981. THE LATER WORKS, 1925-52, will be published in sixteen volumes over the next two decades.

For representative selections of primary works, see THE PHILOSOPHY OF JOHN DEWEY, ed. Paul Schilpp, (Evanston, Ill.: Northwestern University Press, 1939), and INTELLIGENCE IN THE MODERN WORLD: JOHN DEWEY'S PHILOSOPHY, ed. Joseph Ratner (New York: Modern Library, Random House, 1939). Milton A. Thomas, JOHN DEWEY: A CENTENNIAL BIBLIOGRAPHY (Chicago: University of Chicago Press, 1962), contains a listing of the works which occupies 153 pages; it also lists dissertations and theses on Dewey's work. See also JoAnn Boydston, CHECKLIST OF WRITING ABOUT JOHN DEWEY, 1887-1976 (Carbondale: University of Southern Illinois Press, 1978). George R. Geiger, JOHN DEWEY IN PERSPECTIVE (New York: Oxford, 1958), published on the centennial of Dewey's birth, focuses on the aesthetic dimensions of his philosophy. Sidney Hook, JOHN DEWEY, AN INTELLECTUAL PORTRAIT (New York: John Day, 1939), is an engagingly written appraisal of the man and the thinker by one of his most respected students; Robert J. Roth, JOHN DEWEY AND SELF-REALIZATION (Englewood Cliffs, N.J.: Prentice-Hall, 1963), discusses aesthetic aspects of technological experience.

W[ILLIAM] E[DWARD] B[URCHARDT] DuBOIS (1868-1963)

Generally recognized as the most important black intellectual leader in American history, W.E.B. DuBois did pioneering studies of American blacks in history, anthropology, and sociology. DuBois was an activist who was instrumental in founding the National Association for the Advancement of Colored People (NAACP) and in organizing the first Pan-African Congress in 1921. His writing career, distinguished by its volume, its combination of passion and intelligence, and its exploration of the various genres, including poetry, fiction, and history, began with the publication in the Harvard Historical Series of his Ph.D. dissertation, THE SUPPRESSION OF THE AFRICAN SLAVE TRADE TO THE UNITED STATES (1896). THE PHILADELPHIA NEGRO (1899) is a sociological study which is regarded as a classic of urban sociology. THE SOULS OF BLACK FOLK (1903) is a collection of essays ranging from a study of the Negro population in the Black Belt of Georgia to an essay on Negro folk music. DUSK OF DAWN (1940), subtitled "An Essay Toward an Autobiography of a Race Concept," traces the evolution of DuBois' thought from his days as a child in a white New England town through the first half of this century. In this work DuBois develops the idea, opposed to that of Booker T. Washington, that while ignorance must be eliminated, the real causes of racial oppression are economic and political; hence it needed to be clearly demonstrated that the cultural tradition of the Western world included a long and bitter history of racial and colonial exploitation. COLOR AND DEMOCRACY: COLONIES AND PEACE (1945), a scholarly study, and AUTOBIOGRAPHY (1965) develop the arguments concerning racial oppression which DuBois first advanced in DUSK OF DAWN. Ultimately, DuBois despaired of ever seeing meaningful progress in the United States under the present system; he joined the Communist party, gave up his American citizenship, and moved to Ghana a few years before his death.

There are two bibliographies: Herbert Aptheker's ANNOTATED BIBLIOGRAPHY OF THE PUBLISHED WRITINGS OF W.E.B. DuBOIS (Millwood, N.Y.: Kraus-Thomson Organization, 1973) is a substantial work by an important Marxist historian who has also edited THE CORRESPONDENCE OF W.E.B. DuBOIS (2 vols., Amherst: University of Massachusetts Press, 1973-1976). Paul Partington's W.E.B. DuBOIS: A BIBLIOGRAPHY OF HIS PUBLISHED WRITINGS (Whittier, Calif.: Paul Partington, 1973) is the most complete list of the works available, including editions and translations, but it lacks annotations and index. An important critical study of DuBois as a writer, claiming for him a "poetic vision," is Arnold Rampersad's THE ART AND IMAGINATION OF W.E.B. DuBOIS (Cambridge: Harvard University Press, 1976).

LEWIS MUMFORD (1895-)

It is not yet certain that Mumford has been the giant of modern thought that many admirers believe him to be, but no one can dispute his persistent and eloquent contributions, spanning half a century, as a commentator on architectural history, education, and social planning. While his views are vigorously disputed by some authorities who question the appropriateness of Emersonian idealism for public policy, his major works are models of well-documented research and lucid argumentation. They include STICKS AND STONES (1924), which examines American architecture from colonial times onward as demonstrations of the spirit of American civilization; a four-volume work entitled THE RENEWAL OF LIFE, which is a study of the emergence of modern science and technology, starting with TECHNICS AND CIVILIZATION (1934) and continuing with THE CULTURE OF CITIES (1938), THE CONDITION OF MAN (1944), and THE CONDUCT OF LIFE (1951).

Mumford's chief concern was with the relations between man's changing view of the world and the techniques that he uses for his welfare as he sees it within his particular historical context. In THE CITY IN HISTORY (1961), he examines the history of man as an urban creature; THE MYTH OF THE MACHINE (1967), perhaps his most controversial work, argues that the effect of machinery upon modern society has been essentially negative; the companion volume to the previous work appeared in 1971 under the same title, and is subtitled THE PENTAGON OF POWER. GREEN MEMORIES (1947) is an account of the childhood of Mumford's son, Geddes, who was killed in World War II.

Considering the quantity and importance of Mumford's work, there has not been much written about him. The most interesting essay is by his contemporary, Van Wyck Brooks, "Lewis Mumford: American Prophet," HARPER'S MONTHLY, 204 (1952), 46-53. For a list of Mumford's writings to 1970, see Elmer S. Newman, LEWIS MUMFORD: A BIBLIOGRAPHY 1914-1970 (New York: Harcourt, Brace, 1971); criticism is not included. David R. Conrad, EDUCATION FOR TRANSFORMATION: IMPLICATIONS IN LEWIS MUMFORD'S ECOHUMANISM (Palm Springs, Calif.: ETC Publications, 1976), considers Mumford in the light of educational theory and its relation to ecology. Unfortunately, all the jargon and tunnel vision that Mumford himself eschewed for fifty years found its way into this volume.

GEORGE SANTAYANA (1863-1952)

Unlike some of his major contemporaries whose ideas have proved more lasting than their literary styles--Dewey and Veblen in particular--Santayana has achieved more lasting distinction as a prose stylist than as an influential thinker; for, according to Abraham Kaplan in THE NEW WORLD OF PHILOSOPHY (New York: Random House, 1961), he has had "few followers, even within the academy." Born in Spain, Santayana was raised and educated in Boston and taught philosophy at Harvard until 1912, when an inheritance allowed him to resign and devote his time to writing. Santayana wrote verse and drama as well as an interesting novel, THE LAST PURITAN (1935), but his major works were in philosophy. His early major work, a five-volume study called THE LIFE OF REASON (1905-06), developed the idea that matter is the only reality and that all mankind's institutions and myths were descriptions or expressions of matter. In his later works Santayana modified his ideas to include the advocacy of faith in intuitive essences which could be opposed to complete skepticism, and he wrote widely about British and American culture as well.

Something of the flavor of Santayana's lucid yet elegant talent for generaliza-
tion and definition--and of the style for which he was admired--may be seen
in this passage from THE LIFE OF REASON: "The human race, in its intellectual life, is organized like the bees; the masculine soul is a worker, sex-
ually atrophied, and essentially dedicated to impersonal and universal arts; the
feminine is a queen, infinitely fertile, omnipresent in its brooding industry,
but passive and abounding in intuitions without method and passions without
justice."

An excellent summation of Santayana's importance as an American writer despite
his foreign birth and citizenship is provided in Cleanth Brooks et al., eds.,
AMERICAN LITERATURE: THE MAKERS AND THE MAKING (New York: St.
Martin's, 1973), Vol. 2, 1537-41. M.M. Kirkwood, SANTAYANA: SAINT
OF THE IMAGINATION (Toronto: University of Toronto Press, 1961), employs
extensive quotation from the writings to show the values Santayana found in
the imagination. Irving Singer, SANTAYANA'S AESTHETICS: A CRITICAL
INTRODUCTION (Cambridge: Harvard University Press, 1957), is a close
analysis of the concepts underlying Santayana's approach to the arts and his
criticism. Gary R. Stolz, "Santayana in America," NEW ENGLAND QUAR-
TERLY, 50 (1977), 53-67, is an excellent, abundantly annotated survey for
the interested nonspecialist in American attitudes regarding Santayana. Stolz
concludes that Santayana reached his peak only after "he had made his break
with the society that had nurtured his genius."

LINCOLN STEFFENS (1866-1936)

The most important of the muckrakers, Lincoln Steffens was a national
figure from 1904, when THE SHAME OF THE CITIES appeared, until his death
three decades later. His reputation for probity suffered greatly for a time with
the general populace after his notoriously favorable reaction in 1919 to newly
Communist Russia--"I have seen the future and it works"--and he was virulently
attacked long after his death as a Communist dupe or agent, especially during
the cold war years. Only recently have such critics as Justin Kaplan in his
excellent biography begun to remind us that whatever his faults, Steffens "consistently asked the right questions." He represented a "thoroughly native tradition of grass-roots, down-home pragmatic radicalism" independent of foreign
ideologies. His abilities allowed him to become a journalist of great influence,
a respected voice in Franklin D. Roosevelt's first New Deal administration, and
the predecessor in style and tone of such later muckrakers as Ralph Nader.

In addition to Kaplan's LINCOLN STEFFENS: A BIOGRAPHY (New York:
Simon and Schuster, 1974), which is ever better than the author's better-known
book on Mark Twain, see Russell Norton, LINCOLN STEFFENS (New York:
Twayne, 1974), an excellent summary of the life and works. Christopher Lasch,
THE NEW RADICALISM IN AMERICA (New York: Knopf, 1965), provides a
good corrective to the attacks on Steffens in the 1950s as a dogmatic, naive,

and deceptive apologist for communism. The standard work on Steffens and other similar literary activists--including Ray Stannard Baker, Ida Tarbell, S.S. McClure, and Frederick Howe--is Louis Filler, THE MUCKRAKERS: CRUSADERS FOR AMERICAN LIBERALISM (Chicago: Regnery, 1968).

THORSTEIN VEBLEN (1857-1929)

Though often an obscure stylist, Veblen enlivened what he called the "dismal science" of economics with his insights into the foibles of mass society, and especially the faults of capitalism as he saw them. "Conspicuous consumption," "leisure class," "absentee ownership," and "price system," among other phrases coined by him, have become part of our language; and the ideas that they reflect have figured largely in the work of Sinclair Lewis and the later iconoclastic political scientist, C. Wright Mills. Irony and satire were Veblen's means of getting and holding attention in his major work, THE THEORY OF THE LEISURE CLASS (1899), in which his intent was sometimes more to disconcert than to explain. As his fellow social critic Lewis Mumford once noted, Veblen was "one of the half-dozen important figures in scholarship that America has produced since the Civil War," but he was particularly unusual in being "grimly whimsical" like "a stick of dynamite wrapped up to look like a stick of candy." Veblen's audience diminished with his later books, THE THEORY OF BUSINESS ENTERPRISE (1904), THE INSTINCT OF WORKMANSHIP (1914), and THE ENGINEERS AND THE PRICE SYSTEM (1921). Today, he continues to be more talked about than read by the general public, but his influence on thinkers like Mumford is important.

A good, brief introduction with critical bibliography is Douglas Down, THORSTEIN VEBLEN (New York: Washington Square Press, 1964). The basic reference is still Joseph Dorfman, THORSTEIN VEBLEN AND HIS AMERICA (New York: Viking, 1930), which includes a complete bibliography of the subject's works and places him in his epoch. Dorfman also, in "The 'Satire' of Thorstein Veblen's THEORY OF THE LEISURE CLASS," POLITICAL SCIENCE QUARTERLY, 47 (1932), 363-409, shows Veblen using Herbert Spencer's terminology to define modern society in terms of the military and feudal aspects of modern capitalism. The one book on Veblen to combine scholarly insight with lucid style is David Riesman, THORSTEIN VEBLEN: A CRITICAL INTERPRETATION (New York: Scribner's, 1953), which celebrates "the recurrent charm of his intellect, the bite of his sarcasm, the period flavor of his hatreds and affections."

BOOKER T[ALIAFERRO] WASHINGTON (1856-1915)

Satirized as President Bledsoe in Ralph Ellison's famous novel, INVISIBLE MAN (1952), and rejected later by militant blacks as an "oreo" whose primary concern was with black acceptance by whites, Washington's once-illustrious reputation has suffered in recent years. He has been seen as out of step with modern principles of civil-rights activism for his insistence on such bourgeois qualities as industry, thrift, and order, and criticized by Ellison and others for his benevolent despotism as president of Tuskegee Institute for thirty-four years. More recently, though, Washington's insistence on economic self-sufficiency and education as the keys to real integration of the races has been recognized by many as a reasonable alternative to civil disobedience, replacing the appeal to moral indignation which later black leaders often substituted for Washington's belief in accommodation.

Washington's books all date from the turn of the century, beginning with THE FUTURE OF THE AMERICAN NEGRO (1899); his most famous work, and the one most often excerpted for anthologies, is UP FROM SLAVERY (1903), which describes his own extraordinary climb from ignorant servitude to national prominence. In WORKING WITH THE HANDS (1904), PUTTING THE MOST INTO LIFE (1906), and THE NEGRO IN BUSINESS (1907), he stresses the potential for blacks to develop themselves as mechanics, farmers, and artisans. Other works include FREDERICK DOUGLASS (1907) and MY LOWER EDUCATION (1911).

An annotated bibliography is included in a collection of his writings, BOOKER T. WASHINGTON, ed. Emma Lou Thornbrough (New York: Prentice-Hall, 1909); the best recent treatment of the life and works is Louis R. Harlan, BOOKER T. WASHINGTON: THE MAKING OF A BLACK LEADER (New York: Oxford University Press, 1972). THE BLACK AMERICAN REFERENCE BOOK, ed. Mabel M. Smythe (Englewood Cliffs, N.J.: Prentice-Hall, 1976), is a valuable comprehensive view of black American history in all its aspects, and contains numerous references to Washington.

WILLIAM ALLEN WHITE (1865-1944)

Despite his relatively unimpressive post as editor of a newspaper whose subscription list never exceeded seven thousand, in a town famed primarily for being in the geographical center of the country, William Allen White became one of the most admired and respected public figures of his time. "The sage of Emporia" expanded into "the colossus of the prairie," becoming the intimate friend of Franklin D. Roosevelt, an emissary from America's heartland to the corridors of national power. The vitality of his personality is still evident in the pages of his AUTOBIOGRAPHY (1946), one of the most compellingly readable accounts of its kind in our literature. A life-long Republican, but a liberal in the nineteenth-century sense of the word, White celebrated individual initiative and hard work, balanced by generous compassion and good humor, and mourned the passing of preindustrial America when men could take personal satisfaction in their work.

His extraordinary energy resulted in a huge quantity of work, and White's editorials on topics ranging from labor relations to Soviet politics were read with respectful attention by important people in high places. But the most memorable single piece today, and one which gives touching insight into White's own moral strength, compassion, and style, is the obituary he wrote for his daughter Mary, who died in 1921 at the age of fourteen. A model of controlled sentiment, it has been reprinted in hundreds of high school anthologies as an elegy without parallel. It is included in FORTY YEARS ON MAIN STREET, ed. and comp. by Russell H. Fitzgibbon from the files of the EMPORIA GAZETTE (1937). The full listing of his works is A BIBLIOGRAPHY OF WILLIAM ALLEN WHITE (2 vols., Emporia, Kans.: Teachers College Press, 1969). There have been three biographies, of which the latest, John Dewitt McKee, WILLIAM ALLEN WHITE: MAVERICK ON MAIN STREET (Westport, Conn.: Greenwood Press, 1975), is the most useful. It supersedes Everett Rich, WILLIAM ALLEN WHITE: THE MAN FROM EMPORIA (New York: Farrar, 1941), and David Hinshaw, A MAN FROM KANSAS: THE STORY OF WILLIAM ALLEN WHITE (New York: Putnam, 1954).

PHILIP WYLIE (1902-72)

Philip Wylie, an angry moralist who reached a peak of invective with GEN-ERATION OF VIPERS (1944), attacked with equally vehement scorn the "Lib-eral Intellectual Establishment," which he called LIE, and the Communists; organized religion, labor, and big business; sexual promiscuity and sexual re-pression; and, most notoriously, Mom, the great American mother. He thereby managed to offend and entertain almost everyone. Wylie was rewarded for a time--from the early 1930s through the 1940s--with astonishing popularity; he claimed to have received over sixty thousand letters from readers of GENERA-TION OF VIPERS, 95 percent of them admiring; and there is little doubt that Wylie, an extremely prolific writer, reached with his ideas millions of people who were indifferent to more temperate or subtle stylists. His social satire, FINNLEY WREN (1934), and his science-fiction novel, WHEN WORLDS COL-LIDE (with Edwin Balmer, 1933), are still vivid and readable essays in fiction on the frailties of human nature. Wylie has recently found an able advocate in Truman Frederick Keefer, whose PHILIP WYLIE (New York: Twayne, 1977) is a forthright argument that attention should be paid.

Category 2

TEACHERS: GROUP C

Category 2
TEACHERS: GROUP C

JAMES TRUSLOW ADAMS (1879-1949) won the Pulitzer Prize for THE FOUND-ING OF NEW ENGLAND (1921); two of his other best-selling and critically applauded historical works were THE ADAMS FAMILY (1930) and THE EPIC OF AMERICA (1931).

MORTIMER ADLER (1902--), philosopher and educator, is best known to the general public for his best-selling HOW TO READ A BOOK (1940); he has also been closely associated with the ENCYCLOPEDIA BRITANNICA and the Aspen Institute, Aspen, Colorado. Adler published an account of his career entitled PHILOSOPHER AT LARGE: AN INTELLECTUAL BIOGRAPHY (1977).

FREDERICK LEWIS ALLEN (1890-1954) was a popular historian and gifted re-dactor of facts and ideas with an engaging literate style that allows his books to be read today with no diminution of pleasure. ONLY YESTERDAY (1931) was a best-selling examination of the 1920s; it was followed by SINCE YESTER-DAY (1940), a similar book on the 1930s. His last book, THE BIG CHANGE (1952), covers the period from 1900 to 1950.

MARY AUSTIN (1868-1931) was a novelist (SANTA LUCIA, 1908) and a na-turalist (THE LAND OF LITTLE RAIN, 1903) who lived most of her life in California and New Mexico. Her autobiography, EARTH HORIZON (1932), is an account of her literary career.

CURTIS BOK (1865-1930), an immigrant Dutch boy who became the editor of the LADIES HOME JOURNAL when that magazine had literary ambitions, de-scribed his rise to fame and fortune in a curiously naive, self-serving, and charming autobiography, THE AMERICANIZATION OF EDWARD BOK (1920).

CATHERINE DRINKER BOWEN (1897-1973), author of the excellent biography of Oliver Wendell Holmes, YANKEE FROM OLYMPUS (1939), and of JOHN ADAMS AND THE AMERICAN REVOLUTION (1950), was a good friend of

Bernard DeVoto. Like him, she saw the potential for history in the use of narrative and character portrayal, and she had the stylistic tools to do justice to her large themes and subjects.

GAMALIEL BRADFORD (1868-1932) developed a biographical technique which he called the "psychograph," consisting of a montage of significant moments in the subject's life. He wrote widely on the Civil War (LEE THE AMERICAN, 1912, and CONFEDERATE PORTRAITS, 1914). Van Wyck Brooks edited his journal of more than one million words to manageable length in THE JOURNAL OF GAMALIEL BRADFORD (1933).

CARL CARMER (1893-1976) wrote STARS FELL ON ALABAMA (1934), a collection of legends, tales, and myths of that region, and was later general editor of The Rivers of America Series, for which he wrote THE HUDSON (1939).

WILL DURANT (1885--) is still actively working on his popular histories of ideas and social movements; he found the key to public acceptance of, and hunger for, knowledge and ideas in his best-selling THE STORY OF PHILOSOPHY (1926). Will and Ariel Durant's account of their marriage and their long intellectual collaboration was published as A DUAL BIOGRAPHY (New York: Simon and Schuster, 1977). Margaret Schoon, in an untitled essay-review of this volume (MAGILL'S LITERARY ANNUAL: BOOKS OF 1977, Englewood Cliffs, N.J.: Salem Press, 1977, I, 280-82), notes that the Durants' famous enthusiasm for their subject would have come to nothing "were he not a very good and hard-working writer."

STEWART HOLBROOK (1893-1964) found a large audience for his entertaining and accurate accounts of the American past in a number of books, of which LOST MEN OF AMERICAN HISTORY (1946) is a typical example.

MARK ANTHONY DE WOLFE HOWE (1864-1960) was a prolific biographer whose subjects included THE LIFE AND LETTERS OF GEORGE BANCROFT (1908) and BARRETT WENDELL AND HIS LETTERS (1924); the latter won the Pulitzer Prize.

MABEL DODGE LUHAN (1879-1962) is best known for her life with D.H. Lawrence in Taos, New Mexico, recounted in her book, LORENZO IN TAOS (1932). Her autobiography, INTIMATE MEMORIES (3 vols., 1936), is a well of information about American social and literary life during the early twentieth century. Emily Hahn, MABEL: A BIOGRAPHY OF MABEL DODGE LUHAN (Boston: Houghton Mifflin, 1977), traces her life from the salons of New York and Paris to Florence and Greenwich Village and finally to Taos, detailing her acquaintance with Gertrude Stein, John Reed, and, of course, D.H. Lawrence.

THOMAS MERTON (1897-1958) described the circumstances leading to his con-
version to Catholicism in THE SEVEN STOREY MOUNTAIN (1948), a bestseller. Dennis Q. McInerney, THOMAS MERTON: THE MAN AND HIS
WORKS (Spencer, Mass.: Cistercian Publications, 1974) is a brief but pro-
vocative study. See also William Bly, "The Hermit Days of Henry Thoreau
and Thomas Merton," THOREAU SOCIETY BULLETIN, 130 (1975), 2-5.

HENRY PRINGLE (1897-1958) won the Pulitzer Prize for his biography THEO-
DORE ROOSEVELT (1931); a revised edition in 1956 found a new and enthusiastic general audience, and it continues to be a stimulating survey of our
first modern president's life and times.

JAMES HARVEY ROBINSON (1863-1936) was a historian who was influenced
by William James's studies in pragmatism and psychology and wrote a well-
received account of these interests in THE MIND IN THE MAKING (1921).

CONSTANCE ROURKE (1885-1941) wrote AUDUBON (1936), a biography of
the great painter and naturalist which was praised by Henry Seidel Canby as
a "narrative essay upon the life of a wanderer of genius." Her book AMERI-
CAN HUMOR (1921) remains one of the best studies of that subject.

IRVING STONE (1903--) popularized a new genre, the biographical novel,
with his life of Jack London, SAILOR ON HORSEBACK (1938). For an interesting account of the continuing controversy which this book aroused, see
Richard W. Etulain, "The Lives of Jack London," WESTERN AMERICAN LIT-
ERATURE, 11, No. 2 (1976), 149-64.

HENDRIK VAN LOON (1882-1944), born in Holland, came to the United
States as a young man and graduated from Cornell. He was the first and still
remains the most successful popularizer of scientific subjects, most notably in
his best-selling THE STORY OF MANKIND (1921).

Category 3

REPORTERS

Category 3

REPORTERS

Writers who observe and record their impressions of what they see chiefly to inform, rather than to entertain or to teach, range from the glamorous foreign correspondent to the solitary bird-watcher. While they may seem to have little in common, they share an interest in conveying their sense of the way things--including nature, politics, and human relationships--work. Relatively few writers in this category in the period from 1900 to 1950 have been awarded the kind of recognition given their peers in the first two categories of this present guide. Only James Agee seems to be accepted as a reporter of major importance, and there are not many others in the second rank, group B. There are, however, a number of interesting writers who deserve mention and are described briefly in group C.

It should be noted that one reason for the relative lack of major writers in this category is that the marked increase of interest in natural history and ecology which we now note seems to have developed for the most part after 1950. Loren Eiseley's THE IMMENSE JOURNEY (1957) and Edwin Way Teale's NORTH WITH THE SPRING (1951) and his subsequent narratives of his travels are works of considerable literary merit which do not quite fall within the confines of this volume. Similarly, Joseph Wood Krutch's THE DESERT YEAR (1952), Rachel Carson's THE SEA AROUND US (1951), Paul Horgan's GREAT RIVER: THE RIO GRANDE IN NORTH AMERICAN HISTORY (1954), David Lavender's BENT'S FORT (1954), Robert Murphy's PEREGRINE FALCON (1963), and J. Frank Dobie's THE MUSTANGS (1952) are excluded. It is worth remembering that two of the most popular nonfiction books in recent years have been Robert Ardrey's THE TERRITORIAL IMPERATIVE (1966) and Alvin Toffler's FUTURE SHOCK (1970), works by an amateur anthropologist and a sociologist which suggest that the trend toward nature writing and interpretive reportage is becoming increasingly strong. This trend was anticipated by the writers included below. For further information see also:

Borland, Hal, ed. OUR NATURAL WORLD: THE LAND AND WILDLIFE OF AMERICA AS SEEN AND DESCRIBED BY WRITERS SINCE THE COUNTRY'S DISCOVERY. New York: Doubleday, 1966.

> This 850-page collection by one of our most distinguished contemporary writers on nature includes selections from the well-known (Paul Horgan, Loren Eiseley) to the obscure-but-worth-knowing (Aldo Leopold, John Kieran).

Lamar, Howard R., ed. THE READER'S ENCYCLOPEDIA OF THE AMERICAN WEST. New York: Crowell, 1977.

> One of the major bibliographical efforts in recent years, this is an exhaustive and engrossing account of Western history, biography, and letters; it contains information on John Muir and some of the other writers mentioned in this present guide.

Teale, Edwin Way, ed. GREEN TREASURY. New York: Dodd Mead, 1952.

> Ranging widely, from Aristotle to Tao Yung Ming, this collection includes selections from several writers noted in this present guide, including William Beebe and Mary Austin.

Ternes, Alan, ed. ANTS, INDIANS, AND LITTLE DINOSAURS. New York: Scribner's, 1975.

> The selections here are from the American Museum of Natural History's magazine, NATURAL HISTORY, and span the last seventy-five years; they are as eclectic as the title indicates, reflecting the reputation of the magazine as "off-beat," a product of the museum's "bewildering, glorious diversity."

True, Webster P., ed. SMITHSONIAN TREASURE OF SCIENCE. 3 vols. New York: Simon and Schuster, 1960.

> Selections have been culled from three thousand articles which have appeared in the series called SMITHSONIAN REPORTS (from 1846-1958). The fifty articles selected represent observations on significant events in the physical and natural sciences, including anthropology, for the general reader. Ranging from Einstein on Newton to Wendell Stanley on "The Nature of Viruses, Genes, and Life"--that is, from the eminent to the unknown, the large to the small--the essays are distinguished by an earnest clarity rather than by ease of style; but taken as a whole they constitute at least the beginning of a liberal education in the modern history of science.

Category 3

REPORTERS: GROUP A

JAMES AGEE (1909-55)

Commonly considered a "genius with words," James Agee achieved lasting distinction with his autobiographical novel, A DEATH IN THE FAMILY (1957). For the purposes of this volume, however, he is important as the journalist who created art out of the documentary form in his text for LET US NOW PRAISE FAMOUS MEN (1941), on the plight of southern sharecroppers. The book grew out of an assignment for FORTUNE magazine in 1936, which required Agee and the photographer Walker Evans to spend several weeks living with Alabama sharecropper families to get accurate background information for a magazine article. The editors of FORTUNE decided not to publish the resulting article, and it first appeared as a book in 1941.

As a movie reviewer (for TIME, primarily) who saw the artistic potential of film and did much to help develop it, Agee combined a fan's enthusiasm, a poet's sense of language, and a scriptwriter's sense of structure and dialogue. His reviews and articles have been collected in AGEE ON FILM (1958). An eclectic writer (he did the lyrics for CANDIDE and the screenplay for THE AFRICAN QUEEN in addition to his other works) with an interest in stylistic form, Agee conveys a sense of nostalgic melancholy in much of his work. The consequent depth which it sometimes displays accounts for his continuing popularity today.

PRINCIPAL WORKS

PERMIT ME VOYAGE, 1934
LET US NOW PRAISE FAMOUS MEN, 1941
THE MORNING WATCH, 1951 (Novel)
A DEATH IN THE FAMILY, 1957 (Novel)
AGEE ON FILM: REVIEWS AND COMMENTS, 1958
AGEE ON FILM: FIVE FILM SCRIPTS, 1960
FOUR EARLY STORIES BY JAMES AGEE, 1964
THE COLLECTED SHORT PROSE OF JAMES AGEE. Ed. Robert Fitzgerald, 1968
THE COLLECTED POEMS OF JAMES AGEE. Ed. Robert Fitzgerald, 1968

James Agee

LETTERS

THE LETTERS OF JAMES AGEE TO FATHER FLYE. Ed. James H. Flye. New York: George Brazillier, 1962.

THE LETTERS OF JAMES AGEE TO FATHER FLYE. 2nd ed. Boston: Houghton Mifflin, 1971.

> This edition also contains the letters of Flye to Agee.

BIBLIOGRAPHY

Fabre, Genevieve. "A Bibliography of the Works of James Agee." BULLETIN OF BIBLIOGRAPHY, 24 (1965), 145-48, 163-66.

CRITICAL WORKS

Barson, Alfred T. A WAY OF SEEING: A CRITICAL STUDY OF JAMES AGEE. Amherst: University of Massachusetts Press, 1972.

> The development of Agee's artistic consciousness is traced here.

Broughton, George. "Agee and Autonomy." SOUTHERN HUMANITIES REVIEW, 4 (1970), 101-11.

> This article examines Agee's concept of individualism.

Chase, Richard. "Sense and Sensibility." KENYON REVIEW, 13 (1951), 688-91.

> Chase comments on problems with the symbolism in Agee's minor novel, THE MORNING WATCH.

Chesnick, Eugene. "The Plot Against Fiction." SOUTHERN LITERARY JOURNAL, 4 (1972), 48-67.

> Agee's fictional techniques are attacked.

Gregor, Charles, and William Dorman. "The Children of James Agee." JOURNAL OF POPULAR CULTURE, 9 (1976), 996-1002.

> The authors discuss the "new journalism" and argue that several writers are followers of Agee in their use of "the ideas, the language, and the techniques of fiction." Joan Didion, Tom Wolfe, and Norman Mailer are judged as some of these.

Holder, Alan. "Encounter in Alabama: Agee and the Tenant Farmer." VIRGINIA QUARTERLY REVIEW, 48 (1966), 189-206.

This is an analysis of some of the problems encountered in attempting to establish critical distance, because of Agee's ability to convey his personal sympathy for the farmers in LET US NOW PRAISE FAMOUS MEN.

Hynes, Samuel. "James Agee: LET US NOW PRAISE FAMOUS MEN." In LANDMARKS IN AMERICAN WRITINGS. Ed. Hennig Cohen. New York: Basic Books, 1969, pp. 328-40.

This is an overview of Agee's journalistic method.

Kramer, Victoria. "Agee and Plans for the Criticism of Popular Culture." JOURNAL OF POPULAR CULTURE, 5 (1972), 755-66.

This account is based largely on unpublished manuscript materials describing Agee's interest in the criticism of popular culture.

_____. "Agee's LET US NOW PRAISE FAMOUS MEN: Images of Tenant Life." MISSISSIPPI QUARTERLY, 25 (1972) 405-17.

The author examines Agee's text as an image of American life.

_____. JAMES AGEE. New York: Twayne, 1975.

Agee's fiction receives the most attention, but Kramer argues strongly for consideration of the nonfiction as art.

Larsen, Erling. JAMES AGEE. Minneapolis: University of Minnesota Press, 1971.

This is a useful introduction to Agee's life and major works.

MacDonald, Dwight. "James Agee." In his AGAINST THE AMERICAN GRAIN. New York: Random House, 1965, pp. 143-66.

The journalistic and cultural critic recalls his acquaintance with Agee and surveys the writings.

Madden, David, ed. REMEMBERING JAMES AGEE. Baton Rouge: Louisiana State University Press, 1974.

Agee's widow and other persons who knew him well contributed essays and recollections.

Ohlin, Peter H. AGEE. New York: Obolensky, 1966.

This is one of the more detailed and only partially favorable commentaries about Agee's work.

Oulahan, Richard. "A Cult Grew Around a Many-Sided Writer." LIFE, 1 November 1963, pp. 69-72.

Perry J. Douglas, Jr. "Thematic Counterpoint in A DEATH IN THE FAMILY: The Function of the Six Extra Scenes." NOVEL, 5 (1972), 234-41.

In this analysis, the nonsequential parts of the novel are shown to be parts of an artistically unified whole.

Phillipson, John S. "Character, Theme, and Symbol in THE MORNING WATCH." WESTERN HUMANITIES REVIEW, 15 (1961), 359-67.

The intricate structure of the novella is explicated.

Ramsey, Roger. "The Double Structure of THE MORNING WATCH." STUDIES IN THE NOVEL, 4 (1972), 494-503.

The narrative and the "triptych" structure are shown as balancing and supporting each other.

Ruoff, Gene W. "A DEATH IN THE FAMILY: Agee's 'Unfinished' Novel." In THE FIFTIES. Ed. Warren French. Deland, Fla.: Everett-Edwards, 1970, pp. 121-32.

The introductory essay comments on the predominant ideas in Agee's novel.

Rupp, Richard H. "James Agee: The Elegies of Innocence." In his CELE-BRATION IN POST-WAR AMERICAN FICTION. Coral Gables: University of Miami Press, 1972, pp. 99-111.

This article deals with the lament for lost innocence in THE MORNING WATCH and in A DEATH IN THE FAMILY.

Seib, Kenneth. JAMES AGEE: PROMISE AND FULFILLMENT. Pittsburgh: University of Pittsburgh Press, 1968.

Seib surveys the works, praising the fiction but finding the non-fiction of much less value.

Stott, William. DOCUMENTARY EXPRESSION AND THIRTIES AMERICA. New York: Oxford University Press, 1973.

This is an essential study of the documentary genre, with separate chapters on Evans' photographs and Agee's text of LET US NOW PRAISE FAMOUS MEN.

Townsend, R.C. "The Possibilities of Field Work." COLLEGE ENGLISH, 34 (1973), 481-99.

LET US NOW PRAISE FAMOUS MEN is discussed as one of
several works which relate the study of literature to "life."

Wensberg, Erik. "Celebration, Adoration and Wonder." NATION, 194
(1960), 417-18.

This is a brief but perceptive appreciation of LET US NOW
PRAISE FAMOUS MEN.

Category 3

REPORTERS: GROUP B

WILLIAM BEEBE (1877-1962)

William Beebe gained international attention in 1934 when his bathysphere descended to record-breaking depths in the ocean near Bermuda. An unusually gifted man who combined the attributes of artist and scientist, Beebe was the curator of ornithology for the New York Zoological Society from 1899 until his death, but his range of interests was far greater than this academic title suggests. His chapters on insects in EDGE OF THE JUNGLE (1921) are reminiscent of Thoreau's description of the battle of the ants in WALDEN for their minute observation of nature and for their recognition that man and nature are closely linked. Some of his more familiar titles are THE LOG OF THE SUN (1906), PHEASANT JUNGLES (1927), and HALF MILE DOWN (1934).

Beebe's life and career are ably described by Robert Henry Walker, NATURAL MAN: THE LIFE OF WILLIAM BEEBE (Bloomington: Indiana University Press, 1975). Though the study lacks a critical bibliography, it contains good chaper endnotes, is very well written, and concludes with an excellent chapter called "The Finality of Words," which is helpful not only for its comments on Beebe's style but in placing him among other American naturalists--noting, for example, that Beebe anticipated Rachel Carson's famous SILENT SPRING in his concern for ecological integrity.

RICHARD HARDING DAVIS (1864-1916)

Though he may be "deservedly forgotten" now, in the harsh judgment of a later critic, Richard Harding Davis was the very model of the dashing foreign correspondent during his lifetime. Anticipating Ernest Hemingway's famous adventures in war, Davis was motivated by a similar desire to see the front; he charged up San Juan Hill with Teddy Roosevelt during the Spanish-American War and was almost shot during World War I by the Germans as a spy. Davis' romantic but verified adventures were transformed into popular fiction, of which SOLDIERS OF FORTUNE (1902) is the best known, as well as a number of popular plays. Nonfiction titles include THREE GRINGOS IN VENEZUELA AND CENTRAL AMERICA (1896) and WITH THE FRENCH IN FRANCE AND SALONIKA (1916). Robert Waldon, "Around the World with Swash and Buckle," AMERICAN HERITAGE, 18 (August 1967), 56-59, 71-74, provides a cheerful

survey of Davis' lively career; two earlier books, Fairfax Downey, RICHARD
HARDING DAVIS: HIS DAY (New York: Scribner's, 1933) and Gerald Lansford,
THE RICHARD HARDING DAVIS YEARS (New York: Holt, Rinehart and Winston,
1961), have recently been augmented by Scott Osborne and Robert Phillips,
Jr., RICHARD HARDING DAVIS (New York: Twayne, 1979).

JOHN GUNTHER (1901-70)

A talented, energetic reporter, John Gunther was famous as the author of
"inside" books about different nations and regions, beginning with INSIDE
EUROPE (1936) and continuing until the posthumous INSIDE AUSTRALIA (1972)
was published. Ten of his books were Book-of-the-Month Club selections, and
he wrote a number of books for children. Gunther was not a scholar or a
philosopher, and his books were not noted for depth of insight; but he was able
to convey the particular nature of particular places through a skillful amalga-
mation of data and anecdote in a way that has not been duplicated since his
death. His best book in terms of literary value is his affecting account of his
son's fatal illness, DEATH BE NOT PROUD (1949).

JOHN MUIR (1838-1914)

The dean of nature writers, John Muir was profoundly influenced by his father's
stern Calvinism on the one hand and by Emersonian Transcendentalism on the
other. His works reflect, accordingly, a deep reverence for nature and a
sense of man's duty to find his proper place in it. Muir is memorialized today
by the famous trail through the Sierra Nevada range of mountains that he loved,
in California, and which has as its center the Yosemite Valley described with
incomparable vividness in MY FIRST SUMMER IN THE SIERRA (1961). In addition to this book, the most important of Muir's works are THE STORY OF MY
BOYHOOD AND YOUTH (1965), A THOUSAND-MILE WALK TO THE GULF
(1915), TRAVELS IN ALASKA (1915), and THE CRUISE OF THE CORWIN (1917).

Despite the quality and quantity of his written work, Muir had difficulty thinking
of himself simply as a writer, and with good reason. As the founder of the
Sierra Club, which has become one of the strongest national forces for the
preservation of the wilderness, his contributions are political as well as philosophical and aesthetic. There is as yet no full biography of Muir, but his life
and works are surveyed in Herbert P. Smith, JOHN MUIR (New York: Twayne,
1965), a useful overview which contains a good bibliography. Thomas J. Lyon,
JOHN MUIR (Western Writers Series, No. 3. Boise, Idaho: Boise State Col-,
ege, 1972), shows how Muir rejected his father's Calvinism. Harold P. Simonson,
"The Tempered Romanticism of John Muir," WESTERN AMERICAN LITERATURE,
13 (1978), 227-42, provides an important elaboration of the significance of
Lyon's insight in terms of Muir's idealization of nature.

JOHN REED (1887-1920)

John Reed was a wealthy Harvard graduate whose interest in social problems was heightened by his friendship with Lincoln Steffens and Max Eastman. He visited Mexico during one major revolution and wrote INSURGENT MEXICO (1914). Reed later became a sympathetic supporter and friend of Lenin during the Russian Revolution and provided a still-vivid eyewitness account of the uprising in TEN DAYS THAT SHOOK THE WORLD (1919). Reed enjoyed the sympathetic attention of a number of writers during his short but eventful life and is the subject of a biography, JOHN REED (1936), by Granville Hicks. Robert Rosenstone's ROMANTIC REVOLUTIONARY: A BIOGRAPHY OF JOHN REED (New York: Knopf, 1975) was applauded on its publication by the liberal NEW REPUBLIC and damned by the conservative NATIONAL REVIEW for its lengthy and sympathetic portrayal of its subject.

ERNEST THOMPSON SETON (1860-1946)

Although he was born in England and raised in Canada, Ernest Thompson Seton is usually listed as an American writer and is too important as a popularizer of nature writing to be forgotten. WILD ANIMALS I HAVE KNOWN (1898) was his most famous early book, and LIVES OF GAME ANIMALS (4 vols., 1925-28) won a prize for excellence in nature writing. BIOGRAPHY OF A GRIZZLY (1900), LIVES OF THE HUNTED (1901), and BIOGRAPHY OF AN ARCTIC FOX (1937) are among his other books. Seton was criticized for being a "nature-faker" in his books for younger readers, indulging in sentimental anthropomorphism; but Hal Borland in his anthology OUR NATURAL WORLD (1965) says Seton's "lore is sound and the natural history is well observed."

GEORGE R[IPLEY] STEWART (1895-1980)

George R. Stewart was an unconventional writer whose fiction is essentially documentary narrative about natural phenomena. STORM (1941) describes the path of a typhoon and FIRE (1948) is a similar story about a forest fire. His nonfiction account of the Donner party in the critically acclaimed ORDEAL BY HUNGER (1937) is distinguished by its combination of scholarship (Stewart was an English professor at the University of California) and insight into the emotions of people under stress. NAMES ON THE LAND (1945) is a fascinating account of the derivations of American place names; and MAN, AN AUTO-BIOGRAPHY (1946) examines the cultural career of mankind as though it were one individual.

Category 3

REPORTERS: GROUP C

Category 3

REPORTERS: GROUP C

HENRY BESTON (the pseudonym of Henry Beston Sheahan, 1888-1968) wrote
THE OUTERMOST HOUSE (1928), a description of an Atlantic storm he wit-
nessed from his house on Cape Cod in 1927 which has the vividness of Joseph
Conrad's sea stories. Clarissa M. Lorenz's "Henry Beston: The Outermost
Man," ATLANTIC, 16 (1978), 107-10, is an interview with the poet Elizabeth
Coatesworth, Beston's widow, which deals with the art and craft of the retiring
naturalist and author.

BRUCE BLIVEN (1889-1977) was editor of THE NEW REPUBLIC from 1930 to
1955 and wrote a number of books about modern American politics and culture,
in addition to writing about science. His autobiography is FIVE MILLION
WORDS LATER (1970). He figures interestingly as a minor character in Wallace
Stegner's novel, THE SPECTATOR BIRD (1976).

HEYWOOD BROUN (1888-1939) was recognized as a presence, somewhat like
Dr. Johnson, more than as a writer, even though he wrote widely and well
about sports, the theater, and contemporary events with great gusto. Both his
appeal and his limitations can be inferred from the title of a collection of
dramatic reviews called PIECES OF HATE, AND OTHER ENTHUSIASMS (1922).
See Richard O'Connor, HEYWOOD BROUN (New York: Putnam, 1975) for a
competent journalistic biography.

JANET FLANNER (1892-1978) wrote columns from Paris under the pen name
"Genet" for THE NEW YORKER for half a century. Mary Blume, "The Enduring
Journalism of Janet Flanner," LOS ANGELES TIMES, November 26, 1978,
"Calendar," p. 68, praises Flanner's prose as "sonorous and succinct," com-
bining French rationality with a taste for extravagance.

PAUL GALLICO (1897-1976) wrote the moving war story THE SNOW GOOSE
(1941) and an excellent acrid analysis of athletics in FAREWELL TO SPORT
(1938). He is the subject of an article by V.V.B. Rama, "The Achievement
of Paul Gallico," INDIAN JOURNAL OF AMERICAN STUDIES, 4 (1978), 78-88.

RICHARD HALLIBURTON (1900-1939) was the favorite writer of escape-minded and, later, Depression-grounded readers, in such works as THE ROYAL ROAD TO ROMANCE (1925) and THE FLYING CARPET (1932), books which described his travels around the world. He disappeared at sea in 1939, trying to sail a Chinese junk across the Sea of Japan.

ALDO LEOPOLD (1887-1948) wrote several books while working in the U.S. Forestry Service and in the field of wildlife management. A SAND COUNTY ALMANAC (1949) has become a classic of conservationist literature.

CAREY McWILLIAMS (1905-1980), editor for many years of THE NATION, wrote two essential books about California history, mores, and politics: SOUTHERN CALIFORNIA COUNTRY: AN ISLAND ON THE LAND (1946) and CALIFORNIA: THE GREAT EXCEPTION (1949).

DONALD CULROSS PEATTIE (1898-1964), trained as a botanist, wrote an impressionistic account of Audubon's life, SINGING IN THE WILDERNESS (1935), and two acclaimed histories of America's woodlands, A NATURAL HISTORY OF TREES OF EASTERN AND CENTRAL AMERICA (1950), and A NATURAL HISTORY OF WESTERN TREES (1953).

ROGER TORY PETERSON (1908--) is the birdman of America, credited with doing more than any other writer since Audubon to educate the public about birds. A typical collection is BIRDS OVER AMERICA (1948). John C. Devlin's THE WORLD OF ROGER TORY PETERSON (New York: New York Times Books and Harper and Row, 1978) is an authorized biography which effectively details Peterson's accomplishments in education, conservation, and art.

GRANTLAND RICE (1880-1954) was the country's leading sportswriter for many years. His autobiography is THE TUMULT AND THE SHOUTING (1954).

[JAMES] VINCENT SHEEAN (1899--) wrote biographies of Gandhi (LEAD, KINGLY LIGHT, 1949) and Edna St. Vincent Millay (THE INDIGO BUNTING, 1951) and works on Verdi, Nehru, and Sinclair Lewis, in addition to several novels. His best book may be PERSONAL HISTORY (1936), his autobiographical account of the growing tension in Europe during the years between World Wars I and II. A recent indication of scholarly interest in his life is the Ph.D. dissertation by Carl E. Johnson, "A Twentieth-Century Seeker: A Biography of James Vincent Sheean" (University of Wisconsin, 1975).

JOSHUA SLOCUM (1844-1909) is known to all sailors worth their salt as "the Thoreau of the sea" for his classic travel adventure, SAILING ALONE AROUND THE WORLD (1900). William M. Teller's THE SEARCH FOR CAPTAIN SLOCUM (New York: Scribner's, 1956) is an account of Slocum's life and his disappearance on a voyage in 1909.

LOWELL [JACKSON] THOMAS (1892--), still active as a broadcaster, has written a great number of books since his first, LAWRENCE OF ARABIA (1925). Peripatetic and prolific, he conveys in his books the calm certainty and poise amidst excitement and sometimes danger that still mark his radio broadcasts.

DOROTHY THOMPSON (1894-1961) was a foreign correspondent whose life with Sinclair Lewis is recorded in Vincent Sheean's DOROTHY AND RED (1963). Marion Sanders, DOROTHY THOMPSON: A LEGEND IN HER TIME (Boston: Houghton Mifflin, 1973), makes a persuasive case for her importance.

AMERICAN CRITICISM, 1900-1950

INTRODUCTION: LITERARY CRITICISM

A. SCHOOLS OF CRITICISM

1. Expressionism and Impressionism

Twentieth-century American criticism began with a lecture. Joel Elias Spingarn (1875-1939), a literary historian of Renaissance criticism from Columbia University and one of the founders of the National Association for the Advancement of Colored People, gave an address in 1910 entitled "The New Criticism." Spingarn had been influenced by the Italian aesthetician Benedetto Croce, whose genetic theory of expressionism extolled the experience of the writer during the act of creation. Spingarn's idea of "new" was very different from the textualist and concrete theories of the New Critics who rose to prominence in the early 1940s. "Criticism" is "the study of expression," announced Spingarn, and the best criticism shares the expressive power of what it is judging. "Taste and genius are one." In addition to insisting that the critic must become "at one with the creator," Spingarn maintained that moral standards and literary historicism were unsuitable as criteria for criticism.

James Gibbons Huneker (1860-1921) also had no use for moral criteria. Between 1899 and 1910 he practiced impressionist criticism, the celebration of the affective pleasures of reading. Inspired by Anatole France's "adventures among masterpieces," Huneker's enthusiastic responses to music, art, and books made him a living example of his own doctrine. Literature was not something pallid and genteel but rich in claps of thunder and Wagnerian crescendos--and Huneker vibrated to them all.[1] Huneker's _impressionism_ and Spingarn's _expressionism_, although opposites on the surface, were actually twin muses: a deep look at the reader, a deep look at the writer.

Many years later William Kurtz Wimsatt, Jr. (1907-75), an aesthetician and critic closely identified with the contextualist theories of the New Critics, disturbed by the lack of reliable standards or systematic theory in either impressionism or expressionism, dismissed them both as the "Affective and Intentional Fallacies."[2] Nevertheless, the ultimate effect of both Huneker's and Spingarn's insistence that the critical response mattered, and that it must shake itself free of academic dust and moral preconceptions, was precisely the value the New Critics ultimately methodized into a close look at the text. Despite their strong aversion to what Huneker and Spingarn stood for, the New Critics owe something of their ascendancy in the first half of this century to the forces Huneker and Spingarn set in motion. Spingarn had said criticism was as important as the art it judged. And that idea held, regardless of the theoretical nature of the criticism itself.

2. The New Humanism

Spingarn reserved one of his strongest volleys in the 1910 lecture for the New Humanists (or Neo-Humanists): "We have done with all moral judgment of literature. . . . No critic of authority now tests literature by the standards of ethics." Somewhat ahead of their time, these were provoking words in 1910 when the New Humanists, Irving Babbitt and Paul Elmer More (part 3, sections A and G) were just beginning to make a national impression.[3] By the 1920s, their decade, the New Humanists almost dominated American criticism. In a time of moral laxity and materialistic self-indulgence, they seemed just what the dormant conscience needed. Babbitt and More felt that moral enlightenment was the principal criterion for value in literature. Such enlightenment was to be found primarily in the classical because in this mode the aesthetic of restraint and the celebration of ethical will went hand in hand. It cost them the enmity of expressionists, impressionists, and social reformers, but the New Humanists rejected both Romanticism and Naturalism. The former rested on "Rousseauistic emotionalism" and encouraged democratic vulgarity; the latter flaunted an impiously antireligious, scientific, and philosophical determinism. More's pursuit of the "One in the Many" led him to Plato and, ultimately, a passionate Christian mysticism. T.S. Eliot (part 3, section F) and the New Critics categorically rejected the New Humanist principle that literature must have a moral intention, but they largely accepted the conservative political and religious assumptions underlying the cultural humanism informing the movement as a whole.

In THE GENTEEL TRADITION AT BAY (New York: Scribner's, 1931), George Santayana (1863-1952), who spoke with as much urbanity as any New Humanist, faulted Babbitt and More for their parochial morality and misguided attitude toward Naturalism. This attack represented the culmination of a growing general disillusionment in the critical community with the New Humanism.[4] Only one year before Santayana published his book, the New Humanists had defiantly gathered their views in a symposium edited by Norman Foerster, HUMANISM AND AMERICA: ESSAYS ON THE OUTLOOK OF MODERN CIVILIZATION (New York: Farrar and Rinehart, 1930).[5] In a promptly fired counterblast, C. Hartley Grattan edited THE CRITIQUE OF HUMANISM: A SYMPOSIUM (New York: Brewer and Warren, 1930). The contributors to Grattan's volume constituted a broad cross-section of contemporary critical opinion: social critics with radical leanings, apologists for science, and New Critics in various shades of budding formalism.[6]

3. Liberal and Radical Criticism

The economic and social dislocation of the 1930s did more finally to dislodge the New Humanists than any of the critical blasts directed against them. At the same time, the "Great Depression" provided the leftist critics their last opportunity, perhaps until the 1960s, to capture the critical forum. From approximately 1910 to the beginning of World War II, radical critics produced a great deal of interesting literary journalism, reviews, and polemics, but their ideas about literature did not achieve lasting statement through the thought or theory of any great individual critics.[7]

Long before the 1930s, Van Wyck Brooks (part 3, section D) in AMERICA'S COMING OF AGE (1915) had espoused socialism as both a corrective to Puritan materialism and an inspiration toward reaffirming the democratic ideal, but he moved from socialism to psychological criticism and finally to a literary nationalism. Kenneth Burke and Edmund Wilson (part 3, sections E and K) identified early in their careers with Marxist theory. Although Burke never completely disavowed these leanings, his criticism took a psychological and "dramatistic" direction that obscures, and certainly disguises, any latent Marxism. Wilson's disillusionment with Russian communism led him to a cosmopolitan and left-of-center historicism. At the end of the forties, Lionel Trilling (part 3, section J) eloquently transformed political criticism into cultural criticism with the publication of THE LIBERAL IMAGINATION (1950). Trilling urged the "liberal imagination" to reassert its "awareness of complexity and difficulty."

Radical criticism, all over the world, has always been intimately connected with magazines and journals, the traditional voices of manifesto and agitation. Except for one or two histories (part 1, section C), this is certainly true of American leftist literary criticism. The first important radical magazine was the MASSES, published in Greenwich Village from 1911 to 1917. Although it did not preach doctrinal communism or urge revolutionary violence, it attacked bourgeois institutions with such vigor that the government succumbed to reactionary pressure and closed its doors in 1917. The magazine had been edited by Max Eastman (1883-1969) and Floyd Dell (1887-1969), who promptly started another, the LIBERATOR, which continued the policies of the MASSES from 1918 to 1924 when Communist ties absorbed it into the WORKERS MONTHLY.[8] Both MASSES and LIBERATOR championed writers like Whitman and Dreiser but devoted the bulk of their articles to social and political questions. Contributors from 1912 to 1923 included muckrakers and reformers, popular literary editors and journalist adventurers, Communist poets and novelists. The NEW MASSES, which first appeared in 1926, soon became explicitly Marxist when Michael Gold (1893-1967) took over the editorship in 1928. Ironically echoing Horace Greeley, Gold issued his war cry, "Go Left, Young Writers!" The NEW MASSES attracted writers radicalized by the economic collapse as well as expatriates of the war generation who were returning to America.[9] Another significant journal of this period that published criticism was the MODERN QUARTERLY, A JOURNAL OF RADICAL OPINION, printed in Baltimore between 1923 and 1928. In the early 1930s it changed its title to the MODERN MONTHLY. In the 1920s it was edited by V.F. Calverton (1900-1940) and

S.D. Schmalhausen and in the 1930s, briefly, by Max Eastman and Edmund Wilson. Marxist and Freudian perspectives dominated the criticism.

The last, and the most impressive from a critical point of view, of the radical journals of the 1930s was the PARTISAN REVIEW. Appearing in 1934, the same year that the NEW MASSES became a political weekly, it was committed to communism by its editors, Philip Rahv (1908-1973) and William Phillips. However, its editorials and articles showed sympathy for avant-garde writers who were only vaguely, if at all, to the Left. In December 1937, appalled by the Moscow purges and the growing totalitarianism of international communism, the journal declared itself independent of the Communist party and openly identified with the cultural value of the nonpolitical "aesthetic revolt" characteristic of modern literature. Because they believed that most proletarian literature had oversimplified social problems, the editors of PARTISAN REVIEW encouraged criticism of great novels by bourgeois writers whose work had intentionally or incidentally fed the revolutionary cause. Essay-articles by Edmund Wilson on Flaubert, by Rahv on Dostoyevsky, and by William Troy on D.H. Lawrence established a new standard in American literary criticism by intellectuals identified with the Left. By the 1940s the PARTISAN REVIEW was accepting major pieces by the New Critics, formalists known for their political conservatism. T.S. Eliot's "Notes Towards the Definition of Culture" appeared in 1944. In 1946, when William Barrett joined the staff as editor, the journal introduced American readers to French existentialism.[10]

4. The New Criticism and the Neo-Aristotelians

Both I.A. Richards (1893-1979), the British psychologist and literary theorist, and T.S. Eliot strongly influenced the group of largely southern critics who, under the leadership of John Crowe Ransom (part 3, section H), identified their approach as the "New Criticism" in 1941. Richards' emphasis on the structure and texture of the language of poetry, together with Eliot's traditionalism and orthodoxy, his impersonal theory of art (an aversion to all forms of impressionism and didacticism), and his urging of a technical criticism met and educated the predilections of Ransom, Allen Tate (part 3, section I), Cleanth Brooks (part 3, section C), and, eventually, R.P. Blackmur (part 3, section B).

The founders of the New Criticism developed their early ideas about literature and life in two affiliations: as students and teachers at Vanderbilt University where they discussed one another's verse and then published it in a journal entitled the FUGITIVE, edited by Ransom from 1922 to 1928, and as supporters of the Agrarian movement, a conservative answer to the economic disasters of the Depression. Whereas the radical and Marxist critics championed the working class and condemned capitalism, the Agrarians championed the agricultural class, particularly the small-propertied farmer, and condemned industrialism. In 1930 the Agrarians published their manifesto (the same year Foerster edited HUMANISM AND AMERICA; see this Introduction, above), a symposium entitled I'LL TAKE MY STAND: THE SOUTH AND THE AGRARIAN TRADITION (New York: Harper, 1930).[11] Four of the twelve southern contributors were from the fugitive group (Donald Davidson, Ransom, Tate, and Robert Penn Warren).

The New Critics also contributed articles to the AMERICAN REVIEW (1933-1937), a forum for a variety of conservatives: Hilaire Belloc and G.K. Chesterton's English "Distributionists," the American New Humanists, neoscholastics, and some Fascist sympathizers.[12]

After the publication of UNDERSTANDING POETRY (1938), the textbook by Cleanth Brooks and Robert Penn Warren (1905--), the basic New Critical contextualist principles--that form and content are finally indistinguishable--were soon established in college English departments throughout the nation. Ransom advocated the turning from historical and philological questions to textualism in THE WORLD'S BODY, published the same year as UNDERSTANDING POETRY. In the 1940s the New Criticism continued successfully to challenge the dominance of the literary historians in the academy. The publication by René Wellek (1903--) and Austin Warren (1899--) of THEORY OF LITERATURE (New York: Harcourt, Brace, 1949) firmly established the new ascendancy of criticism over literary history--or, for that matter, over any form of literary inquiry that wandered from textualism. To spell out the relationship of poetics and criticism to research and literary history, Wellek and Warren divided the study of literature into extrinsic and intrinsic approaches; the intrinsic (formalist, textualist) is decidedly favored. While THEORY OF LITERATURE helped secure their position in the graduate schools, the New Critics had added to the prestige of their ideas by editing journals which attracted some of the best English and American critics of the time. Cleanth Brooks and Robert Penn Warren were associate editors of the SOUTHERN REVIEW from 1935 to 1941 and editors from 1941 to 1942; John Crowe Ransom edited the KENYON REVIEW from 1939 to the late 1950s; and Allen Tate edited the SEWANEE REVIEW from 1944 to 1946.

Strong in practice but often considered weak in theory, the New Critics have aroused able defenders and articulate enemies. One of their most impressive champions, W.K. Wimsatt, Jr. (see this INTRODUCTION above), stressed the critical need for their textualist methods: "If we are to lay hold of the poetic art . . . and if it is to pass as a critical object, it must by hypostatized."[13] William Elton published A GLOSSARY OF THE NEW CRITICISM (Chicago: Modern Poetry Association, 1949) to clarify New Critical terms (e.g., irony, paradox, tension, etc.), but Walter E. Sutton believes that Elton's glossary inadvertently exposes contradictions in New Critical theory.[14]

Murray Krieger's THE NEW APOLOGISTS FOR POETRY (Minneapolis: University of Minnesota Press, 1956) was the first and, in the revised edition of 1963, is still the best book-length study of the New Critics. Krieger recognizes the New Critical value of "complexity"[15] but is somewhat disturbed by the absolute formalism implicit in contextualist theory: "How can poetry tell us something about our world when for the contextualist it is not in any obvious way referential?" Krieger's query was voiced in a different way by the Neo-Aristotelians or, as they are often called, the Chicago Critics; they taught at the University of Chicago in the late 1930s and through the 1940s. Without producing any single critic of the stature of a Ransom or Tate, they were ably led by Ronald S. Crane (1886-1967) and Richard McKeon. To combat New

Critical terminology and contextualism, which struck them as responsible for a kind of verbal solipsism, they revived Aristotle's classification of genres in a mimetic theory of their own. The Chicago Critics hoped to provide a model for clear distinctions between descriptive and historical identification. Works of a certain genre permit comparison among themselves, in parts and as wholes; and since genres have a history, they provide a perspective lacking in the linguistic inclusiveness of the New Criticism where every work is its own verbal world.[16]

5. Psychological and Myth Criticism

Van Wyck Brooks, Edmund Wilson, Lionel Trilling, Kenneth Burke, and many other critics of lesser renown have used psychological, specifically Freudian, approaches in their criticism. I.A. Richards, whose elusive psychological theory was rooted in behaviorism, explored the language of poetry and its effect on the modern reader. His ideas, as noted above, had an indirect but important influence on the New Critics. From the early 1920s to the present, critics have turned to psychology for the purposes of drafting theory and elucidating texts. We remember that Spingarn had advocated an "expressionistic" criticism in 1910, and it seems almost inevitable that the nineteenth-century's fascination with the creative personality should evolve into the twentieth-century's absorption with self and the unconscious. The search for the writer's meaning became more and more a search for his mind, his characters' minds, and finally, in formalist terms, the mind of the work itself.

Frederick C. Prescott was one of the first American critics to explore the literary implications of Freud's dream theory. In THE POETIC MIND (New York: Macmillan, 1922), he uses Freud's ideas about the symbolic power of dreams to refurbish Romantic theories of the imagination. A few years later Joseph Wood Krutch (1893-1970) applied the Freudian concept of the Oedipus complex to an analysis of Poe in EDGAR ALLAN POE: A STUDY IN GENIUS (New York: Knopf, 1926). The memory of his mother kept Poe from any normal loving; this conflict, says Krutch, relying on the Freudian principle of sublimation, fueled Poe's art.[17] Freudian assumptions color an entire history of literature in Ludwig Lewisohn's EXPRESSION IN AMERICA (New York: Harper, 1932). His hero is Theodore Dreiser, who, despite crudities of language and form, freed American literature from the sexual self-consciousness which Lewisohn insists permeates the work of Melville, Howells, and Henry James in the previous century.[18]

Despite his condemnation of nineteenth-century sexual repression, Lewisohn's praise of Dreiser as a champion of libido reflects a basically nineteenth-century psychology of art rooted in the Nietzschean or Dionysian celebration of unfettered emotion. Throughout the twentieth century, in contrast to Lewisohn, Freudians interested in literature are usually identified with ego psychology.[19] Hans Sachs, a Viennese psychiatrist and contemporary of Freud, published in 1942 THE CREATIVE UNCONSCIOUS: STUDIES IN THE PSYCHOANALYSIS OF ART, second edition enlarged and edited by A.A. Roboek (Cambridge, Mass.: Sci-Art Publishers, 1951). Sachs states that the superego cannot be threatened by a work of art if it is to be aesthetically successful because the absence of anxiety is an indispensable condition for beauty. Similarly, Ernst Kris's PSYCHOANALYTICAL EXPLORATIONS IN ART (New York: International Universities Press, 1952) maintains that art is subject to ego and has little connection with impulses of the id. Animal impulses may inspire art, but its function, says Kris, is human and social. In his FICTION AND THE UN-CONSCIOUS, with a preface by Ernest Jones (Boston: Beacon Press, 1957), Simon O. Lesser writes that form in literature is associated with the mastery or control identified with the ego. The following journals have included articles on various aspects of ego psychology and literature: THE AMERICAN IMAGO, edited by Hans Sachs from 1939 to 1947 and afterwards by George E. Wilbur, and LITERATURE AND PSYCHOLOGY, edited by Leonard Manheim, which includes a running bibliography of important books and articles.

Two works of scholarship are essential to an understanding of the connections between Freudian psychology and American literature and criticism in the first half of the twentieth century. The first is Frederick J. Hoffman's FREUDIAN-ISM AND THE LITERARY MIND (Baton Rouge: Louisiana State University Press, 1957); the second is Louis Fraiberg's PSYCHOANALYSIS AND AMERICAN LITERARY CRITICISM (Detroit: Wayne State University Press, 1960). Hoffman's book introduces the reader to Freudian theory itself, its history and general influence, and then concentrates on Freud's influence on four great European moderns: Joyce, Lawrence, Kafka, and Mann. Modern fiction's language experiments, designed to represent dream states, are inspired by Freud, says Hoffman; Freud's theories of dream symbolism, first published in 1900, stimulated writers to actualize comparable symbolizations in literature. Hoffman discusses the wide literary influence of Freud's theory of the Oedipus complex; he also stresses Mann's insistence on the ego's dominion over the id, a point of view which put Mann closer to Freud than either Joyce, Lawrence, or Kafka, who were persuaded of the id's undeniable supremacy. Hoffman reminds us that while modern artists continued to glorify the id, in more or less Romantic or Dionysian terms, psychological critics largely outgrew these assumptions. Three American writers connected with Freudianism are analyzed: Sherwood Anderson, Waldo Frank (novelist and critic), and F. Scott Fitzgerald. There is a very useful bibliography surveying criticism with a psychological emphasis.

Fraiberg's study is a survey of six American critics who used psychoanalytical theories: Van Wyck Brooks, Joseph Wood Krutch, Ludwig Lewisohn, Edmund Wilson, Kenneth Burke, and Lionel Trilling. Brooks, Krutch, and Lewisohn do not succeed, says Fraiberg, in properly integrating psychology and criticism, and Edmund Wilson does not do full justice to Freud. No glorifier of the id, Wilson is no clear supporter of ego psychology either. Burke is criticized for assuming that Marxist and psychoanalytical terms are interchangeable; his semantic approach reduces all ideas to the level of terminology and obscures the fact that psychoanalysis is grounded in experience. Trilling is singled out as the critic with the most comprehensive knowledge of Freud. Trilling's belief that by fashioning his works the artist is in the act of coping with his neurosis is at the heart of Fraiberg's praise of Trilling for achieving a "creative extension of Freudian concepts." Fraiberg's book includes a bibliography.

If Freudian ideas monopolize psychological criticism, myth criticism is largely indebted to C.G. Jung's theory of archetypes or primordial images, the "psychic residue of numberless experiences of the same type" inherited by the race. See "On the Relation of Analytical Psychology to Poetic Art," translated by H.G. and Carey F. Baynes, CONTRIBUTIONS TO ANALYTICAL PSYCHOLOGY (New York: Harcourt Brace, 1928). Freud's depth psychology answers questions put by an essentially expressionistic criticism, but Jung's theory of archetypes appeals to generic or descriptive criticism because it locates the work of literature in an anthropological and historical context of evolving symbolizations.

The British critic Maud Bodkin is usually credited with introducing the Anglo-American critical community to Jung's ideas in her ARCHETYPAL PATTERNS IN POETRY: PSYCHOLOGICAL STUDIES OF IMAGINATION (London: Oxford University Press, 1934). Philip Wheelwright's "Poetry, Myth, and Reality," THE LANGUAGE OF POETRY, edited by Allen Tate (Princeton, N.J.: Princeton University Press, 1942, pp. 3-33), and his THE BURNING FOUNTAIN, A STUDY IN THE LANGUAGE OF SYMBOLISM (Bloomington: Indiana University Press, 1954) inject a religious dimension into the mythic archetype by suggesting that the primordial group consciousness provides a basis for a faith that transcends the individual's separateness. A combination of myth and religion, says Wheelwright, can correct the bias of positivistic materialism and revive man's sense of his unity with others and the unknown. Wheelwright's myth criticism seems remote from the New Humanism and the New Criticism, and yet all three have key philosophical assumptions in common: an aversion to materialism and a predilection toward a religious metaphysics.

Joseph Campbell's THE HERO WITH A THOUSAND FACES (New York: Pantheon, 1949) enlarges the concept of myth to define all of literature, which becomes an arrangement of mythic patterns unified in the "monomyth" of the reborn hero who goes through three distinct "rites of passage": separation or departure, trials and victories of initiation, and return or reintegration with society.[20] Campbell's "monomyth" is an important model for Northrop Frye (1912--), the Canadian critic whose "theory of myths" combines a literary taxonomy of greater logical and descriptive severity than the Aristotelian or generic classifications of the Chicago critics with a mythic pattern of the seasons based on archetypal, Jungian ideas. Just as spring, summer, fall, and winter are integral parts of the calendrical year, their corresponding "mythoi"--comedy, romance, tragedy, and irony--are four aspects of one "central unifying myth" in Frye's system.

Northrop Frye's first major articulation of his theory of myths is ANATOMY OF CRITICISM: FOUR ESSAYS (Princeton, N.J.: Princeton University Press, 1957). He is a critic of the first rank whose nationality and dates put him beyond the focus of this guide.[21] Even if he were an American critic working before 1950, his bold integration of "scientific" classification and literary subject matter would seem largely alien to the critical theories of the first half of the twentieth century in America. A firm division between science and art underlies the majority of the critical movements between 1900 and 1950. Kenneth Burke's "dramatistic" system is the obvious exception, but, then, his ideas have always seemed somewhat eccentric. Marxist critics and certain psychological critics were committed to the scientific precision of their analytical principles, but the humanistic values of culture and philosophy held their positivism in check. From the New Humanism through the New Criticism to the religious positions of certain myth critics, traditional humanism still provided a resting place. Not so after Frye. American literary criticism is still reeling from the challenge of his intricate and detailed map of the literary landscape.

6. Beyond 1950

Frye's calm insistence that his "system" has nothing to do with evaluation (as scientific a characteristic of his theory as its taxonomic thoroughness) links him to the French structuralists, who have attracted increasing attention in America in the last twenty years.[22] The trends of the last thirty years have helped to put the first fifty of this century into bolder relief. We can see now that from 1900 to 1950 literary criticism, despite two great wars and a catastrophic world depression, is characterized by a strong rejection of determinism in all its forms. Tradition was conceived by Eliot, Babbitt, and the New Critics as a liberating counterforce to the social and scientific determinism of the modern world. The critic was to replace the historian in the classroom; his subject, poetry, had its own form of knowledge, different and perhaps superior to that of science. Even leftist critics turned from Communist dogma and rigidity in political and literary matters, and culture critics reasserted the autonomy of the mind. Ego psychologists questioned persistent expressions of biological and psychological determinism. Only myth criticism in its later phases and certain trends in Neo-Aristotelianism (see Wayne C. Booth's THE RHETORIC OF FICTION [Chicago: University of Chicago Press, 1961]) can be said to have anticipated the current criticism.

The structuralists and their disciples have revived all the old determinisms, and they have added a new one--language itself. Since the end of the eighteenth century, literary language was considered a rejuvenating and creative force for both cultural traditionalists and liberals. In recent years literary language has been recast by linguistically oriented structuralists into "ecriture," or "writing as an institution."[23] This turns the literary artist into a vehicle for predetermined conventions of linguistic and literary expression. What would Joel Spingarn say to that?

B. STRUCTURE AND AIMS OF THIS GUIDE

Although this research guide is devoted to literary criticism in America from 1900 to 1950, both dates have been interpreted rather loosely. We have already discussed the debut of twentieth-century criticism in 1910, and we have seen that the important movements of the 1930s and 1940s did not really wind down until the 1960s. In short, there is a "tilt" light flashing 1910-1960. If the readers can indulge this chronological difficulty, they can trust in their having a good deal of the first half of this century's criticism before them.

Introduction: Literary Criticism

In this guide an attempt at bibliographical thoroughness is only one principle among several. The main purpose is to introduce beginning researchers to the field, not to try to give them everything that has been done. The great quantity and variety of critical materials, primary and secondary, would frustrate any hopes for a definitive inclusiveness short of a multivolumed encyclopedia approach. What has been attempted here is to give researchers sufficient resources to enable them to make their own way on their own terms.

To help researchers find a clear path, no matter where they choose to enter the wood, the following methodology has been employed:

> 1. A number of key secondary works are mentioned in more than one part of this guide.

> 2. There are numerous cross-references between the introduction and the "Individual Bibliographical Essays: Major Critics," and other sections.

> 3. A long list of important essays (part 2, section B) is provided on the assumption that critics often express the heart of their critical values or systems in relatively short prose works.

> 4. The "Individual Bibliographical Essays: Major Critics" can be read independently of the rest of the guide without fear of overlooking the works most pertinent to the critic in question.

Once familar with general critical trends and the critical approaches to the art of criticism itself that are outlined in this guide, the reader will discover that the future study of criticism in America may well turn to some of the following questions. In pondering them, readers may discover lines of inquiry for their own research in literary criticism.

> 1. Why has American criticism lost its humanist moorings?

> 2. What are the ties between Feminist Criticism (a movement that originated in the 1960s and therefore is not treated in this guide) and the Radical Criticism of the 1920s and 1930s?

> 3. Despite continual attacks on contextualism, why does the New Criticism refuse to die?

> 4. Do structuralism and poststructuralism have any clear ties to the New Criticism? To Neo-Aristotelianism? If so, what are they?

> 5. Will Freudian ego-psychology continue to dominate psychological literary criticism?

> 6. What are the historical origins of American myth criticism? Did it develop from Jungian and/or British anthropological sources, and if so, how?

> 7. In an age of descriptive criticism, what are the chances for a revival of evaluation? Can the humanists and cultural critics of the past be of any use?

8. Like structuralism, phenomenology is beyond the confines of this study. Is there, nevertheless, a connection between the impressionism of the early 1900s and the efforts of the "Critics of Consciousness" and their American disciples (Geoffrey H. Hartman's THE UNMEDIATED VISION [New Haven: Yale University Press, 1954] and J. Hilles Miller's THE DISAPPEARANCE OF GOD: FIVE NINETEENTH CENTURY WRITERS [Cambridge: Harvard University Press, 1963]) to identify their own consciousness as critics with the author's?

9. Finally, is the intentionalism of E.D. Hirsch's VALIDITY OF INTERPRETATION (New Haven: Yale University Press, 1967) totally unrelated to Spingarn's expressionism?

Peter A. Brier

NOTES TO THE INTRODUCTION

1. EXPRESSIONISM AND IMPRESSIONISM

1. Huneker's major works include MEZZOTINTS IN MODERN MUSIC (1899),
VISIONARIES (1905), ICONOCLASTS (1905), EGOISTS (1909), PROMENADES
OF AN IMPRESSIONIST (1910), THE PATHOS OF DISTANCE (1913), IVORY,
APES, AND PEACOCKS (1915), UNICORNS (1917), and STEEPLEJACK (1920).
His LETTERS (New York: Scribner's, 1922), and INTIMATE LETTERS (New York:
Boni and Liveright, 1924) were edited by Josephine Huneker. The best intro-
ductions to Huneker are two essays by H.L. Mencken: "James Huneker," A
BOOK OF PREFACES (New York: Knopf, 1917), pp. 151-94, and "James
Huneker," PREJUDICES, THIRD SERIES (New York: Knopf, 1922), pp. 65-84.
See also Alfred Kazin, ON NATIVE GROUNDS: AN INTERPRETATION OF
MODERN AMERICAN PROSE LITERATURE (New York: Reynal and Hitchcock,
1942), pp. 62-66.

2. William K. Wimsatt, Jr., and Monroe C. Beardsley, THE VERBAL ICON:
STUDIES IN THE MEANING OF POETRY (Lexington: University of Kentucky
Press, 1954), pp. 3-18, 21-39. For a useful "biobibliographical profile" of
Wimsatt, see Grant Webster's THE REPUBLIC OF LETTERS: A HISTORY OF
POSTWAR AMERICAN LITERARY OPINION (Baltimore: Johns Hopkins University
Press, 1979), pp. 369-70.

2. THE NEW HUMANISM

3. A precursor of New Humanism was William Crary Brownell (1851-1928), an
Arnoldian antiimpressionist who had urged "high seriousness," European cosmo-
politanism, and disciplined formal organization in a series of elegant studies at
the turn of the century. His works include FRENCH TRAITS (1889), FRENCH
ART (1892), VICTORIAN PROSE MASTERS (1901), AMERICAN PROSE MASTERS
(1909), CRITICISM (1914), STANDARDS (1917), THE GENIUS OF STYLE (1924),
DEMOCRATIC INSTITUTIONS IN AMERICA (1927), and THE SPIRIT OF SO-
CIETY (1927). Brownell and his place in the literary generation before World
War I are treated in Howard Mumford Jones's introduction to a reissue of
AMERICAN PROSE MASTERS (Cambridge: Harvard University Press, 1963).

See also S.P. Sherman, William Crary Brownell," POINTS OF VIEW (New York: Scribner's, 1924), pp. 89-126.

4. Walter E. Sutton, MODERN AMERICAN CRITICISM (Englewood Cliffs, N.J.: Prentice-Hall, 1963), pp. 39-41. Sutton discusses Stuart Pratt Sherman (1881-1926), one of Babbitt's students at Harvard and an early supporter of the New Humanism. Sherman soon became a wavering disciple. In AMERICANS (1922) he praised nineteenth-century American Romantics for their individualism, satire of Puritanism, and democratic faith. In CRITICAL WOODCUTS (1926), Sherman expressed the fear that the pace of modern life would make it increasingly difficult to honor Babbitt's ideas.

5. A summary of some of the most important pieces in Foerster's symposium provides a distillation of New Humanist thought: Irving Babbitt's "Humanism: An Essay at Definition," pp. 25-51, urges humanists and Christians to unite in opposing behaviorism; and T.S. Eliot's "Religion Without Humanism," pp. 105-12, argues that just as historical humanism united the mystic and ecclesiastic in one church, humanism should now continue to unite parts into a whole. Paul Elmer More's "The Humility of Common Sense," pp. 52-74, establishes the keynote for the New Humanist attack on science by questioning the "self-contradicting monisms" which have sprung from the "union of science and metaphysics." More's banner is also raised by his brother, Louis Trenchard More, in "The Pretensions of Science," pp. 3-24. Robert Shafer's "An American Tragedy," pp. 149-69, attacks Dreiser's Naturalism for its onesided emphasis on the animal in man.

6. The following summaries of the essays in Grattan's book reveal the broad range of opinion marshaled against the New Humanists: The defense of science is the theme of the opening essay, Grattan's "The New Humanism and the Scientific Attitude," pp. 3-36, and the closing essay, Lewis Mumford's "Toward an Organic Humanism," pp. 337-59. Edmund Wilson's "Notes on Babbitt and More," pp. 39-60, and Yvor Winters' "Poetry, Morality, and Criticism," pp. 301-33, both attack the New Humanists for confusing literary traditionalism with moral discipline; Wilson is particularly indignant at More's unwillingness to grant Joyce an ethical perspective. Both R.P. Blackmur's "The Discipline of Humanism," pp. 237-54, and Malcolm Cowley's "Humanizing Society," pp. 63-84, take issue with various forms of New Humanist arrogance and insensitivity to art and society. Allen Tate argues, in "The Fallacy of Humanism," pp. 131-66, that without a clear basis in religion, the New Humanism is doomed to failure.

3. LIBERAL AND RADICAL CRITICISM

7. The best single work on left-wing and radical writers in America is Daniel Aaron's WRITERS ON THE LEFT (New York: Harcourt, Brace and World, 1961). In revealing detail it recounts the attraction to and withdrawal from communism by important American writers and critics of the Left. The notes, pp. 409-68, form a rich addition to the text. Aaron also moderated a symposium with Kenneth Burke, Malcolm Cowley, Granville Hicks, and William Phillips entitled "Thirty Years Later: Memories of the First American Writers Congress," published in AMERICAN SCHOLAR, 35 (1966), 495-516.

8. Floyd Dell's INTELLECTUAL VAGABONDAGE: AN APOLOGY FOR THE INTELLIGENTSIA (New York: George M. Doran, 1926), based on articles originally published in the LIBERATOR, interpreted English literature as the result of social forces but refrained from urging any immediate revolutionary action. Dell was at heart a Romantic individualist, a critic very much in Spingarn's mold. Michael Gold, the radical novelist and editor, held Dell in scorn for having grown rich on sex treatises. Max Eastman also retreated from the radicalism of his youth and wrote books on laughter and other affective themes. Since science is concerned with fact, he came to believe that art should pursue fantasy and thus heighten the reader's sensitivity to life. See his THE LITERARY MIND: ITS PLACE IN AN AGE OF SCIENCE (New York: Scribner's 1931).

9. For background information on the founding and editorial policies of both the MASSES and the NEW MASSES, see Daniel Aaron, WRITERS ON THE LEFT, pp. 37-40, 35-58 passim, 114-20, 216-22, and Malcolm Cowley's EXILES RETURN: A LITERARY ODYSSEY OF THE 1920'S (New York: Norton, 1934), pp. 66-67, 221-24.

10. Sutton, MODERN AMERICAN CRITICISM, p. 74. Also see Grant Webster, THE REPUBLIC OF LETTERS, pp. 355-57, for a "biobibliographical profile" of Philip Rahv. A moving and informative tribute to Rahv is Mary McCarthy's "Philip Rahv, 1908-1973," NEW YORK TIMES BOOK REVIEW, 17 February 1974, pp. 1-2.

4. THE NEW CRITICISM AND THE NEO-ARISTOTELIANS

11. This famous manifesto was reprinted with a useful introduction by Louis D. Rubin and biographical essays on the twelve contributors by Virginia Rock (New York: Harper and Row, 1962), pp. vi-xviii, 360-85.

12. Although a somewhat polemical piece, the best essay on the political and intellectual history underlying the conservative and often reactionary elements in both the New Humanism and the New Criticism is Robert Gorham Davis' "The New Criticism and the Democratic Tradition," AMERICAN SCHOLAR, 19 (1949-50), 9-19.

13. Wimsatt, THE VERBAL ICON, p. xvii. The New Criticism soon stretched "poetic art" to include drama and fiction, and it became necessary to persuade the literary community that New Critical methods could "hypostatize," or support, the analysis of these genres as well as of poetry. Robert B. Heilman's THIS GREAT STAGE: IMAGE AND STRUCTURE IN KING LEAR (Baton Rouge: Louisiana State University Press, 1948) demonstrated the validity of textualist approaches to Shakespeare; and William Handy, influenced by Cleanth Brooks and Robert Penn Warren's UNDERSTANDING FICTION (1943), wrote "Toward a Formalist Criticism of Fiction," TEXAS STUDIES IN LITERATURE AND LANGUAGE, 3 (1961), 81-88.

14. Sutton, MODERN AMERICAN CRITICISM, p. 148, suggests that New Critical terminology is more "incantatory" than "analytical"; terms like "heresy of paraphrase" (Cleanth Brooks) and "intentional and affective fallacies" (W.K. Wimsatt) are compared to E.A. Poe's "epic mania" and "heresy of the didactic." Richard Foster, in THE NEW ROMANTICS: A REAPPRAISAL OF THE NEW CRITICS (Bloomington: Indiana University Press, 1962), like Sutton, argues

that the New Critics pursued the meaning of poetry as if it were a unique form of knowledge with revelatory powers. Douglas Day, in "The Background of the New Criticism," JOURNAL OF AESTHETICS AND ART CRITICISM, 24 (1966), 429-40, surveys the influences from Spingarn to Eliot on the New Critics and concludes that the Romantic element in their work prevented the New Critics, who professed classicism, from achieving agreement in a realized critical theory. William J. Handy's KANT AND THE SOUTHERN NEW CRITICS (Austin: University of Texas Press, 1963) asserts that Ransom, Tate, and Brooks owe a considerable debt to Kant's distinction between the understanding and the imagination. For a contemporary dialogue which looks back at the strengths and weaknesses of the New Criticism, see René Wellek's "The New Criticism: Pro and Contra," CRITICAL INQUIRY, 4 (1978), 611-24, and Gerald Graff's "New Criticism Once More," CRITICAL INQUIRY, 5 (1979), 569-75, and Wellek's "A Rejoinder to Gerald Graff," CRITICAL INQUIRY, 5 (1979), 576-79.

15.   John Crowe Ransom, "Introduction," in his THE KENYON CRITICS: STUDIES IN MODERN LITERATURE FROM THE KENYON REVIEW (Cleveland and New York: World Publishing, 1951), pp. vii-x.

16.   Crane collected his own and McKeon's essays together with important work by their colleagues at the University of Chicago (W.R. Keast, Norman Maclean Elder Olson, and Bernard Weinberg) in CRITICS AND CRITICISM: ANCIENT AND MODERN (Chicago: University of Chicago Press, 1952). McKeon's essay, "The Philosophic Bases of Art and Criticism," is the most extensive dis-cussion of theory. McKeon divides criticism into dialectical (what the New Critics do) and scientific modes and gives his own Aristotelian criticism high marks for scientific objectivity. Crane's THE LANGUAGE OF CRITICISM AND THE STRUCTURE OF POETRY (Toronto: University of Toronto Press, 1953) con-tinues the attack on the New Critics by questioning the validity of their critical terms. Aristotelian terms and theory are presented as superior to the semantic and reductive terminology of the New Critics. For a New Critical rebuttal, see W.K. Wimsatt, Jr.'s. "The Chicago Critics," COMPARATIVE LITERATURE, 5 (1953), 50-74. Elder Olson recently published ON VALUE JUDGMENTS IN THE ARTS AND OTHER ESSAYS (Chicago: University of Chicago Press, 1976).

5. PSYCHOLOGICAL AND MYTH CRITICISM

17.   Edmund Wilson felt Krutch's book to be "incomplete, depending too much on Freudian oversimplification" (CLASSICS AND COMMERCIALS [New York: Farrar, 1950], p. 245).

18.   Sutton, MODERN AMERICAN CRITICISM, pp. 1-26. Sutton provides a very useful summary of the early years of American psychological criticism in his survey of Prescott, Krutch, and Lewisohn.

19.   The best introduction to the uses of ego psychology in literary criticism may very well be Henry A. Murray's sensitive essay on MOBY DICK, "In Nomine Diaboli," NEW ENGLAND QUARTERLY, 24 (1951), 435-52. Sutton, MODERN AMERICAN CRITICISM, pp. 204 ff., notes that in contrast to the ego-psychologist-critics, who credit literature with the power to embody ra-tionalism and health, there are psychoanalytically oriented critics who condemn the writer to neurotic illusion. Sutton points out Edmund Bergler's THE WRITER

AND PSYCHOANALYSIS (1950; 2nd ed. revised, New York: Bruner, 1954) which labels literary composition the "defense mechanism of a psycho masochist."

20. Campbell's "monomyth" is closer to the work of the British anthropological school than it is to Jung's theory of archetypes. British anthropology had produced its own mythic or archetypal criticism, quite apart from Jung's theories, rooted in the researches of Sir James Frazer's THE GOLDEN BOUGH (many various editions from 1890). Frazer's discovery of the "essential similarity of man's chief wants everywhere and at all times," as reflected in ancient mythology, led to such British scholarly works as Gilbert Murray's "Hamlet and Orestes," a lecture given in 1914 and published in THE CLASSICAL TRADITION IN POETRY (Cambridge, Mass.: Harvard University Press, 1927). Murray's essay had a strong influence on the American work, Francis Fergusson's THE IDEA OF A THEATER (Princeton, N.J.: Princeton University Press, 1949) which argues that HAMLET follows the same ritual pattern as Sophocles' OEDIPUS. For a concise summary of Jungian and British contributions to myth criticism, see Wilfrid Guerin, Earle Labor, Lee Morgan, and John R. Willingham, A HANDBOOK OF CRITICAL APPROACHES TO LITERATURE (New York: Harper and Row, 1979), pp. 153-73.

21. Although only chronologically marginal to this present research guide, Frye is too important to American criticism to leave entirely unannotated. Fortunately there is an excellent volume of essays introducing his work from several points of view: NORTHROP FRYE IN MODERN CRITICISM, edited with an introductory essay by Murray Krieger (New York: Columbia University Press, 1966). This volume includes essays by Krieger, Frye, Angus Fletcher, W.K. Wimsatt, Jr., and Geoffrey Hartman, as well as a forty-two-page check-list of writings by and about Frye compiled by John E. Gaunt.

6. BEYOND 1950

22. Readers desiring an introduction to structuralist poetics and theory can turn to several texts. STRUCTURALISM, edited by Jacques Ehrmann (Garden City, N.Y.: Doubleday, 1970), includes essays applying structuralist approaches in linguistics, anthropology, art, psychiatry, and literature; this work contains a bibliography on "Structuralism and Literary Criticism" by T. Todorov, pp. 260-62. Robert Scholes's STRUCTURALISM IN LITERATURE: AN INTRODUCTION (New Haven: Yale University Press, 1974) is designed expressly for American readers schooled in New Critical values. It has a bibliographical appendix with annotated titles, pp. 201-17. Jonathan Culler's STRUCTURALIST POETICS: STRUCTURALISM, LINGUISTICS, AND THE STUDY OF LITERATURE (Ithaca, N.Y.: Cornell University Press, 1975) seems to be the best-written introduction to date; it contains an international bibliography, pp. 267-93.

23. Roland Barthes, WRITING DEGREE ZERO AND ELEMENTS OF SEMIOLOGY (Boston: Beacon, 1970). See Hugh M. Davidson's English Institute paper of 1971, "Sign, Sense, and Roland Barthes," in LITERARY CRITICISM: IDEA AND ACT, THE ENGLISH INSTITUTE, 1939-1972, SELECTED ESSAYS, ed. W.K. Wimsatt, Jr. (Berkeley and Los Angeles: University of Calif. Press 1974), pp. 228-41, for a lucid explication of Barthe's critical theories.

Part 1

GENERAL BIBLIOGRAPHICAL AIDS

A. BIBLIOGRAPHIES OF CRITICISM

The following titles supply the most ample checklists and bibliographies of criticism and works on criticism available. The reader should also consult my coauthor's bibliographical aids and James Woodress, ed., "Background Source Material," AMERICAN FICTION, 1900-1950: A GUIDE TO INFORMATION SOURCES. American Literature, English Literature, and World Literatures in English Information Guide Series, vol. 1 (Detroit: Gale Research Co., 1974), pp. 3-12. For journalistic sources of critical prose, the reader should consult Edward E. Chielens, ed., THE LITERARY JOURNAL IN AMERICA, 1900-1950: A GUIDE TO INFORMATION SOURCES. American Literature, English Literature, and World Literatures in English Information Guide Series, vol. 16 (Detroit: Gale Research Co., 1977).

Brown, Clarence Arthur, ed. THE ACHIEVEMENT OF AMERICAN CRITICISM. New York: Ronald Press, 1949.

> This collection of essays includes a selected bibliography of American criticism of which part 4, "Trends in Modern Criticism," includes one section of nine pages on "Primary Works" and two other sections, "Secondary Works: General" and "Secondary Works: On Individual Authors." The secondary lists are only five pages in length and are unannotated, but they enumerate the major materials written from the 1920s to the mid-1950s.

Leary, Lewis, ed. ARTICLES ON AMERICAN LITERATURE: 1900-1950. Durham, N.C.: Duke University Press, 1954.

> This standard unannotated bibliography has seven pages of entries on literary criticism in general and approximately one- or one-half-page entries on individual critics.

_____. ARTICLES ON AMERICAN LITERATURE: 1950-1967. Durham, N.C.: Duke University Press, 1970.

> This work has the same format as the earlier volume. There are five pages on literary criticism in general.

_____. AMERICAN LITERATURE: A STUDY AND RESEARCH GUIDE. New York: St. Martin's Press, 1976.

> This guide includes an eighteen-page chapter "Types and Schools of Criticism," which has brief and often misleading descriptions of major critical schools. Some important books are mentioned and briefly annotated.

Spiller, Robert E., et al., eds. LITERARY HISTORY OF THE UNITED STATES: BIBLIOGRAPHY. 2 vols. 4th ed., rev. New York: Macmillan, 1974.

> In addition to the original section in the earlier editions, "The Twentieth Century: Studies of Critical Movements," the reader is urged to consult the new supplement in the 1974 edition and read the chapter with the same title in that volume. By tracing the changing emphases, the reader gets not only a capsule history of American critical prose but also critical reactions to it from 1900 to approximately 1970. Deeper into the bibliography are entries for individual critics; these are usually very reliable: primary publications, important dates, and secondary sources are amply provided. Secondary sources are seldom annotated.

Stallman, Robert Wooster, ed. CRITIQUES AND ESSAYS IN CRITICISM: 1920-1948. New York: Ronald Press, 1949.

> With fifty pages devoted in large part to secondary works (un-annotated articles and books), this well-known collection of essays provides, to this day, one of the most reliable bibliographies of British and American criticism for the years concerned.

Webster, Grant. THE REPUBLIC OF LETTERS: A HISTORY OF POST-WAR AMERICAN LITERARY OPINION. Baltimore: Johns Hopkins University Press, 1979.

> This recently published historical survey of American criticism from 1945 to the present ends with a useful thirty-three pages of biographical and bibliographical information entitled "Profiles: The Lives and Works of Selected American Men of Letters." The critics described are R.P. Blackmur, Cleanth Brooks, Kenneth Burke, Richard Chase, R.S. Crane, T.S. Eliot, Irving Howe, Alfred Kazin, Murray Krieger, Philip Rahv, John Crowe Ransom, Allen Tate, Lionel Trilling, Austin Warren, René Wellek, Edmund Wilson, W.K. Wimsatt, Jr., and Yvor Winters.

Woodress, James, ed. AMERICAN LITERARY SCHOLARSHIP: ANNUAL. Durham, N.C.: Duke University Press, 1963-- .

> Consult this work for in-depth reviews of major studies of American criticism done after 1965. In the early volumes Harry Finestone does the reviewing in a section entitled "Literary History and Criticism"; in the later volumes G.R. Thompson and Michael J. Hoffman cover the topic in "Themes, Topics and Criticism."

B. GENERAL HISTORIES OF CRITICISM

Baym, Max. A HISTORY OF LITERARY AESTHETICS IN AMERICA. New York: Ungar, 1973.

> This book has useful chapters on psychological criticism and the New Critics. Documentation is very thorough.

Foerster, Norman. AMERICAN CRITICISM: A STUDY IN LITERARY THEORY FROM POE TO THE PRESENT. Boston: Houghton Mifflin, 1928.

> With a New Humanist emphasis, this study confines analysis largely to nineteenth-century figures.

Goldsmith, Arnold L. AMERICAN LITERARY CRITICISM: 1905-1965. Boston: Twayne, 1979.

> This is one of a three volume history of American literary criticism from 1800-1965. John W. Rathbun authored the 1800-1860 volume and, together with Harry Hayden Clark, the 1860-1905 volume. Goldsmith's study is a reliable summary of the main critical trends, but it lacks the insights and synthesizing power of Walter E. Sutton's MODERN AMERICAN CRITICISM (see below). There is a useful selected bibliography.

Hyman, Stanley Edgar. THE ARMED VISION: A STUDY IN THE METHODS OF MODERN LITERARY CRITICISM. New York: Knopf, 1948. Revised and abridged. New York: Vintage, 1955.

> The 1948 edition included essays on Wilson, Winters, Eliot, Van Wyck Brooks, Blackmur, and Burke; the 1955 edition omitted the Wilson essay. Hyman set out to describe the methodologies of modern criticism and provide a sense of their historical development. He also hoped "to suggest some possibilities for an integrated and practical methodology that would combine and consolidate the best procedures of modern criticism." His book was one of the first attempts at a survey of modern literary criticism to mid-century. Too polemical and subjective to live up to its purported intentions, it is nevertheless a pioneering work that cannot be ignored. The essays on Blackmur and Burke are the best. In conclusion, Hyman stresses the value of synthesis in criticism: "the ideal . . . critic" should incorporate all the theories and procedures of his "flesh and blood colleagues."

O'Connor, William Van. AN AGE OF CRITICISM: 1900-1950. Chicago: H. Regnery, 1952.

> This historical survey has a strongly formalist point of view. The concluding chapter maintains that New Criticism is a continuation of nineteenth-century English criticism. Chapter headings include "The Genteel Tradition," "Sophistication and Impressionism,"

"Realism and the Aegis of Science," "Organic and Expressive Form," "The New Awareness of America," "The New Humanism," "Social and Activist Criticism," "Psychoanalysis and Myth," and "Analytical Criticism." There is a good index.

Peyre, Henri. WRITERS AND THEIR CRITICS. Ithaca, N.Y.: Cornell University Press, 1944.

A well-known French intellectual and professor at Yale surveys modern literary criticism. Chapter 2 is on America. Peyre faults American criticism for not subjecting contemporary writers to a probingly comparative and historical evaluation.

Pritchard, John Paul. CRITICISM IN AMERICA: AN ACCOUNT OF THE DEVELOPMENT OF CRITICAL TECHNIQUES FROM THE EARLY PERIOD OF THE REPUBLIC TO THE MIDDLE YEARS OF THE TWENTIETH CENTURY. Norman: University of Oklahoma Press, 1956.

This is the first book-length historical survey of American criticism from its beginnings to mid-century. Pritchard shows how criticism has moved from regional to national perspectives, a trend set by E.A. Poe. Chapters dealing with modern criticism are "The New Humanists and Their Opponents," "The New Criticism," and "Recent Practicing Critics" (T.K. Whipple, Edmund Wilson, Van Wyck Brooks, and the Chicago critics). The "Bibliographical Notes" include many secondary sources.

Smith, Bernard. FORCES IN AMERICAN CRITICISM. New York: Harcourt, Brace, 1939.

This Marxist study rejects all aspects of formalism and regrets the loss of the socially conscious criticism that had originated with Whitman and Howells.

Stovall, Floyd, ed. THE DEVELOPMENT OF AMERICAN LITERARY CRITICISM. Chapel Hill: University of North Carolina Press, 1955.

All contributors to this collection of historical essays assert the genuinely American quality of our criticism. John H. Raleigh's "Revolt and Revaluation in Criticism: 1900-1930" maintains that Woodberry and Brownell tried to preserve historical approaches and Victorian morality, but were followed by Babbitt, Spingarn, Mencken, Sherman, Van Wyck Brooks, and Eliot--who, despite their differences, had in common a rejection of the nineteenth century and the need "to get down to first principles in everything." C. Hugh Holman's "The Defense of Art: Criticism Since 1930" finds the New Criticism too partisan in its taste (Eliot and Yeats) and stresses its lack of success with the novel and drama.

Sutton, Walter E. MODERN AMERICAN CRITICISM. Englewood Cliffs, N.J.: Prentice-Hall, 1963.

This important work surveys American literary criticism from approximately 1910 to the late 1950s. The chapter titles are "Early Psychological Criticism," "The New Humanism," "Liberal and Marxist Criticism," "The New Criticism," "The Neo-Aristotelians," "Psychological and Myth Criticism," "Histories," "Theories and Critiques of Criticism," and "Criticism as a Social Art."

A contribution to the Princeton Studies in Humanistic Scholarship in America, this work subjects all of the major critical schools to a tough-minded Socratic inquiry. Sutton is not afraid to expose weaknesses in theory whenever he finds them, and he is usually persuasive when he does. His last chapter elaborates a point of view developed throughout the book: criticism must find a way of synthesizing social and aesthetic values. He calls for an "open organic form" that would be a corrective to the bias against "extra-literary" thought in the holistic organicism of theories like Wellek's "Perspectivism" (see below). "Open organic form," writes Sutton, "recognizes not only the interconnectedness of the verbal elements of a poem, but also their dependence upon a larger order of experience."

These ideas do not, however, constrict the book to the point of vitiating its historical inclusiveness. No marked bias informs the many useful summaries of dozens of important primary and secondary works. His is the most useful book available to anyone desiring a truly informed condensation of modern American literary criticism. Those doing research in the field are heavily in his debt.

Webster, Grant. THE REPUBLIC OF LETTERS: A HISTORY OF POST-WAR AMERICAN LITERARY OPINION. Baltimore: Johns Hopkins University Press, 1979.

Committed to what he calls a "theory of charters," Webster tendentiously traces the New Criticism and the social and cultural criticism of the postwar period (giving each group a reductive label: the New Critics becoming "Tory Formalists" and the others, "New York Intellectuals") through a predictable series of hoops: ideology, revolution, "Normal" criticism, obsolescence of charter, and "Eponymous" criticism. His "theory of charters" is based, by analogy and loosely, on Thomas S. Kuhn's THE STRUCTURE OF SCIENTIFIC REVOLUTIONS (Chicago: University of Chicago Press, 1970). "Kuhn's conception of the development of a paradigm in science," says Webster, "seems useful to humanists not as a model to be slavishly followed but as a theory that poses the right sequence of questions about the rise and fall of intellectual ideas and groups." Webster's suggestion that literary movements have a predictable paradigm is in the spirit of literary structuralism.

Wellek, René. CONCEPTS OF CRITICISM. New Haven: Yale University Press, 1963.

This book contains useful bibliographical-historical essays on various aspects of modern criticism--couched within the framework of Wellek's "Perspectivism," his theory of intrinsic organicism. Essay titles are "Concepts of Form and Structure in Twentieth-Century

Criticism," "American Literary Scholarship," "Philosophy and Postwar American Criticism," and "The Main Trends of Twentieth Century Criticism." Wellek is coauthor with Austin Warren of THEORY OF LITERATURE (New York: Harcourt, Brace, 1949), which is mentioned in the introduction above.

Wimsatt, William K., Jr., and Cleanth Brooks. LITERARY CRITICISM: A SHORT HISTORY. New York: Knopf, 1957.

A selective history with an admittedly "argumentative" approach by two major representatives of the New Criticism, this work tends to interpret historical literary criticism from Plato to the present as either confirming or questioning New Critical theories. Brooks is responsible for the seven chapters dealing with modern criticism, and Wimsatt deals with the aesthetic problems of contextualist theory in the epilogue. It is there that Wimsatt drives an analogy between "the religious dogma of the Incarnation" and the metaphysical values that various New Critical ideas have adumbrated--tension, irony, paradox, and contextualist meaning itself.

C. SPECIALIZED HISTORIES AND STUDIES OF MAJOR SCHOOLS AND MOVEMENTS: A SELECTIVE CHECKLIST

1. The New Humanism

Boynten, Percy. THE CHALLENGE OF MODERN CRITICISM. Chicago: Thomas S. Rockwell, 1931.

Elliott, G.R. HUMANISM AND IMAGINATION. Chapel Hill: University of North Carolina Press, 1938.

Foerster, Norman. TOWARD STANDARDS: A STUDY OF THE PRESENT CRITICAL MOVEMENT IN AMERICAN LETTERS. New York: Farrar and Rinehart, 1931.

Munson, Gorham B. THE DILEMMA OF THE LIBERATED: AN INTERPRETATION OF TWENTIETH CENTURY HUMANISM. New York: Coward-McCann, 1930.

Ruland, Richard. THE REDISCOVERY OF AMERICAN LITERATURE: PREMISES OF CRITICAL TASTE 1900-1940. Cambridge: Harvard University Press, 1967.

Santayana, George. THE GENTEEL TRADITION AT BAY. New York: Scribner's, 1931.

2. The New Criticism

Cowan, Louise. THE FUGITIVE GROUP: A LITERARY HISTORY. Baton Rouge: Louisiana State University Press, 1959.

Foster, Richard. THE NEW ROMANTICS: A REAPPRAISAL OF THE NEW CRITICS. Bloomington: Indiana University Press, 1962.

Krieger, Murray. THE NEW APOLOGISTS FOR POETRY. Rev. ed. Bloomington: Indiana University Press, 1963.

Weinman, Robert. "NEW CRITICISM" UND DIE ENTWICKLUNG BÜRGERLICHER LITERATURWISSENSCHAFT. Halle, W. Ger.: Universitäts Druckeri, 1962.

3. Psychological Criticism

Fraiberg, Louis. PSYCHOANALYSIS AND AMERICAN LITERARY CRITICISM. Detroit: Wayne State University Press, 1960.

Hoffman, Frederick J. FREUDIANISM AND THE LITERARY MIND. Rev. ed. Baton Rouge: Louisiana State University Press, 1957.

Morrison, Claudia C. FREUD AND THE CRITIC: THE EARLY USE OF DEPTH PSYCHOLOGY IN LITERARY CRITICISM. Chapel Hill: University of North Carolina Press, 1968.

4. Radical Criticism

Aaron, Daniel. WRITERS ON THE LEFT: EPISODES IN AMERICAN LITERARY COMMUNISM. New York: Harcourt, Brace and World, 1961.

Freeman, Joseph. AN AMERICAN TESTAMENT: A NARRATIVE OF REBELS AND ROMANTICS. New York: Farrar, 1936.

Gilbert, James H. WRITERS AND PARTISANS: A HISTORY OF LITERARY RADICALISM IN AMERICA. New York: Wiley, 1968.

D. LITERARY HISTORIES OF SIGNIFICANCE TO LITERARY CRITICISM

Calverton, V[ictor] F[rancis] (George Goetz). THE NEWER SPIRIT: A SOCIOLOGICAL CRITICISM OF LITERATURE. New York: Boni and Liveright, 1925.

> Aesthetic judgments are entirely conditioned by the environment and "sociological" reality of the reader.

_____. THE LIBERATION OF AMERICAN LITERATURE. New York: Scribner's, 1932.

American literature is the result of the conflict between Puritan myth and frontier spirit. A new collectivist faith based on the nineteenth-century hopes of Emerson and Whitman may inspire the twentieth-century "proletariat" to "remake the modern world."

Chielens, Edward E., ed. THE LITERARY JOURNAL IN AMERICA, 1900-1950: A GUIDE TO INFORMATION SOURCES. American Literature, English Literature, and World Literatures in English Information Guide Series, vol. 16. Detroit: Gale Research Co., 1977.

This is a recent valuable research resource which updates previous studies of the same subject. The introduction, pages 1-13, is particularly valuable in defining literary journals in relation to such subjects and interests as regionalism, political factionalism, editorial policies, and major writers and literary periodicals.

Fishman, Solomon. THE DISINHERITED OF ART: WRITERS AND BACKGROUND. Berkeley and Los Angeles: University of California Press, 1953.

This cultural history touches on all the major critical movements since World War I. There are interesting juxtapositions of Marxism and Agrarianism.

Hicks, Granville. THE GREAT TRADITION: AN INTERPRETATION OF AMERICAN LITERATURE SINCE THE CIVIL WAR. Rev. ed. New York: Macmillan, 1935.

This Marxist literary history traces proletarian literature to its nineteenth-century roots.

Hoffman, Daniel, ed. HARVARD GUIDE TO CONTEMPORARY WRITING. Cambridge, Mass.: Belknap Press, 1979.

A. Walton Litz's essay "Literary Criticism" is a skillful condensation of trends in literary criticism from 1945 to the present. He is particularly good in tracing the fading power of the New Criticism as the emphasis shifted from practical to theoretical criticism in the 1950s.

Hoffman, Frederick J., with Charles Allen and Carolyn F. Ulrich. THE LITTLE MAGAZINE: A HISTORY AND BIBLIOGRAPHY. Princeton, N.J.: Princeton University Press, 1946.

This is an important guide to all modern literary periodicals and indispensable for those interested in the radical criticism of the 1920s and 1930s.

Janssens, G.A.M. THE AMERICAN LITERARY REVIEW: A CRITICAL HISTORY 1920-1950. The Hague: Mouton, 1968.

This book surveys the history of the literary review and has individual chapters on the DIAL (1920-29), the HOUND AND HORN (1927-34), the SYMPOSIUM (1930-1933), and the SOUTHERN REVIEW (1935-42).

Kazin, Alfred. ON NATIVE GROUNDS: AN INTERPRETATION OF MODERN AMERICAN PROSE LITERATURE. New York: Reynal and Hitchcock, 1942.

> Chapter 14, "Criticism at the Poles," provides a dramatic and polemical account of the collapse of the literary Left and the rise of the New Critics. Kazin objects to "scientific" aridity and "Talmudic" love of exegesis in the New Critics. He praises Trilling and Wilson who, "in a bad time for criticism, did their part to feed the hunger for critical leadership."

Knight, Grant C. THE STRENUOUS AGE IN AMERICAN LITERATURE: 1900–1910. Chapel Hill: University of North Carolina Press, 1954.

> Knight captures the elusive and transitional nature of literature and criticism at the turn of the century.

Lewisohn, Ludwig. EXPRESSION IN AMERICA. New York: Harper, 1932.

> In this Freudian interpretation of Melville, Howells, Henry James, and Dreiser, Lewisohn argues that nineteenth-century American literature suffers from acute sexual repression.

Matthiessen, F[rancis] O[tto]. AMERICAN RENAISSANCE: ART AND EXPRESSION IN THE AGE OF EMERSON AND WHITMAN. New York: Oxford University Press, 1941.

> An interest in tragedy, myth, organic form, and symbolism (as well as textualist principles of analysis through the influence of I.A. Richards, T.S. Eliot, and the New Critics) make this elegant critical history of America's five major writers (Emerson, Thoreau, Hawthorne, Melville, and Whitman) a reflection of the critical theories strong in the 1930s and early 1940s. Matthiessen was deeply identified with Christianity and the political Left. Despite his tragic vision of American literature, he maintained that all five of his nineteenth-century greats shared a "devotion to the possibilities of democracy."

Parrington, V[ernon]. L[ouis]. MAIN CURRENTS IN AMERICAN THOUGHT. 3 vols. New York: Harcourt, Brace, 1927-30.

> Parrington insists that democratic values permeate American literary thought. His work anticipates the literary nationalism of Van Wyck Brooks's last phase and, in its own time, balanced the radical criticism of the 1930s.

Part 2

COLLECTIONS OF CRITICAL ESSAYS

A. COLLECTIONS CONCENTRATING ON THE FIRST FIFTY YEARS OF THE CENTURY

There are many textbook collections, but the following are particularly useful. Despite the broad range of selections, which often reach back to the nineteenth century, all of the following either take us up to mid-century or focus sharply on the period 1900-1950 itself. Editorial aids such as introductions, bibliographies, and biographies are of a high quality.

Beaver, Harold. AMERICAN CRITICAL ESSAYS: TWENTIETH CENTURY. London: Oxford University Press, 1959.

> Edited from a British point of view, this book's introduction calls the New Criticism the most significant phenomenon in American criticism of this century--an "orthodoxy" that captured the American university. The textualist emphasis in the New Criticism is traced back to Coleridge in BIOGRAPHIA LITERARIA (1817).

Brown, Clarence Arthur. THE ACHIEVEMENT OF AMERICAN CRITICISM. Foreword by Harry Hayden Clark. New York: Ronald Press, 1954.

> This is the first collection to offer criticism from the seventeenth through the twentieth centuries. A detailed but condensed introduction to modern criticism is strengthened by lengthy footnotes providing information on primary and leading secondary sources.

Glicksberg, Charles Irving. AMERICAN LITERARY CRITICISM: 1900-1950. New York: Hendricks House, 1951.

> In a penetrating introduction, psychoanalytical, humanist, and formalist points of view are carefully traced. Selections from early twentieth-century critics like Huneker, Spingarn, Brownell, and Sherman are more ample than in most modern collections. Every critic represented is given an informative intellectual biography.

Hyman, Stanley Edgar. THE CRITICAL PERFORMANCE: AN ANTHOLOGY OF AMERICAN AND BRITISH LITERARY CRITICISM OF OUR CENTURY. New York: Vintage, 1956.

> THE ARMED VISION (see part 1, section B, above) was intended by Hyman to serve as an "introduction" to this collection of essays.

Ransom, John Crowe. THE KENYON CRITICS: STUDIES IN MODERN LITERATURE FROM THE KENYON REVIEW. Cleveland: World Publishing Co., 1951.

> In his introduction, Ransom writes that literature tends to be "cryptic, Delphic" and requires critics who can discover its "hidden" or less visible meaning. His editorial policy is reflected in the essays.

Salzman, Jack. YEARS OF PROTEST: A COLLECTION OF AMERICAN WRITINGS OF THE 1930'S. New York: Pegasus, 1967.

> James Farrell's debate with the Marxists is included. There is a bibliography on the literature and criticism of the 1930s and one devoted specifically to "Literary Memoirs, Studies and Collections."

Stallman, Robert Wooster. CRITIQUES AND ESSAYS IN CRITICISM 1920-1948: REPRESENTING THE ACHIEVEMENT OF MODERN BRITISH AND AMERICAN CRITICS. Foreword by Cleanth Brooks. New York: Ronald Press, 1949.

> Brooks writes in the foreword that "the attempt to drive a wedge between close reading of the text and evaluation of the work seems to me confused and confusing." Although this well-known collection includes essays reflecting all of the major twentieth-century approaches, its editorial apparatus leans heavily toward the formalistic principles central to new critical doctrine. The appendix includes biographical notes and an excellent primary and secondary bibliography (good to 1948).

_____, comp. THE CRITIC'S NOTEBOOK. Minneapolis: University of Minnesota Press, 1950.

> This is a collection of statements--excerpts from their essays and books--by British and American critics (1920-1950), classified according to the following chapter headings: "The Nature and Function of Criticism," "Life and Art," "Form," "The Problem of Meaning," "The Concept of the Objective Correlative," "The Problem of the Personal Element," "The Problem of Belief in Poetry," and "The Problem of Intentions." There is a detailed bibliography for each of the above chapter headings. Stallman's attempt to arrange all these "excerpts" is impressive, but the reader must be wary of interpreting them solely in the light of Stallman's organization. His predilection for formalist theory is, however, under control.

Van Nostrand, Albert D. LITERARY CRITICISM IN AMERICA. New York: Liberal Arts Press, 1957.

> Two-thirds of this collection is devoted to nineteenth-century critics. However, the introduction makes an interesting comparison between New Humanists and New Critics: the former movement stressing morality and tradition in art but ironically motivating the rise of Marxist criticism in the late 1930s; the latter, despite its distrust of the nineteenth century, anticipated by various shades of formalism in earlier critics like Bryant, Emerson, Poe, Henry James, Santayana, and Howells.

Zabel, Morton Dauwen. LITERARY OPINION IN AMERICA: ESSAYS ILLUS-TRATING THE STATUS, METHODS, AND PROBLEMS OF CRITICISM IN THE UNITED STATES IN THE TWENTIETH CENTURY. Rev. ed. New York: Harper's, 1951.

> Zabel's is perhaps the most generous, prestigious, and gracefully edited of all the criticism collections focusing on the twentieth century. There is a second revised edition (2 vols., New York: Harper's, 1962), but the 1951 edition is the best for 1900-1950. The introduction, "Criticism in America," supplies a chrono-logically arranged portrait gallery of important critics from Henry James to Irving Babbitt and then closes with a summation of cur-rent trends at mid-century: aestheticism and the New Humanism challenging the liberalism of an earlier era; Socialist and Marxist criticism rising in the aftermath of the Depression; the simultaneous development of formalism (New Criticism) and interdisciplinary approaches (literary criticism joining forces with psychology, an-thropology, semantics, and history.

> The essays in the 1951 edition are mostly nuggets: e.g., Burke's "Psychology and Form," Trilling's "Freud and Literature," and Edmund Wilson's "Marxism and Literature." Important appendixes include bibliographies of collections of critical writing and of American journals publishing critical prose, as well as a useful note on contemporary British criticism. Spiller's LITERARY HIS-TORY OF THE UNITED STATES: BIBLIOGRAPHY (see part 1, section A, above) calls Zabel's bibliography on twentieth-century criticism the "best" of those available in collections of criticism.

B. NOTEWORTHY CRITICAL ESSAYS BY MAJOR AND OTHER CRITICS APPEARING IN THE COLLECTIONS LISTED IN PART 2, SECTION A

The following essays by major and other critics of the first part of this century represent a cross section of critical theory and practice. Many of these essays can be found in the standard editions of the critics' works which are identified, below, in part 3 of this guide: "Individual Bibliographical Essays." However, the collections described above are often more readily available. The reader is, thus, here referred to them as sources. When a critic is represented by more than one essay, the sequence of listing suggests an order for reading.

Babbit, Irving
"The Critic and American Life"
Glicksberg, p. 291; Van Nostrand, p. 254; Zabel, p. 133.

Blackmur, R.P.
"A Critic's Job of Work"
Glicksberg, p. 380; Zabel, p. 770
"The Enabling Act of Criticism"
Stallman (hereafter, CRITIQUES AND ESSAYS IN CRITICISM 1920-1948),
      p. 412.
"Languages as Gesture"
Van Nostrand, p. 311
"The Later Poetry of W.B. Yeats."
Stallman, p. 358.
"A Rage of Goodness: THE IDIOT of Dostoyevsky"
Hyman, p. 235.

Brooks, Cleanth
"Modern Criticism"
Brown, p. 678; Stallman, p. xv.
"What Does Poetry Communicate?"
Beaver, p. 249.
"Irony as a Principle of Structure"
Zabel, p. 729.
"The Language of Paradox"
Glicksberg, p. 517; Stallman, p. 66.

Brooks, Van Wyck
"The Literary Life in America"
Glicksberg, p. 146.
"The Critical Movement in America"
Zabel, p. 80.

Brownell, William Crary
"Criterion"
Glicksberg, p. 113.
"Method"
Glicksberg, p. 123.

Burke, Kenneth
"Psychology and Form"
Stallman, p. 224; Zabel, p. 667.
"Lexicon Rhetoricae"
Stallman, p. 234.

"Applications of the Terminology"
Glicksberg, p. 310.
"Symbolic Action in a Poem of Keats"
Hyman, p. 259.

Chase, Richard
"The Broken Circuit: Romance and the American Novel"
Beaver, p. 313.

Dupee, F.W.
"The Americanism of Van Wyck Brooks"
Stallman, p. 460; Zabel, p. 561.

Eliot, T.S.
"Tradition and the Individual Talent"
Glicksberg, p. 133; Stallman, p. 377; Van Nostrand, p. 229; Zabel, p. 91.
"The Metaphysical Poets"
Brown, p. 614; Stallman, p. 47.
"Hamlet and His Problems"
Brown, p. 609; Stallman, p. 384.
"Poetry and Propaganda"
Zabel, p. 97.
"The Social Function of Poetry"
Stallman, p. 105.

Farrell, James T.
"The Categories of 'Bourgeois' and 'Proletarian'"
Glicksberg, p. 429.
"A Note on Literary Criticism"
Salzman, p. 277.

Fergusson, Francis
"Oedipus Rex: Tragic Rhythms of Action"
Hyman, p. 317.

Frank, Waldo
"Values of the Revolutionary Writer"
Glicksberg, p. 442.

Hicks, Granville
"Literature and Revolution"
Glicksberg, p. 408.

Huneker, James Gibbons
"The Great American Novel"
Zabel, p. 73.

Hyman, Stanley Edgar
"Attempts at an Integration"
Zabel, p. 757.

Kazin, Alfred
"Ishmael and Ahab"
Beaver, p. 332.

Krutch, Joseph Wood
"The Function of Criticism"
Glicksberg, p. 334.

Levin, Harry
"Observations on the Style of Ernest Hemingway"
Beaver, p. 286.
"Literature as an Institution"
Zabel, p. 655.

More, Paul Elmer
"Criticism (1910)"
Brown, p. 575.
"The Demon of the Absolute"
Glicksberg, p. 258.
"How to Read 'Lycidas'"
Zabel, p. 146.

Olson, Elder
"An Outline of Poetic Theory"
Stallman, p. 264.

Rahv, Philip
"Paleface and Redskin"
Beaver, p. 280; Ransom, p. 12.

Ransom, John Crowe
"Criticism, Inc."
Glicksberg, p. 453.
"Criticism as Pure Speculation"
Zabel, p. 639.
"Poetry: A Note on Ontology"
Stallman, p. 30.
"Poetry Without Laurels"
Van Nostrand, p. 273.
"Yeats and His Symbols"
Hyman, p. 191.

Schwartz, Delmore
"The Literary Dictatorship of T.S. Eliot"
Zabel, p. 573.
"Poetry and Belief in Thomas Hardy"
Stallman, p. 334.

Sherman, Stuart P.
"The Point of View in American Criticism"
Glicksberg, p. 164.

Spingarn, Joel E.
"The New Criticism (1910)"
Brown, p. 525; Glicksberg, p. 76.
"The American Critic"
Zabel, p. 123.

Tate, Allen
"The Present Function of Criticism"
Glicksberg, p. 471.
"Tension in Poetry"
Stallman, p. 55.
"The Man of Letters in the Modern World"
Beaver, p. 129.
"Narcissus as Narcissus"
Hyman, p. 175.

Trilling, Lionel
"Reality in America"
Brown, p. 655; Zabel, p. 404.
"Freud and Literature"
Zabel, p. 677.
"Art and Neurosis"
Glicksberg, p. 550.
"Wordsworth and the Iron Time"
Ransom, p. 233.

Vivas, Eliseo
"The Objective Correlative of T.S. Eliot"
Stallman, p. 389.
"Kafka's Distorted Mask"
Ransom, p. 58.

Warren, Robert Penn
"Pure and Impure Poetry"
Ransom, p. 17; Stallman, p. 85.

Wellek, René
"The Mode of Existence of a Literary Work of Art"
Stallman, p. 210.

Wilson, Edmund
"The Historical Interpretation of Literature"
Brown, p. 654; Glicksberg, p. 485; Stallman, p. 449.
"Marxism and Literature"
Zabel, p. 693.
"Philoctetes: The Wound and the Bow"
Van Nostrand, p. 294.

Wimsatt, W.K., Jr., and Monroe C. Beardsley
"The Affective Fallacy"
Stallman, p. 401.

Winters, Yvor
"Preliminary Problems"
Glicksberg, p. 536; Stallman, p. 201.
"Maule's Curse: or, Hawthorne and the Problem of Allegory"
Beaver, p. 143.
"Robert Frost: or, The Spiritual Drifter as Poet"
Zabel, p. 417.

C. SPECIALIZED AND MORE RECENT COLLECTIONS

Crane, Ronald S. CRITICS AND CRITICISM: ANCIENT AND MODERN. See the introduction to this guide, note 16 (p. 127).

> This book is the primary source for Neo-Aristotelian essays.

Foerster, Norman, ed. AMERICAN CRITICAL ESSAYS. London: Oxford University Press, 1930.

> This collection has a New Humanist perspective.

_____. HUMANISM AND AMERICA: ESSAYS ON THE OUTLOOK OF MODERN CIVILIZATION. New York: Farrar, 1930.

> This famous pro-New Humanism symposium is described in detail in the introduction to this guide, above.

Grattan, C. Hartley, ed. THE CRITIQUE OF HUMANISM: A SYMPOSIUM. New York: Brewer and Warren, 1930.

> A wide variety of critics respond harshly to HUMANISM AND AMERICA (see Foerster above). The introduction to this guide, above, also describes Grattan's collection in detail.

Handy, William J., and Max Westbrook. TWENTIETH CENTURY CRITICISM: THE MAJOR STATEMENTS. New York: Free Press, 1974.

> Handy and Westbrook forge beyond the chronological span of this guide to include Frye, Claude Levi-Strauss, Susan Sontag, and others. Nevertheless, this collection contains three important essays that fall within the spectrum of 1900-1950: R.S. Crane, "The Multiplicity of Critical Languages"; Mark Schorer, "Technique as Discovery" (one of the most influential of all New Critical pronouncements); Lionel Trilling, "The Sense of the Past."

Hicks, Granville, Michael Gold, Isidor Schneider et al., eds. With Critical Introduction by Joseph Freeman. PROLETARIAN LITERATURE IN THE UNITED STATES. New York: International Publishers, 1935.

Howe, Irving. MODERN LITERARY CRITICISM: AN ANTHOLOGY. Boston: Beacon Press, 1958.

Litz, Walter A., and Lawrence I. Lipking. MODERN LITERARY CRITICISM: 1900-1970. New York: Athenuem, 1971.

> This collection ranges from Pound to Frye.

Malen, Irving, ed. PSYCHOANALYSIS AND AMERICAN FICTION. New York: Dutton, 1965.

> Fifteen carefully chosen essays by critics such as Richard Chase, Edmund Wilson, and Leon Edel make this the best collection devoted to psychoanalytical criticism of the first half of the century.

O'Neill, William L., ed. With Introduction by Irving Howe and Afterword by Max Eastman. ECHOES OF REVOLT: THE MASSES, 1911-1917. Chicago: Quadrangle Books, 1966.

Stallman, Robert Wooster. See his collections (part 2, section A); they have a strong New Critical emphasis.

Part 3

INDIVIDUAL BIBLIOGRAPHIC ESSAYS
MAJOR CRITICS

The critics' primary works are listed chronologically (cited as The Critical Works). Major secondary material is discussed thematically (cited as Representative Secondary Sources). Supplementary secondary works are arranged alphabetically (cited as Resources for Further Research). Bibliographical sources are listed preceding The Critical Works (cited as Bibliography). Cross-references to works cited in this present guide but discussed more fully elsewhere appear within parenthesis following the name of the author or the title of the work--for example, Zabel (part 2, section A), THE ARMED VISION (part 1, section B).

A. IRVING BABBITT (1865-1933)

Irving Babbitt (hereafter B or IB) was born in Ohio. In addition to his studies at Harvard, he spent two years at the Sorbonne where, among other things, he studied Sanskrit. He used his learning and strong convictions to formulate the New Humanism, a critical credo for the reestablishment of historical humanism as a counterforce to the "Naturalism" he believed had gradually undermined ethics and faith through the influence of Bacon's scientific rationalism and Rousseau's sentimental subjectivity. B's platform remained for some forty years his professorship in comparative literature at Harvard. It was his dream to make the university a voice of critical power, not just of scholarly authority. Yet no one stressed the importance of knowing the facts as much as he. His primary quality was intensity; it helped make him one of the greatest teacher-critics of the century. Dogmatic? Crusaders usually are.

BIBLIOGRAPHY

The editors of B's posthumous publication, SPANISH CHARACTER, AND OTHER ESSAYS (see below), included a list of his published articles and books as well as an index to his works. Also consult Fred B. Millett's CONTEMPORARY AMERICAN AUTHORS (New York: Harcourt, Brace, 1940), pp. 231-34.

THE CRITICAL WORKS

LITERATURE AND THE AMERICAN COLLEGE: ESSAYS IN DEFENSE OF THE HUMANITIES (1908), THE NEW LAOKOON: AN ESSAY ON THE CONFUSION OF THE ARTS (1910), THE MASTERS OF MODERN FRENCH CRITICISM (1912), ROUSSEAU AND ROMANTICISM (1919), DEMOCRACY AND LEADERSHIP (1924), ON BEING CREATIVE AND OTHER ESSAYS (1932), and SPANISH CHARCTER, AND OTHER ESSAYS (1940).

REPRESENTATIVE SECONDARY SOURCES

Without a standard biography, the reader's best source for a portrait of B is

Irving Babbitt

IRVING BABBITT: MAN AND THINKER (New York: Putnam, 1941) edited by Frederick Manchester and Odell Shepard with a sketch by B's widow, Dora D. Babbitt, to whom he dictated his later works. The contributors to this volume include many of the best known literary personalities of the age, many of whom had been his students. Stuart P. Sherman notes that B's "students couldn't keep up with his thoughts. . . . You felt he was a Coleridge, a Carlyle, a Buddah." T.S. Eliot thought he was at his best with small groups and that the generation's debt to him would be "obvious to posterity." Austin Warren writes that B "felt pain at the defection of every disciple." Theodore Spencer compares him to Dr. Johnson; each inspired awe and love. John Livingston Lowes (B's great Harvard rival) praises him as "grandly promotive for gain of the intellectual life." Paul Elmer More, who became his partner in the New Humanism, credits him with a born love and mastery of the Roman and Greek poets, "according to his own accent." More feels that B was "better as a talker than writer."

T.S. Eliot--in "The Humanism of Irving Babbitt," FORUM, 80 (1928), 37-44-- is less charitable than in his contribution to the portrait noted above. He feels that B's humanism was weakened by its vague Christianity, principle without dogma. Leary, Stallman, Pritchard, and Spiller (see part 1, section A) provide many titles dealing with B's conservatism, classicism, and moralism. The reviews and scholarship dealing with him in his own time are full of extremes of glorification and vilification. The reader is advised to begin with the more recent studies noted below.

A.C. Brown (part 1, section B) is good for a short background study of B's thought. In THE MORAL MEASURE OF LITERATURE (Denver: Swallow, 1961), Keith McKean concludes that he was, finally, too much a moralist; B found, says McKean, that literature was only incidental to his ethical ideas about the dualism of man and nature, the higher will, and the inner check. When appointed to the IB professorship of comparative literature at Harvard in 1960, Harry Levin gave an important lecture which was published in a pamphlet the following year: IRVING BABBITT AND THE TEACHING OF LITERATURE (Cambridge, Mass.: Harvard University Press, 1961). Levin maintains that in his teaching B stressed the principle of "cultural relatedness," the interrelationships of all great cultural traditions, including the Asian. Formal analysis without historical consciousness constituted a betrayal of empirical objectivity. B's famous ethicism, says Levin, was based on a fervid mistrust of the naturalism and materialism that had reduced man to being a slave of the "law for thing" when he could be living according to the precepts of "law for man." Rousseau's romanticism had led to a sentimental humanitarianism, "which he considered a travesty of humanism." Levin also provides information about B's childhood and youth, which were not without difficulties.

Walter E. Sutton (part 1, section B) gives a good survey of B's critical and historical education. His New Humanism, in its idealizing tendencies, is closer to Romanticism, says Sutton, than B realized. But René Wellek, in comparing B with Paul Elmer More, concludes that although both relied on Emerson's transcendentalism, B was uneasy with Emerson's symbolic metaphysics which reminded him of Rousseau's sentimentalism and optimism ("Irving Babbitt, Paul Elmer More and Transcendentalism," TRANSCENDENTALISM AND ITS LEGACY, ed. Myron Simon and Thornton H. Parsons [Ann Arbor: University of Michigan Press, 1966]).

RESOURCES FOR FURTHER RESEARCH

Blackmur, R.P. "Humanism and Symbolic Imagination: Notes on Rereading IB." SOUTHERN REVIEW, 7 (1941), 309-25.

Crocker, Leslie G. "Professor Babbitt Revisited." STUDIES IN ROMANTICISM, 10 (1971), 260-82.

Eliott, G.R. "T.S. Eliot and Irving Babbitt." AMERICAN REVIEW, 7 (1936), 442-54.

Mercier, Louis J.A. LE MOUVEMENT HUMANISTE. Paris: The Sorbonne, 1928.

More, Paul Elmer. "Irving Babbitt." AMERICAN REVIEW, 3 (1934), 23-40.

Pritchard, John P. RETURN TO THE FOUNTAINS: SOME CLASSICAL STUDIES OF AMERICAN CRITICISM. Durham, N.C.: Duke University Press, 1942.

Wilson, Edmund. "Notes on Babbitt and More." NEW REPUBLIC, 63 (1930), 115-20.

B. R[ICHARD] P[ALMER] BLACKMUR (1904-65)

As one of the editors of HOUND AND HORN: A HARVARD MISCELLANY from 1927 to 1934, R.P. Blackmur (hereafter B or RPB) developed the give and take that grew into a broadly tolerant critical sensibility. Born and educated in Massachusetts, he left New England to teach creative writing at Princeton. Eventually identified with the New Criticism, he was at one time sympathetic to the social position of the leftist critics. But as early as the 1940s he urged "extrinsic" approaches and warned the New Critics that the linguistic method alone was not enough. B was a cosmopolitan spirit whose critical methods and the subjects he considered ranged far wider than his contextualist peers. While they exalted the metaphysical poets and generally condemned the nineteenth century, he wrote essays on such authors as Henry James, Mann, Tolstoy, Dostoyevsky, and Flaubert. His progressively more impenetrable style added to his uniqueness, but it also made him seem remote and even mystical. The contradiction between his open mind and his sealed and difficult style puzzles the contemporary reader. Indeed, B's opacity does seem to be withholding the immortality that so many admirers felt would be his in spite of his oftentimes almost impenetrable prose. But it is as yet too early to make a final judgment. Henry James's "late phase," much admired by B, is now accepted by many, and the weight of B's thought may yet redeem the difficulty of his syntax.

BIBLIOGRAPHY

Consult Carlos Baker's "R.P. Blackmur: A Checklist," PRINCETON UNIVERSITY LIBRARY CHRONICLE, 3 (1942), 99-106, and Allen Tate's checklist of two pages in the revised edition of SIXTY AMERICAN POETS, 1896-1944 (Washington, D.C.: U.S. Library of Congress, 1954). Gerald J. Pannick has done a primary and secondary bibliography in the BULLETIN OF BIBLIOGRAPHY, 13 (1974), 165-69, which concentrates more heavily on B's criticism than does Baker or Tate. Grant Webster, however (part 1, section A), finds Pannick's list inaccurate.

R[ichard] P[almer] Blackmur

THE CRITICAL WORKS

T.S. ELIOT (1928), THE DOUBLE AGENT (1935), THE EXPENSE OF GREAT-
NESS (1940), LANGUAGE AS GESTURE (1952), FORM AND VALUE IN MODERN
POETRY (1952), THE LION AND THE HONEYCOMB (1955), ANNI MIRABILES
1921-1925: REASON IN THE MADNESS OF LETTERS (1956), NEW CRITICISM
IN THE UNITED STATES (1959), ELEVEN ESSAYS IN THE EUROPEAN NOVEL
(1964), and A PRIMER OF IGNORANCE (1967).

REPRESENTATIVE SECONDARY SOURCES

John Crowe Ransom hailed B's commitment to close textualist analysis in "Mr.
Blackmur's Essays," KENYON REVIEW, 3 (1941), 95-100, but it was S.E. Hyman's
strongly positive portrait in THE ARMED VISION (part 1, section B) that called
general attention to B's criticism. Hyman notes that although B seems eclectic
in his methods, he has a "capacity for painstaking investigation." B does his
homework; his close look at background material, not just the text, gives his
criticism added power. Hyman also finds B good at classifying, as is evident
in B's well-known introduction to Henry James's preface (THE ART OF THE
NOVEL: PREFACES BY HENRY JAMES. New York: Scribner's, 1934). Hyman
bestows his own idea of highest praise by comparing B favorably to Kenneth
Burke, Hyman's model for the "integrative critic."

B's admirers tend to sound similar notes throughout the 1950s and 1960s. Walter
E. Sutton (part 1, section B) comments on B's high degree of organization, his
readiness to deal with all of the evidence, textual and otherwise. For B, says
Sutton, criticism constitutes a mysterious "burden" or responsibility requiring one
to "make bridges between society and the arts"; and although B fastens "on the
work itself," unlike Ransom or Brooks he approaches his task without any abso-
lutes or prescribed theories. Sutton sees him as always aware of the subtlety
of an author's psychological orientation; this accounts for the tentative quality
of B's own language.

The question of B's language figures prominently in the commentary of those who
tend to qualify or withhold praise. One of the earliest important essays on his
style is by Delmore Schwartz, "The Critical Method of R.P. Blackmur," PO-
ETRY, 53 (1938), 28-39 (reprinted in SELECTED ESSAYS OF DELMORE SCHWARTZ,
ed. Donald A. Dike and David H. Zucker [Chicago: University of Chicago
Press, 1970]): "Sometimes the syntactical arrangement of the sentence or the
formal succession of the argument becomes so slippery that it requires several
readings." Alfred Kazin, in ON NATIVE GROUND (part 1, section D), writes
a purple passage on the clinical ardity of B's style. More recently the English
critic John Wain, in his essay on B in ESSAYS ON LITERATURE AND IDEAS
(London: Macmillan, 1964), uses B's style to reaffirm the virtues of British
critical writing which Wain insists is less technical and clearer than its American
counterpart: B "deliberately refuses to reduce his meaning to simple terms . . .
he inflates it, surrounding it with a numbus of uncaught and uncatchable
meaning rather than let any possible nuance escape him." Wain supports his
accusation with a highly detailed analysis of B's style.

Perhaps the most suggestive and ingenious discussion of B's style is by R.W.B. Lewis, "Casella as Critic: A Note on R.P. Blackmur," KENYON REVIEW, 13 (1951), 458-74. Lewis concedes that B's style makes him "obscure . . . irritating . . . [the] least engaging of contemporary critics." Nevertheless, he seems one of the two or three likely to endure. Lewis sees B, like Kenneth Burke, as moving toward theology, and believes that this may guarantee them both "continuing attention." The ease with which B's critical preferences move from one epoch or writer to another strikes Lewis as "Emersonian" and distinctly American. B's early admiration of Eliot and his abiding love for the work of Henry James stem from a belief that both of them were trying to bridge the Christian and "post-Christian" realities. Sensitive to contradiction, but hungry for synthesis, B was driven to desperate ruses, argues Lewis. B uses the "hidden ball play," says Lewis, and grammatically omits the objective case, which is often "the paradox lurking in the syntax." B usually prefers veiled or submerged illuminations, and Lewis concludes that B's style intentionally disguises them.

RESOURCES FOR FURTHER RESEARCH

Foster, Richard. THE NEW ROMANTICS. Bloomington: University of Indiana Press, 1962.

Frank, Joseph. "R.P. Blackmur: The Later Phase." In his THE WIDENING GYRE. Rutgers, N.J.: Rutgers University Press, 1963, pp. 229-50.

Pritchard, William H. "R.P. Blackmur and the Criticism of Poetry." MASSA-CHUSETTS REVIEW, 8 (1967), 633-49.

Tate, Allen. "R.P. Blackmur and Others." SOUTHERN REVIEW, 3 (1937), 183-98.

Wellek, René. "R.P. Blackmur Re-Examined." SOUTHERN REVIEW, 7 (1971), 825-45.

C. CLEANTH BROOKS (1906-)

As the driving force behind the dissemination of New Critical formalism in the universities, Cleanth Brooks (hereafter B or CB) has done more than any other American critic to change the emphasis from literary history to literary criticism in the classroom. By translating his contextualism and organicism into stunningly effective critical terms--"irony," "paradox," "the heresy of paraphrase"--this master rhetorician won the minds of students and teachers alike. The close textualist analysis of poetry (and later fiction) and the pursuit of symbolic patterns in imagery, tone, characterization, and action are all attributable largely to his influence and the very wide adaptation in the university classroom of his famous text, UNDERSTANDING POETRY, written together with Robert Penn Warren (1905--).

B's victory in the English departments of the nation was almost too complete, and the failure of his fellow New Critics to supply a strong theory of poetry or aesthetics to support his tactical gains as explicator and pedagogue led in the late 1950s to a decline in the prestige of his methods. Nevertheless, to this day, teachers of literature at all levels of instruction continue to be drawn to his approach.

BIBLIOGRAPHY

CONTEMPORARY AUTHORS, edited by Clare D. Kinsman, rev. ed., vols. 17-20 (Detroit: Gale Research Co., 1976), 102-03, provides a reliable list of B's writings and edited texts and works through 1972. There is a checklist, very much dated now, by R.W. Stallman in the UNIVERSITY OF KANSAS CITY REVIEW, 14 (1948), 317-24.

THE CRITICAL WORKS

UNDERSTANDING POETRY: AN ANTHOLOGY FOR COLLEGE STUDENTS (with Robert Penn Warren, 1938; 4th ed., 1976); MODERN POETRY AND THE TRADITION (1939); THE WELL WROUGHT URN (1947); MODERN RHETORIC (with Robert Penn Warren, 1949; 3rd ed., 1970); LITERARY CRITICISM: A

SHORT HISTORY (with William K. Wimsatt, Jr., 1957); THE HIDDEN GOD: STUDIES IN HEMINGWAY, FAULKNER, YEATS, ELIOT AND WARREN (1963); WILLIAM FAULKNER: THE YOKNAPATAWPHA COUNTY (1963); and A SHAPING JOY: STUDIES IN THE WRITER'S CRAFT (1972).

REPRESENTATIVE SECONDARY SOURCES

Ronald S. Crane, one of the founders of the Neo-Aristotelian or Chicago critics (see the introduction to this present guide, above), attacked B in a now famous essay entitled "Cleanth Brooks: or, The Bankruptcy of Critical Monism." MODERN PHILOLOGY, 45 (1948), 226-45. According to Crane, B's proclaiming "irony," or the reconciliation of opposites, the distinguishing feature of poetry ignores the fact that Coleridge had extended the synthesizing imagination to include science and indeed all of knowledge. B, on the other hand, fails to persuade us, says Crane, that what he calls "irony" is not at the heart of science as well. "E-MC^2 . . . is the greatest 'ironical' poem written so far in the twentieth century."

Both Murray Krieger, THE NEW APOLOGISTS FOR POETRY (see the introduction to this present guide, above), and René Wellek, in his CONCEPTS OF CRITICISM (part 1, section B), call attention to the difficulty of reconciling B's contextualist theory--the "self-containedness" or "organicity" of a work of art--with a "meaningful relation to reality." These words are Wellek's, but nevertheless he rises to B's defense by insisting that he has not ignored history. Walter Sutton (part 1, section B) does an able job of summarizing B's major essays and concludes that "the contextualist critic like Brooks is himself the victim of an ironic dilemma in asserting the cognitive function of poetry while denying that statements of truth can be abstracted from it." In other words, B does not provide a means of validating the significance of the "knowledge" he finds in poetic "symbols."

Lewis P. Simpson has edited a rich collection of essays on B, THE POSSIBILITIES OF ORDER: CLEANTH BROOKS AND HIS WORK (Baton Rouge: Louisiana State University Press, 1976). In this collection, for example, Robert Penn Warren's "A Conversation with Cleanth Brooks" provides in one hundred pages a dramatic recreation of the lifelong dialogue between the authors of UNDERSTANDING POETRY. "There are between us," says Warren, "vast differences in temperament, character, and sense of the world. So every agreement has . . . to be regarded in the dramatic context of such differences, and every difference, in the context of sometimes hard won agreement." Allen Tate's "What I Owe to Cleanth Brooks" maintains that although B dedicated his MODERN POETRY AND THE TRADITION to him, Tate "during all those years learned more from B" than B "could possibly have learned" from Tate himself. B, says Tate, persuaded him of the centrality of the metaphysical poets. In "Cleanth Brooks: Some Snapshots, Mostly from an Old Album," the former chairman of the English department at the University of Washington, Robert B. Heilman, praises B for his dedication to teaching and his "lucidity of mind and style."

Walter J. Ong, S.J., in "From Rhetorical Culture to New Criticism: The Poem as a Closed Field," maintains in his contribution to Simpson's collection that B's close readings, which fix "the eye unflinchingly on chirographic and typographic expression," signaled a "final break" with the rhetorical (oral) tradition that had prevailed from antiquity to Romanticism. Thomas Daniel Young's "A Little Divergence: The Critical Theories of John Crowe Ransom and Cleanth Brooks" argues that B and Ransom agreed that poetry "contains a unique kind of knowledge" but differed on the nature of poetry. Ransom, says Young, questioned B's insistence that wit, paradox, and irony are "essential elements of poetry"; and B felt that Ransom's argument for the "logical structure" of poetry threatened to destroy "its essential unity by suggesting a split between form and content." In two other essays in the collection, René Wellek makes a "plea for B as a historian of criticism," and Monroe K. Spears discusses B's literary ethics.

RESOURCES FOR FURTHER RESEARCH

Coughlin, Phyllis F. "Aspects of Literary Form in Three Contemporary Theorists: Cleanth Brooks, R.S. Crane, W.K. Wimsatt Jr." DISSERTATION ABSTRACTS, 34 (1973), 5096A (Fordham).

Graff, Gerald. "Cleanth Brooks: New Critical Organicism." In POETIC STATEMENT AND CRITICAL DOGMA. Evanston, Ill.: Northwestern University Press, 1970, pp. 87-111.

Hardy, John Edward. "The Achievement of Cleanth Brooks." In SOUTHERN RENASCENCE: THE LITERATURE OF THE MODERN SOUTH. Ed. Louis D. Rubin, Jr., and Robert D. Jacobs. Baltimore: Johns Hopkins University Press, 1953, pp. 413-26.

Strauss, A.B. "The Poetic Theory of Cleanth Brooks." CENTENARY REVIEW, 1 (1949), 10-22.

Strozier, Robert M. "Roger Asham and Cleanth Brooks, Renaissance and Modern Critical Thought." ESSAYS IN CRITICISM, 22 (1972), 396-407.

D. VAN WYCK BROOKS (1866-1963)

Educated at Harvard, for two years an instructor at Stanford, and an editorial writer for a short period in New York, Van Wyck Brooks (hereafter B or VWB) soon settled down to his life's work: literary criticism and literary history. His first book appeared when he was only twenty-two. From then until his death, he published a great deal of work--almost all of it on American literature and its social and historical background. He began as a Jeremiah and ended as something of a Pollyana. AMERICA'S COMING OF AGE (1915) and LETTERS AND LEADERSHIP (1918) were a call to arms. Writers must overcome the materialism and financial greed of the time and dedicate themselves to discovering and embodying the native genius, the cultural identity unique to America.

B later turned from the harsh portrait of American society characteristic of his early work. His condemnation of Puritanism gave way to a glorification of the New England literary heritage; the psychological methods with which he had pilloried Twain and James were abandoned for a bland biographical interest. By 1941, for example, in OPINIONS OF OLIVER ALLSTON, all was right with America's literary past; this attitude pervades his four-volume history of American literature (1936-47). The idealistic Socialist of the post-World War I period had become the favorite of the book clubs. B attributed the change in his thinking to the evolution of his mind. Although he struggled with mental illness, it would be unjust to dismiss entirely the drift of his canon. His dedication to preserving the literary past, even at the intellectual cost of turning literary history into entertainment, was his response to the hatred of the past posed by the narcissism of our time.

BIBLIOGRAPHY

Millet's CONTEMPORARY AUTHORS (New York: Harcourt, Brace, 1940), pp. 262-64, lists all of B's writings including his edited and translated works up to 1936. William Wasserstrom's pamphlet VAN WYCK BROOKS (Minneapolis: University of Minnesota Press, 1968) has a brief primary and secondary bibliography, good up to B's death; so does James R. Vitelli's VAN WYCK BROOKS (New York: Twayne, 1969). Vitelli's VAN WYCK BROOKS: A REFERENCE GUIDE (Boston: G.K. Hall, 1977) is now the definitive secondary bibliography.

Van Wyck Brooks

THE CRITICAL WORKS

THE WINE OF THE PURITANS: A STUDY OF PRESENT-DAY AMERICA (1908), THE MALADY OF THE IDEAL: SENANCOUR, MAURICE DE GUERIN, AND AMIEL (1913), JOHN ADDINGTON SYMONDS: A BIBLIOGRAPHICAL STUDY (1914), THE WORLD OF H.G. WELLS (1914), AMERICA'S COMING OF AGE (1915), LETTERS AND LEADERSHIP (1918), THE ORDEAL OF MARK TWAIN (1920), THE PILGRIMAGE OF HENRY JAMES (1925), EMERSON AND OTHERS (1927), SKETCHES IN CRITICISM (1932), THE LIFE OF EMERSON (1932), THREE ESSAYS ON AMERICA (1934), THE FLOWERING OF NEW ENGLAND 1815-1865 (1936), NEW ENGLAND: INDIAN SUMMER, 1865-1915 (1940), OPINIONS OF OLIVER ALLSTON (1941), THE WORLD OF WASHINGTON IRVING (1944), THE TIMES OF MELVILLE AND WHITMAN (1947), A CHIL-MARK MISCELLANY (1948), THE CONFIDENT YEARS, 1885-1915 (1952), THE WRITER IN AMERICA (1953), SCENES AND PORTRAITS: MEMORIES OF CHILD-HOOD AND YOUTH (1954), JOHN SLOAN: A PAINTER'S LIFE (1955), HELEN KELLER: SKETCH FOR A PORTRAIT (1956), DAYS OF THE PHOENIX: THE NINETEEN-TWENTIES I REMEMBER (1957), DREAMS OF ARCADIA: AMERICAN WRITERS AND ARTISTS IN ITALY, 1760-1915 (1958), FROM A WRITER'S NOTE-BOOK (1958), HOWELL: HIS LIFE AND WORLD (1959), FROM THE SHADOW OF THE MOUNTAIN: MY POST-MERIDIAN YEARS (1961), and FENOLLOSA AND HIS CIRCLE, WITH OTHER ESSAYS IN BIOGRAPHY (1962)

REPRESENTATIVE SECONDARY SOURCES

The authoritative biography is now James Hoopes's VAN WYCK BROOKS IN SEARCH OF AMERICAN CULTURE (Amherst: University of Massachusetts Press, 1977) which in scope and detail supersedes Wasserstrom and Vitelli (see above). Hoopes is critical of B's insistence that nationalism "is the force best suited to promote American high culture"; but he does agree with B on "two fundamental points: (1) that the United States did not have in his time (and still lacks in ours) a culture adequate to its needs and (2) that such a culture must not be genteely removed from, or merely reflective of social reality, but rather, criti-cally engaged with it."

Anyone looking into secondary works on B should refer to James R. Vitelli's VAN WYCK BROOKS: A REFERENCE GUIDE (see above). It provides sub-stantial annotation for seemingly all commentary, articles, and books on B up to 1977. The organization is chronological, year by year in fact, and major secondary works are not distinguished from minor in any key or index.

The best introduction to B is still, however, F.W. Dupee's "The Americanism of Van Wyck Brooks," PARTISAN REVIEW, 6 (1939), 69-85, reprinted in Zabel (part 2, section A, above). Dupee carefully connects the social and psycho-logical strands in B's work: "The effort to reconcile art and society in terms of our national experience has dominated all his work. . . . But in deriving his ethical ideas from the new psychology of the Unconscious, he broke in part with the philosophy of traditional moral individualists." Dupee also comments on B's tendency to dissolve literature into biography, to dilute art and society, finally, into popularizations of American literary history.

Stanley Edgar Hyman's chapter on B in THE ARMED VISION (part 1, section B) finds B full of contradictions for which his socialism provides a convenient blanket. Like Dupee, Hyman stresses B's biographical approach and finds it the one consistent thing in his work. Hyman sees THE ORDEAL OF MARK TWAIN as B's best achievement in "intuitions of personality," thereby indirectly acknowledging the effectiveness of B's psychological criticism. Also like Dupee, Hyman ends by coming down hard on the lowbrow direction of B's literary history of the United States, the volumes beginning with THE FLOWERING OF NEW ENGLAND: 1815-1865: "no point of view, no standards, no depth, no ideas."

William Wasserstrom in his pamphlet (see above) sums up the contradiction at the heart of B's achievement: "Perhaps the most succinct way to crystallize the meaning of B's double career is to note that the first half of his life was spent in demonstrating the ulcerous effects of America on the human spirit and that the second half was spent in an effort to prove that America, in its root meaning, signified the very spirit of health."

Students of B should also consult THE VAN WYCK BROOKS-LEWIS MUMFORD LETTERS, THE RECORD OF A LITERARY FRIENDSHIP 1921-1963, ed. Robert E. Spiller (New York: Dutton, 1970). Family backgrounds of the two are contrasted, and B reveals his revulsion against and attraction to bourgeois traditions.

RESOURCES FOR FURTHER RESEARCH

Colum, M.M. "An American Critic: Van Wyck Brooks." DIAL, 76 (1924), 33-41.

Jones, Howard Mumford. "The Pilgrimage of Van Wyck Brooks." VIRGINIA QUARTERLY REVIEW, 8 (1932), 439-42.

Kohler, Dayton. "Van Wyck Brooks." COLLEGE ENGLISH, 2 (1941), 629-39.

Leavis, F.R. "The Americanness of American Literature: A British Demurrer to Van Wyck Brooks." COMMENTARY, 14 (1952), 466-74.

Rosenfeld, Paul. "Van Wyck Brooks." In his PORT OF NEW YORK: ESSAYS ON FOURTEEN AMERICAN MASTER. New York: Harcourt, Brace, 1924. Rpt. Urbana: University of Illinois Press, 1961, pp. 19-63.

Trilling, Lionel. "The Sense of the Past." PARTISAN REVIEW, 9 (1942), 229-41.

Wasserstrom, William. THE LEGACY OF VAN WYCK BROOKS: A STUDY OF MALADIES AND MOTIVES. Carbondale: University of Southern Illinois Press, 1971.

Wellek, René. "Van Wyck Brooks and a National Literature." AMERICAN PREFACES, 7 (1942), 292-306.

E. KENNETH BURKE (1897-)

A participant in many of the critical movements of the century, Kenneth Burke (hereafter B or KB), born in Pittsburgh and educated at Ohio State and Columbia, remains an elusive phenomenon. Identified in his youth with the social radicals of the twenties and thirties, in the early days of the New Critics he was sometimes included in their ranks as well by reviewers and critics. His chameleon-like reputation is a reflection of his many interests (not a reflection on his sincerity) and vindicates his refusal to trade polymathic joy for the crumbs of a specialized or limited point of view. Literature is a "semantic strategy for encompassing a situation," says Burke, and the "situation" is often better defined by psychology, Marxism, linguistics, symbolic logic, politics, sociology, or any one of a dozen ways of knowing, than by traditional literary norms.

However, the strategy is "semantic," and B busily coined a series of terms that rivaled, and in some cases resembled, the terminology of the New Critics: "Perspective through incongruity" echoed Allen Tate's "tension" and Cleanth Brooks's "irony and paradox"; "symbolic form" gave theoretical support to the "organicism" and formalism the New Critics kept illustrating in their practical criticism; and finally, B's "dramatism" was reflected in Cleanth Brooks's theory of the dramatized persona in lyric poetry (THE WELL WROUGHT URN, 1947). But if the two rhetorics sounded somewhat similar, they were actually at cross purposes. Brooks and company were dedicated to what René Wellek and Austin Warren (THEORY OF LITERATURE, 1949; see the introduction to the present guide) called "intrinsic criticism." Their eye was on the object, the work itself. But B has always practiced "extrinsic" criticism; his eye is less on the object than on its psychological and social ambiance. His "open" organicism embraces all intellections, and his impressive system-building and theorizing anticipate not only the anthropological references of myth criticism but certain aspects of contemporary structuralist criticism. KB is forever young.

BIBLIOGRAPHY

The most comprehensive checklist of B's writings is by Amim Paul Frank and Mechtild Frank at the back of William H. Rueckert's CRITICAL RESPONSES TO KENNETH BURKE: 1924-1966 (Minneapolis: University of Minnesota Press,

Kenneth Burke

1969). It includes uncollected literary criticism, music criticism, translations, and numerous reviews--some five hundred titles in all. A shorter primary bibliography (about half the number of titles) can be found in Rueckert's KENNETH BURKE AND THE DRAMA OF HUMAN RELATIONS (Minneapolis: University of Minnesota Press, 1963).

THE CRITICAL WORKS

COUNTER-STATEMENT (1931), PERMANENCE AND CHANGE: AN ANATOMY OF PURPOSE (1935), ATTITUDES TOWARD HISTORY (1937), THE PHILOSOPHY OF LITERARY FORM: STUDIES IN SYMBOLIC ACTION (1941), A GRAMMAR OF MOTIVES (1945), A RHETORIC OF MOTIVES (1950), THE RHETORIC OF RELIGION: STUDIES IN LOGOLOGY (1961), LANGUAGE AS SYMBOLIC ACTION: ESSAYS ON LIFE, LITERATURE, AND METHOD (1966).

REPRESENTATIVE SECONDARY SOURCES

Austin Warren describes B's intellectual development in the thirties and forties in "Sceptic's Progress," AMERICAN REVIEW, 6 (1936-37), 193-213, and thereby gives us a kind of biographical introduction. This essay, like so many other valuable pieces on B, can be found in William H. Rueckert's CRITICAL RESPONSES TO KENNETH BURKE 1924-1966 (see above). Rueckert supplies essays, reviews, and excerpts from longer works--all about B--by a variety of literary figures: William Carlos Williams writes "for me his life itself is a design." Sidney Hook questions B's principle that a "key metaphor is a better clue to understanding an author than his arguments." John Crowe Ransom clarifies B's use of "dramatistic." R.P. Blackmur notes the central position of rhetoric in B's "dramatistic" system and the inwardness of his mind, his tendency to reduce reality to self. Among the many other contributors to critical responses are Malcom Crowley, Granville Hicks, Harold Rosenberg, Allen Tate, Francis Fergusson, Richard Chase, Louis Fraiberg, and Joseph Frank.

In his book-length study of Burke, KENNETH BURKE AND THE DRAMA OF HUMAN RELATIONS (see above), Rueckert includes a six-page secondary bibliography in which he supplies paragraph-long descriptions of some of the pieces in CRITICAL RESPONSES and of important articles appearing elsewhere by W.H. Auden, Randall Jarrell, and others. Rueckert's own idea of B is summed up by the following: "B is the only writer I know of who has ever developed an inclusive system (his dramatistic system) out of a theory of literature." Arnim Paul Frank's KENNETH BURKE (New York: Twayne, 1969) should be read in conjunction with Rueckert's book. Frank also provides a short, but useful and descriptive, secondary bibliography.

One of B's earliest and most enthusiastic admirers was Stanley Edgar Hyman, whose essay in THE ARMED VISION (part 1, section B) praises him as the critic who most nearly realizes Hyman's ideal of "inclusiveness." Hyman does a lucid exposition of B's thought: Central to all of B's criticism is his "concept of works of art as 'strategies' for encompassing situations; that is, symbolic form." B, says Hyman, expanded his literary theories by adding rhetorical and grammatical categories to his analysis of symbolic action; this enabled him to develop sociological and psychological analogues to symbolic form in art.

Walter Sutton (part 1, section B) reminds us that throughout all of his criticism, B locates the "formal matrix of the work in the collective social consciousness of the audience rather than the private consciousness of the writer" (see B's COUNTER-STATEMENT). Sutton also believes that B's idiosyncratic Marxism, his interest in promoting social reorganization, explains his strategies of scrambling disciplines and of elaborate terminology: B's theory of "symbolic action" combines dramatic, religious, and psychological terms to identify "ritual drama" with the dialectic of history. However, "B's use of dramatic techniques and image patterns--together with his concern for ritual and myth--places him closer to the emerging formalist and myth rather than to Marxist criticism." Sutton does not take B's playful Marxism very seriously; B's is, after all, a verbal universe.

Merle E. Brown, KENNETH BURKE (Minneapolis: University of Minnesota Press, 1969), does not take B's philosophical ambitions any more seriously than Sutton does his Marxism. B's commitment to rhetoric and classification, says Brown, transcends any obligation to a coherent or directed dialectic. Brown also questions the intellectual seriousness of B's reckless pursuit of "oneness" but is charmed by his willingness to embrace the world as it is. B, says Brown, followed his own advice to the leftist American Writers Congress in 1935: "a propagandizer [must] plead with the unconvinced, which requires him to use 'their' vocabulary, 'their' values, 'their' symbols."

RESOURCES FOR FURTHER RESEARCH

Booth, Wayne C. "Kenneth Burke's Way of Knowing." CRITICAL INQUIRY, 1 (1974), 1-22.

Burke, Kenneth. "Dancing with tears in my eyes." CRITICAL INQUIRY, 1 (1974), 23-31.
    A reply to Booth and a discussion of his own critical approach.

Hamlin, William J., and Harold J. Nichols. "The Interest Value of Rhetorical Strategies Derived from Kenneth Burke's Pentad." WESTERN SPEECH: JOURNAL OF THE WESTERN SPEECH COMMUNICATION ASSOCIATION, 37 (1973), 97-102.

Knox, George. CRITICAL MOMENTS: KENNETH BURKE'S CATEGORIES AND CRITIQUES. Seattle: University of Washington Press, 1957.

F. T[HOMAS] S[TERNS] ELIOT (1888-1965)

Although born in St. Louis and a graduate of Harvard, where he studied under Santayana and Babbitt, T.S. Eliot (hereafter E or TSE) lived in England from 1914 until his death. Unlike Henry James, who is the "other" distinguished expatriate of American literary history and who became a British subject only shortly before his death, E assumed British citizenship in 1927, thirty-eight years before his death. Nevertheless, E never denied his American heritage, and most commentators, including many English critics, attribute much of his craft and tone to his American background. He is credited with being the most powerful single influence toward establishing the formalist direction of modern criticism; his interest in structural analysis, aesthetic criteria, and a close examination of the text all became the principal concerns of modern criticism itself.

It is ironic that E--perhaps the last of the literary dictators--himself never subscribed to any firmly-held theory of literature; throughout his long career as poet, critic, and editor, he always insisted that although theories help define poetry and criticism, evaluation rests solely on the mental resources of a truly informed, well-read, and sensitive reader. His own famous formulations, such as the "objective correlative" and the "dissociation of sensibility," led to theories of poetry and literary history in the work of other critics; but for E himself, they were the result of his own "empirical" criticism, his attempts to account for his admiration of Dante, the later plays of Shakespeare, and the metaphysical poets. This helps to explain his many contradictions and changes of taste, or at best offers a rationale for the flexibility and open-mindedness of his purported conservatism. If he was a "classicist" and a champion of the "impersonal" response, he was so because he felt deeply that such values promoted the highest humanity. His place may well be among the great poet-critics of our literary tradition: Johnson, Coleridge, and Arnold.

BIBLIOGRAPHY

The standard bibliography is Donald Gallup's T.S. ELIOT: A BIBLIOGRAPHY (New York: Harcourt, 1969), a thorough revision of the 1953 volume, which superseded a checklist by Gallup for the Yale University Library in 1947. There is a good checklist by Frances Cheney, originally compiled in 1945 and revised for Allen Tate's SIXTY AMERICAN POETS 1896-1944 (Washington, D.C.: Library of Congress, 1954). For the years 1952 to 1964, Beryl York Malawsky's checklist in the BULLETIN OF BIBLIOGRAPHY, 25, No. 3 (1967), 59-61, is a readily available source for E's writings; this checklist includes articles and translations. Northrop Frye's T.S. ELIOT (rev. ed.; New York: Grove Press,1968) has a working bibliography of E's major writings. Bradley Gunter recently compiled THE MERRILL CHECKLIST OF T.S. ELIOT (Columbus: Ohio University Press, 1970).

Richard Ludwig has done a bibliographical essay, which includes a survey of important secondary sources in FIFTEEN MODERN AMERICAN AUTHORS, ed. Jackson R. Bryer (Durham, N.C.: Duke University Press, 1969), pp. 139-74. The major source now for annotated secondary materials is Mildred Martin's A HALF CENTURY OF ELIOT CRITICISM: AN ANNOTATED BIBLIOGRAPHY OF BOOKS AND ARTICLES IN ENGLISH, 1916-1965 (Lewisburg, Pa.: Bucknell University Press, 1972). It includes more than 2,500 items in English on Eliot and covers to the year of his death.

THE CRITICAL WORKS

EZRA POUND: HIS METRIC AND POETRY (1917), THE SACRED WOOD: ESSAYS ON POETRY AND CRITICISM (1920), HOMAGE TO JOHN DRYDEN (1924), SHAKESPEARE AND THE STOICISM OF SENECA (1927), FOR LANCELOT ANDREWS: ESSAYS ON STYLE AND ORDER (1928), DANTE (1929), THOUGHTS AFTER LAMBETH (1931), CHARLES WHIBLEY: A MEMOIR (1931), SELECTED ESSAYS: 1917-1932 (1932), JOHN DRYDEN, THE POET, THE DRAMATIST, THE CRITIC (1932), THE USE OF POETRY AND THE USE OF CRITICISM (1933), AFTER STRANGE GODS (1934), ELIZABETHAN ESSAYS (1935), ESSAYS ANCIENT AND MODERN (1936), THE IDEA OF A CHRISTIAN SOCIETY (1939), THE CLASSICS AND THE MAN OF LETTERS (1942), THE MUSIC OF POETRY (1942), WHAT IS A CLASSIC? (1945), ON POETRY (1947), MILTON (1947), NOTES TOWARD THE DEFINITION OF CULTURE (1949), FROM POE TO VALERY (1948), THE AIMS OF POETIC DRAMA (1949), TALK ON DANTE (1950), POETRY AND DRAMA (1951), THE THREE VOICES OF POETRY (1953), AMERICAN LITERATURE AND THE AMERICAN LANGUAGE (1953), RELIGIOUS DRAMA: MEDIEVAL AND MODERN (1954), THE LITERATURE OF POLITICS (1955), THE FRONTIERS OF CRITICISM (1956), ON POETRY AND POETS (1957), GEORGE HERBERT (1962), KNOWLEDGE AND EXPERIENCE IN THE PHILOSOPHY OF F.H. BRADLEY (1964), and TO CRITICIZE THE CRITIC, AND OTHER WRITINGS (1965).

REPRESENTATIVE SECONDARY SOURCES

So much has been written about every aspect of E's poetry and prose that even a limited and particularized secondary bibliography for this present guide is no simple task. Readers must understand that what follows is solely in the realm of suggestion; prescription would be foolish. As a preliminary it may be useful to define the connections between E's poetry and his criticism in order to place his criticism within the total context of his thought. M.C. Bradbrook's essay, "Eliot's Critical Method," T.S. ELIOT: A STUDY OF HIS WRITING BY SEVERAL HANDS, ed. Balachandra Rajan (London: Dobson, 1971), demonstrates that E's "equipment as a critic is congruent with his equipment as a poet." The social and artistic disintegration of post–World War I Europe reflected in THE WASTE LAND's fragmentation is a pendant, says Bradbrook, to E's search for a meaningful "structural pattern" in his criticism--exhibited in the essays on Jonson, Dryden, and Marlowe, all writers who achieved a congruence with the "structure of tradition." The later poetry, adds Bradbrook, includes reflections on poetry and language that preclude the need to restate them in criticism. "Tradition" is the leitmotif of E's criticism, sounded most eloquently in his early and still influential essay, "Tradition and the Individual Talent" (1919). His enemies usually ride it as hard as his friends.

Stanley Edgar Hyman (part 1, section B), who accesses E of incipient fascism and sees in his "traditional" criticism the props of a "defeated and suffering" man, begins somewhat more subtly than his angry conclusions would indicate: E's "tradition" becomes a highly exclusive term by seeking out the classic and excluding the romantic; E's prose style is an "eighteenth century style larded with twentieth century terminology." Is this, asks Hyman, "traditional"? However, Walter Sutton (part 1, section B) maintains that the moralistic and authoritarian tone in E's cultural criticism of the thirties and forties recalls the traditionalist values of the New Humanists. The real E is hard to find in the conflicting opinions of his hundreds of critics.

Although Mildred Martin's annotated secondary bibliography (see above) is cross-indexed by subject, author, and title, its chronological arrangement makes it difficult to use unless one already knows what the significant books and articles on E are. The reader may find it more congenial to move from essays like Bradbrook's (above) to one of the following collections of essays and excerpts from important books and journals by major critics on Eliot's writings in general and his criticism in particular. The collections are listed chronologically.

Ungar, Leonard. T.S. ELIOT: A SELECTED CRITIQUE. New York: Rinehart, 1948.

> Mark Van Doren writes that "Mr. E has suggested rather than substantiated a human world order, and his humility in doing so is perhaps more exquisite than it should be." Paul Elmer More wonders whether E is a "lyric poet of chaos" or "classicist." Harold J. Laski agrees E is right when he says "moral decay" is the result of the "glorification of power," but "Christianity" cannot, says Laski, liberate us from a situation it has brought about. John Crowe Ransom calls E a "historical critic," and Yvor Winters calls him a "theorist who has repeatedly contradicted himself." Edmund Wilson believes that "TSE has undertaken a kind of scientific study of human values," and F.O. Matthiessen

insists that at the center of all of E's work one finds the "necessary union of intellect and emotion."

Tate, Allen, ed. T.S. ELIOT: THE MAN AND HIS WORK, A CRITICAL
EVALUATION BY TWENTY-SIX DISTINGUISHED WRITERS. New York: Delacorte Press, 1966.

> This volume has excellent photographs, some from E's childhood.
> It includes important reminiscences by I.A. Richards, Stephen
> Spender, Bonamy Dobrée, Ezra Pound, John Crowe Ransom, Cleanth
> Brooks, and others. Mario Proz writes a useful essay, "T.S. Eliot as
> a Critic," in which he argues E is an "empirical" rather than a
> "theoretical" critic. Austin Warren's "Eliot's Literary Criticism"
> offers a provocative juxtaposition of E and Emerson. Robert
> Giroux and Allen Tate write about E's humor, with Tate insisting
> that it was distinctly American.

Martin, Graham, comp. ELIOT IN PERSPECTIVE: A SYMPOSIUM. London:
Macmillan, 1970.

> A group of British critics respond to E's prose. John Chalker in
> "Authority and Personality in Eliot's Criticism" states "the criticism
> deals with problems that have arisen because E is creating a
> particular kind of verse, but the poetry would, on its own, have
> demanded a special critical response, and it consequently encourages
> the acceptance of his critical ideas." In John Porter's "Eliot and
> the CRITERION" we learn that despite E's displeasure with Matthew
> Arnold's belief that poetry would replace religion, Arnold provided
> the ideas and style that gave E's journal its continuity. Peter also
> provides an interesting comparison of CRITERION and SCRUTINY,
> the critical organ of F.R. Leavis. Ian Gregor's "Eliot and Mat-
> thew Arnold" argues that E became increasingly unsure of the
> distinction between religion and poetry. Two other essays are
> Richard Wollheim's "Eliot and F.H. Bradley: An Account" and
> Adrian Cunningham's "Continuity and Coherence in Eliot's Religious
> Thought."

Two book-length studies of interest to students of E's criticism are Northrop
Frye's T.S. ELIOT (see above) and John D. Margolis' T.S. ELIOT'S INTEL-
LECTUAL DEVELOPMENT: 1922-1939 (Chicago: University of Chicago Press,
1972). Frye's own importance as a critic who revolutionized myth criticism
with his famous "map" of literary kinds, ANATOMY OF CRITICISM (see the
introduction to this present guide), lends a particular interest to his chapter
on E's criticism, "The Dialect of the Tribe." Margolis' study is one of the
most recent attempts to trace the development of E's critical ideas in the context of his deep social and cultural concerns.

RESOURCES FOR FURTHER RESEARCH

Spiller's LITERARY HISTORY OF THE UNITED STATES: BIBLIOGRAPHY (part 1, section A) throughout its original and revised entries on E provides an extremely comprehensive list of secondary works, special editions, some collections of letters, and important reprints. In the 1974 entry (good to 1971), works of monograph- or pamphlet-length to be recommended to the reader new to Eliot's criticism include the following:

Headings, Philip R. T.S. ELIOT. New York: Twayne, 1964.

Pearce, T.S. T.S. ELIOT. London: Evans, 1967.

A more specialized, but importantly focused book for students of E's criticism is Austin Allen's T.S. ELIOT: THE LITERARY AND SOCIAL CRITICISM (Bloomington: Indiana University Press, 1971). Two advanced but indispensable studies are Bernard Bergonzi's T.S. ELIOT (rev. ed.; New York: Macmillan, 1978), the first critical biography, and Hugh Kenner's THE INVISIBLE POET: T.S. ELIOT (New York: McDowell, 1959).

G. PAUL ELMER MORE (1864-1937)

Like his brother-in-arms, Irving Babbitt, Paul Elmer More (hereafter M or PEM) was born in the Midwest, but unlike Babbitt he did not identify with the university or teaching as vehicles for humanism. At the age of thirty-three he retired to the village of Shelburne, New Hampshire, to lead a studious life, through which he hoped to achieve a "unifying religious faith." Hermit and seer, his studies included all the European literatures, American literature, and the philosophies and religions of the East and the West. Despite his leaving Shelburne, only three years after he arrived, to become a literary editor in New York, he never quite lost the aura of a mind dedicated to ideals of conduct and learning beyond the capacities of the bulk of his fellow human creatures. Eventually, he became editor-in-chief of THE NATION. Later, he moved again, this time to establish himself at Princeton, where he turned more devotedly than ever to his religious studies. Most scholars concur that the religious zeal behind More's moralism often made him seem more inflexible than he really was and that his firmly held convictions should not obscure the range, insight, learning, and stylistic power of his "oeuvre"--which is historically unique in American letters.

BIBLIOGRAPHY

Malcolm Young's PAUL ELMER MORE: A BIBLIOGRAPHY (Princeton, N.J.: Princeton University Press, 1941) was the first important listing of M's works, but it has been superseded by the two checklists compiled by Arthur Hazard Dakin in his A PAUL ELMER MORE MISCELLANY (Portland, Maine: Anthoensen Press, 1950). Dakin provides not only a complete record of M's writings, but also all major criticism of M up to 1950. Those preferring a shorter and simpler bibliographical introduction to M should consult the brief primary and secondary bibliography appended to Robert M. Davies' THE HUMANISM OF PAUL ELMER MORE (New York: Bookman Associates, 1958).

THE CRITICAL WORKS

SHELBURNE ESSAYS (Eleven volumes, 1904-1921). The last four carry individual titles: THE DRIFT OF ROMANTICISM (1913), ARISTOCRACY (1915), WITH THE WITS (1919), and A NEW ENGLAND GROUP AND OTHERS (1921).

NEW SHELBURNE ESSAYS (1928-1936)
    THE DEMON OF THE ABSOLUTE (1928)
    THE SKEPTICAL APPROACH TO RELIGION (1934)
    SELECTED SHELBURNE ESSAYS (1935)
    ON BEING HUMAN (1936)

THE GREEK TRADITION (1921-1927)
    THE RELIGION OF PLATO (1921)
    HELLENISTIC PHILOSOPHIES (1923)
    THE CHRIST OF THE NEW TESTAMENT (1924)
    CHRIST THE WORLD (1927)

BENJAMIN FRANKLIN (1900), NIETZSCHE (1912), PLATONISM (1917), THE CATHOLIC FAITH (1931)

REPRESENTATIVE SECONDARY SOURCES

The standard biography is by M's major bibliographer, Arthur Hazard Dakin, and stresses M's religious and philosophical ideas: PAUL ELMER MORE (Princeton, N.J.: Princeton University Press, 1960). Other biographical sources include the chapter on M by J. Oates Whitney in THE LIVES OF EIGHTEEN FROM PRINCETON, ed. Willard Thorp (Princeton, N.J.: Princeton University Press, 1946), and Louis T. More's "Shelburne Revisited: An Intimate Glimpse of Paul Elmer More," SEWANEE REVIEW 48 (1940), 457-60. For an entertaining but revealing introduction to M's personality and thought see Edmund Wilson's lead essay, "Mr. More and the Mithraic Bull," in THE TRIPLE THINKERS (New York: Harcourt, Brace, 1938), in which Wilson recalls a visit to M's Princeton home in the company of Christian Gauss in 1929. Wilson shows respect for M's independent learning and his insistence that aesthetic or intellectual values were not enough to establish the greatness of a literary work; it must be intimately connected with moral problems. Wilson, however, expresses irritation at M's flippant dismissal of T.S. Eliot.

Robert Shafer, PAUL ELMER MORE AND AMERICAN CRITICISM (New Haven: Yale University Press, 1935), believes that M's work transcends Matthew Arnold's. Although such praise seems excessive, most of M's champions have continued to insist on his philosophical, generalizing power. Convinced that M ultimately achieved a synthesis of Platonic idealism, Christian theology, and his own form of literary humanism, Robert M. Davies (see above) praises M for his "catholicity of interest." Keith E. McKean, THE MORAL MEASURE OF LITERATURE (Denver: Swallow, 1961), also stresses M's literary range and focus in comparison to Irving Babbitt, who was more of a social than a literary critic. M managed, McKean says, to theorize more forcefully than Babbitt about the connections between literature and ethics. McKean maintains that in M's critical system, literary form provides a moral restraint and protects the writer from the kind of excessive reliance on symbolism which encourages escape from moral responsibility. René Wellek, on the other hand, stresses M's close identification with the "symbolic tradition of German Romanticism and its Neo-Platonic ancestry" in "Irving Babbitt, Paul Elmer More and Transcendentalism," TRANSCENDENTALISM AND ITS LEGACY, ed. Myron Simon and Thornton H. Parsons (Ann Arbor: University of Michigan Press, 1966).

Walter E. Sutton (part 1, section B) seems to disagree with McKean's assessment of M's "catholicity." M's religiosity, says Sutton, ultimately made him far more conservative than the socially sensitive Babbitt while M's denial of democratic values cut him off from his literary model, Thoreau. But Sutton does confirm McKean's view that M was more surely identified with literary values than was Babbitt. M's stress of the "withdrawal theme"--Milton and Wordsworth offer us places of imaginative retirement--anticipates, says Sutton, the rebirth archetype of the myth critics. For M's general view of American literature, consult Daniel Aaron's useful introduction to his collection of SHELBURNE ESSAYS ON AMERICAN LITERATURE (New York: Harcourt, Brace, 1963).

RESOURCES FOR FURTHER RESEARCH

Duggan, Francis X. PAUL ELMER MORE. New York: Twayne, 1967.

Dunham, Barrows. "Paul Elmer More." MASSACHUSETTS REVIEW, 7 (1966), 157-64.

Gregory, Horace. "On Paul Elmer More And his Shelburne Essays." ACCENT, 4 (1944), 140-49.

Mercier, Louis J. THE CHALLENGE OF HUMANISM: AN ESSAY IN COMPARATIVE CRITICISM. New York: Oxford University Press, 1933.

Sherman, Stuart P. AMERICANS. New York: Scribner's, 1922.

Tanner, Stephen L. "Paul Elmer More: Literary Criticism as the History of Ideas." AMERICAN LITERATURE, 45 (1973), 390-406.

Zabel, Morton Dauwen. "An American Critic." POETRY, 50 (1937), 330-36.

H. JOHN CROWE RANSOM (1888-1974)

Except for an important three years at Oxford as a Rhodes scholar, John Crowe Ransom (hereafter R or JCR) spent the first forty-nine years of his life in Tennessee. He graduated from Vanderbilt University in 1909 and later taught there for twenty-three years. His influence on students like Robert Penn Warren and Allen Tate was great. As one of the founders of the Fugitives, a literary circle at Vanderbilt, and one of the leaders of the Agrarian Movement, Ransom has often been called the father of the Southern Literary Renascence. His literary values were decidedly classical: a turning from Romantic expressionism to a pre-Romantic sense of craft and form. In 1937 he was appointed professor of English at Kenyon College in Ohio where he founded the KENYON REVIEW.

R's theorizing up and through the 1940s seemed to insist on a severe distinction between "structure" and "texture" from which it was possible to infer that he did not feel himself bound to an organistic aesthetics. R's position drew ridicule from Yvor Winters and concern from Cleanth Brooks, the latter an active soldier in the New Criticism that R himself had called into being (1941). But in his last major critical statement on the "concrete universal" (1954), R strengthened the organic dimension to his critical theory. More effectively than Eliot, and in opposition to Burke, R consistently demonstrates the superiority of poetry to science as a revealer of reality, of the "World's Body." He rejects what he calls "Platonic poetry," which contributes to the abstraction of experience through political or intellectual allegories and plays into the hands of scientific determinism. The "Metaphysical poetry" he wrote as a poet and advocated as a critic is ultimately supported by a "post-scientific" theoretical foundation stronger than any offered by other American formalists.

BIBLIOGRAPHY

There is a checklist of R's works by R.W. Stallman in the SEWANEE REVIEW, 56 (1948), 442-76, but the definitive primary and secondary bibliography is now Mildred Brooks Peters' sixty-page annotated bibliography in Thomas Daniel Young's JOHN CROWE RANSOM: CRITICAL ESSAYS AND A BIBLIOGRAPHY (Baton Rouge: Louisiana State University Press, 1968). Young's "John Crowe Ransom: A Checklist 1967-1976," MISSISSIPPI QUARTERLY, 30 (1977), 155-68, brings the bibliographical record for R more-or-less up to date.

John Crowe Ransom

THE CRITICAL WORKS

GOD WITHOUT THUNDER: AN UNORTHODOX DEFENSE OF ORTHODOXY (1930); THE WORLD'S BODY (1938); THE NEW CRITICISM (1941); and "The Concrete Universal: Observations on the Understanding of Poetry," KENYON REVIEW, 16 (1954), reprinted in POEMS AND ESSAYS (1955).

REPRESENTATIVE SECONDARY SOURCES

John Paul Pritchard's CRITICISM IN AMERICA (part 1, section B) provides the clearest and shortest introduction to R's three principal books of criticism. Walter E. Sutton's analysis (part 1, section B) is more incisive and brings out sharply the dualism in R's theory "between structure and texture" and compares it to the "ancient form-content dichotomy." Sutton also compares R to Eliot because of their mutual concern with tradition. Despite the importance of his rather spare critical canon to American formalism, most of his commentators are devoted primarily to R's poetry, which seems to strike many as a perfect illus-tration of his critical theories. The best essay in this vein is Graham Hough's "John Crowe Ransom: The Poet and the Critic," SOUTHERN REVIEW, 1 (1965), 1-21. Hough gives a very clear definition of what R meant by "irrelevant texture."

Thomas Daniel Young's introduction to his useful collection of essays on R (see above) notes that by 1925 R's "career as a practicing poet was almost over." The rest of his long career as teacher and critic was devoted largely to social and literary criticism. He contributed the leading essay to the famous Agrarian manifesto I'LL TAKE MY STAND: THE SOUTH AND THE AGRARIAN TRADITION (New York: Harper, 1930) because he thought the social reform which the movement advocated would break the shackles of science and industrialism; similarly, he thought poetry might provide a specific knowledge different from and more humanizing than science. Young sums up the essence of R's critical approach: "'To define the structure-texture procedure of poets' he [R] writes, is to define poetic strategy.' The 'indeterminate final meaning' of a poem results from the interaction of structure and texture, and the understanding of this meaning is the 'vocation par excellence of criticism.'"

Young has published a great deal on R's criticism. He edited THE NEW CRITICS AND AFTER: JOHN CROWE RANSOM MEMORIAL LECTURES (Charlottesville: University of Virginia Press, 1977), to which he contributed "The Evolution of R's Critical Theory: Image and Idea." In addition to the checklist mentioned above, he did another short piece for the same issue of the MISSISSIPPI QUARTERLY entitled "Ransom's Critical Theories, Structure and Texture" in which he con-tinued the analysis begun in his introduction to the 1968 collection of essays. Young has also published GENTLEMAN IN A DUSTCOAT: A BIOGRAPHY OF JOHN CROWE RANSOM (Baton Rouge: Louisiana State University Press, 1976).

The following essays, with their original place of publication noted, are collected in Young's 1968 volume and deal specifically with R's criticism. Robert Penn Warren, "John Crowe Ransom: A Study in Irony," VIRGINIA QUARTERLY, 11 (1935), 93-112, defines the mythic alternative to rationality in R's criticism and then demonstrates the way his poetry provides an illustration. Edwin Berry Burgum, "An Examination of Modern Critics; John Crowe Ransom," ROCKY MOUNTAIN REVIEW, 7 (1944) 87-93, calls R more of a humanist than the New Humanists ever were. His criticism stresses the concern of art with "the whole man," but, says Burgum, he is too contemptuous of "the aid which history and psychology" might bring to criticism. Donald A. Stauffer, "Portrait of the Critic-Poet as Equilibrist," SEWANEE REVIEW, 56 (1948), 426-34, praises R because, for a critic whose prime interest is the metaphysics of aesthetics, "he almost miraculously avoids swollen systems of thought and . . . technical jargon." Morgan Blum, "The Fugitive Particular: John Crowe Ransom, Critic," WESTERN REVIEW, 14 (1950), 85-102, notes that no contemporary critics have a "terminology" as "scrupulous," an "aesthetic" as "subtle and precise." F.P. Jarvis, "F.H. Bradley's Appearance and Reality and the Critical Theory of John Crowe Ransom," PAPERS ON ENGLISH LANGUAGE AND LITERATURE, 1 (1965), 187-91, provides a lucid clarification of R's metaphysics.

No discussion of R's criticism would be complete with mention of Yvor Winters' famous retaliation for R's remarks on Winters in THE NEW CRITICISM (part 3, section L). In THE ANATOMY OF NONSENSE (1943) Winters' essay "John Crowe Ransom, Thunder Without God" attacks R's idea of poetry without abstraction as a lack of common sense; furthermore, says Winters, the limitation of the rational content of a poem to a core about which the "irrelevant texture" is arranged is sheer antiintellectualism and also ignores the organic nature of literary expression. Another attack on R worth looking at is Winifred Lynskey's "A Critic in Action: Mr. Ransom," COLLEGE ENGLISH, 5 (1944), 239-49: literature (e.g., Milton's "Lycidas"), argues Lynskey, is distorted to fit R's theories.

RESOURCES FOR FURTHER RESEARCH

Cowan, Louise. THE FUGITIVE GROUP: A LITERARY HISTORY. Baton Rouge: Louisiana State University Press, 1959.

Elliot, Emory B., Jr. "Theology and Agrarian Ideology in the Critical Theory of John Crowe Ransom." XAVIER UNIVERSITY STUDIES, 10, No. 3 (1971), 1-7.

McDonald, Marcia. "The Function of the Persona in Ransom's Critical Prose." MISSISSIPPI QUARTERLY, 30 (1977), 87-100.

Magner, James E., Jr. JOHN CROWE RANSOM: CRITICAL PRINCIPLES AND PREOCCUPATIONS. The Hague: Mouton, 1971.

Rubin, Louis D., Jr. "A Critic Almost Anonymous: John Crowe Ransom Goes

North." In THE NEW CRITICISM AND AFTER. Ed. T.D. Young. Charlottes-ville: University of Virginia Press, 1977, pp. 1-21.

Stewart, John L. "Ransom's Theories of Poetry and Criticism." In his THE BURDEN OF TIME: THE FUGITIVES AND AGRARIANS. Princeton: Princeton University Press, 1965, pp. 257-306.

I. [JOHN ORLEY] ALLEN TATE (1899-1979)

For Allen Tate (hereafter T or AT) to achieve a reputation as a social and literary "reactionary" was a triumph of intention. It was his way of dramatizing a lifelong struggle with "Positivism"--that bulldozer with science at the wheel and social engineers on the running board who think poetry either useless or an exercise in emotional gratification. T's strategy was to turn himself into a giant obstacle, a polemicist for "tradition" and the authority of art, a critic whose high seriousness might shame the scientists' and engineers' great machine to a halt. Positivism rolls on, but T also stands. Indeed, after Edmund Wilson, who was his political opposite, T emerges as one of the most impressive examples of a "Man of Letters" (a phrase he championed) in our time: critic, novelist, poet, teacher, and conservative apologist.

Many of his ideas about poetry originated with T.S. Eliot, Cleanth Brooks, and John Crowe Ransom, his teacher at Vanderbilt. Except for Brooks's, T's style is more effective than that of any of the New Critics: "A critical style," he said, "ought to be as plain as the nose on one's face." Born in Kentucky, he went to Europe on a Guggenheim Fellowship from 1928 to 1930, and despite his southern loyalties he developed important friendships with writers from all over the world. This cosmopolitan traditionalist converted in 1950 to Catholicism, an act that moved him closer to what he felt was "the living center." As a professor of English at the University of Minnesota from 1951 to 1968, T received numerous degrees and awards, many of them international. "Tension" is one of his most famous critical concepts, and it also defines the delicate equilibrium he achieved between a social and literary exclusiveness and a wide intellectual impact and popularity.

BIBLIOGRAPHY

Willard Thorp's "Allen Tate: A Checklist," PRINCETON UNIVERSITY LIBRARY CHRONICLE, 3 (1942), 85-98, is reprinted in "An Issue for Allen Tate," CRITIQUE: STUDIES IN MODERN FICTION, 10, No. 2 (1968), 17-34. The reprint in CRITIQUE is followed by an addendum by James Korge listing works by and about T to 1968. Marshall Fallwell, Jr., with the assistance of Martha Cook and Frances Immler, compiled ALLEN TATE: A BIBLIOGRAPHY (New

York: Lewis, 1969). This work includes twenty-four pages of annotated titles of bibliographical and critical material through 1967. ALLEN TATE AND HIS WORKS: CRITICAL EVALUATIONS, ed. Radcliffe Squires (Minneapolis: University of Minnesota Press, 1972) includes a thirty-four page primary and secondary bibliography, unannotated but good through 1971.

THE CRITICAL WORKS

REACTIONARY ESSAYS ON POETRY AND IDEAS (1936), REASON IN MADNESS, CRITICAL ESSAYS (1941), ON THE LIMITS OF POETRY, SELECTED ESSAYS: 1928-1948 (1948), THE HOVERING FLY AND OTHER ESSAYS (1949), THE FORLORN DEMON, DIDACTIC AND CRITICAL ESSAYS (1953), THE MAN OF LETTERS IN THE MODERN WORLD, SELECTED ESSAYS: 1928-1955 (1955), COLLECTED ESSAYS (1959), ESSAYS OF FOUR DECADES (1968), and MEMOIRS AND OPINIONS: 1926-1974 (1975).

REPRESENTATIVE SECONDARY SOURCES

Consult John Paul Pritchard's short portrait (part 1, section B), which places T next to Ransom in importance among the New Critics. Walter E. Sutton's account (part 1, section B) puts T closer to Cleanth Brooks than to Ransom by virtue of T's "emphasis on the total structure of the poem as a device for uniting and resolving discordant qualities." T's religious and political absolutism, says Sutton, has made him critical of modern critics "languishing in a 'pragmatic vortex.'" George Hemphill's useful pamphlet, ALLEN TATE (Minneapolis: University of Minnesota Press, 1964), maintains that all of T's literary theory and practical criticism "proceed from a single recognition: the imperfectibility of man." T's distrust of all forms of social engineering is matched by his skepticism of critical theory, suggests Hemphill. Ferman Bishop's ALLEN TATE (New York: Twayne, 1967) concentrates on T's poetry but also deals briefly with his criticism: Despite many resemblances to T.E. Hulme and T.S. Eliot, "T is never the servile imitator." Bishop notes that in T's work on American poetry, he glorified Crane, misunderstood Stevens, and ignored Frost.

The standard biography, and the first, is Radcliffe Squire's ALLEN TATE: A LITERARY BIOGRAPHY (New York: Pegasus, 1971). It reviews T's literary career in more or less chronological fashion and closes with a chapter on "works in progress." Squires also provides an elegant six-page summary of T's life and significance in an introduction to a special collection of essays on T edited by Squires, ALLEN TATE AND HIS WORK: CRITICAL EVALUATIONS (see above). This volume collects some of the best essays written on T in the last thirty years. Several of them come from the special issue "Homage to Allen Tate: Essays, Notes, and Verses in Honor of his Sixtieth Birthday," with a foreword by Monroe K. Spears, SEWANEE REVIEW, 67 (1959, 596-631.

In Squires's collection the essays are arranged under the following three headings: "The Man," "The Essayist," and "The Poet." Under "The Essayist" readers will find the following particularly useful:

> Francis Fergusson's "A Note on the Vitality of Allen Tate's Prose" suggests that T's poetic principle of "tension" is at work in his prose at many levels: in contrasted fields of reference, in the conflict between writer and audience and between syntactical and rhetorical elements. In "The Criticism of Allen Tate," Monroe K. Spears surveys T's criticism up to 1948. T "means to vex the world rather than divert it." He does not successfully reconcile art and tradition, says Spears. As a practical critic, T is most admirable, but we need "desperately . . . a satisfactory general theory." Eliseo Vivas, "Allen Tate as Man of Letters," believes that T invests the "man of letters" with a moral and philosophical responsibility far beyond that of a mere writer; T "forges" in his "conscience" an "image . . . through the joint action of knowledge and judgment." R.P. Blackmur, in "San Giovanni in Venere: Allen Tate as Man of Letters," analyzes T's and Ransom's debt to I.A. Richards; Blackmur also wittily places T's position vis-à-vis Brooks and Ransom: "The different temperament of Tate . . . responded by inventing tension, or in-tension--the relation of stress between the halves of irony and paradox--the stress by which structure is united with texture." T can "see beyond the methods of other critics into an insight of what these methods left out," and he is "surpassed only by Eliot at illuminating quotation." George Core's "A Metaphysical Athlete: Allen Tate as Critic" revels that Herbert Read was the first to call T a "metaphysical athlete." In "A Note on Allen Tate's Essays," a review of T's ESSAYS OF FOUR DECADES (1968), Richard Howard maintains that although T's criticism serves the interests of his poetry, he is fiercely committed to making his readers see the marriage between literature and the world as it is.

RESOURCES FOR FURTHER RESEARCH

Amyx, Clifford. "The Aesthetics of Allen Tate." WESTERN REVIEW, 13, No. 3 (1949), 135-45.

Brooks, Cleanth. "Allen Tate and the Nature of Modernism." SOUTHERN REVIEW, 12 (1976), 685-97.

> This essay is part of "A Special Section on Allen Tate," including other articles by George Core and Radcliffe Squires.

Fain, John Tyree, and Thomas Daniel Young, eds. THE LITERARY CORRESPONDENCE OF DONALD DAVIDSON AND ALLEN TATE. Athens: University of Georgia Press, 1974.

Frye, Norhrop. "Ministry of Angels." HUDSON REVIEW, 6 (1953-54), 442-47.

Glicksberg, Charles I.   "Allen Tate and Mother Earth."   SEWANEE REVIEW, 5 (1937), 284-95.

Warren, Austin.   "Homage to Allen Tate."   SOUTHERN REVIEW, 9 (1973), 753-77.

J. LIONEL TRILLING (1905-75)

Lionel Trilling (hereafter T or LT) spent his entire life in New York City, except for a short teaching assignment in Wisconsin, studying and teaching at Columbia University. He is of that city, as the New Critics were of the South. Modern cosmopolitanism glowed from THE LIBERAL IMAGINATION when it appeared in 1950. For ten years T had been writing able and elegant essays on the modern imagination, its cultural and psychological function and nature, but once they were printed together the full power of their intellectual range and substance was startling. T had successfully crowned himself as, what years later Alfred Kazin was to call, "Emersonian teacher." His mission was the continuing liberation of man's spirit, and like Emerson he belabored the distinction between "law for man" and "law for thing."

That teaching had been one of the guiding principles of Irving Babbitt's New Humanism some twenty years earlier. But although T was deeply disturbed by the same materialism and solipsism that had caused Babbitt so much anguish, T could not move toward a social or cultural conservatism. He was too much a man of our own time to retreat toward the thinking of another era. Although he insisted there was no explicitly Jewish direction to his thought, he was a Jewish intellectual of the twentieth century and profoundly aware of the liberalizing forces that had swept his own people from medieval isolation to a passionate involvement in the matter of the moment. Perhaps one of the last children of the Enlightenment, T stretched his cultural ancestry to include Romanticism, the very movement the New Humanists and the New Critics had found so threatening.

T was both rational and emotional, his own Voltaire and Rousseau, and therein lay his unique strength for dealing with the problems of modern alienation. Unlike so many moderns--Yeats, D.H. Lawrence, Babbitt, and More--who coveted a lost center, who still yearned for Eden, T patiently carried forward the undeniable burden of his individuality and freedom, a precious responsibility bequeathed to him by the intellectual heroes of the modern life. Arnold, E.M. Forster, and preeminently Freud, but also Wordsworth and Keats, were all minds great enough to shoulder the polarities T felt defined the "liberal imagination." They all struggled with the conflicting demands of poetry and duty, self and society, biology and mind, sensation and thought, and reverie and philosophic attention. At various times, for different critical purposes, T engaged all these tensions. His refusal to ignore the complexity of his insights made it impossible to fashion a literary theory. He would not risk oversimplification or distortion. His sensibility or "opposing self" had to assume the entire burden of his insights; no critical terminology or system would do. This is why some thought him abstract and contemplative to a fault. But those able to follow his style and tone, instruments he perfected to do his delicate work, testify to his power.

BIBLIOGRAPHY

The first published bibliography of T's work that includes a list of reviews and essays about him (approximately 175 unannotated titles) is the checklist compiled by Marianne Gilbert Barnaby for BULLETIN OF BIBLIOGRAPHY, 31, No. 1 (1974), 37-44. It has coverage to 1972. The Festschrift, ART, POLITICS AND WILL: ESSAYS IN HONOR OF LIONEL TRILLING, ed. Quentin Anderson, Stephen Donadio, and Steven Marcus (New York: Basic Books, 1977), includes a brief chronology of T's life and works.

THE CRITICAL WORKS

MATTHEW ARNOLD (1939), E.M. FORSTER (1943), THE LIBERAL IMAGINA-
TION: ESSAYS ON LITERATURE AND SOCIETY (1950), THE OPPOSING
SELF: NINE ESSAYS IN CRITICISM (1955), A GATHERING OF FUGITIVES
(1956), FREUD AND THE CRISIS OF OUR CULTURE (1956), BEYOND CULTURE:
ESSAYS ON LITERATURE AND LEARNING (1960), SINCERITY AND AUTHEN-
TICITY (1972), MIND IN THE MODERN WORLD (1972), and THE UNCERTAIN
FUTURE OF THE HUMANISTIC IDEAL (1974).

REPRESENTATIVE SECONDARY SOURCES

Edmund Wilson reviewed MATTHEW ARNOLD in the NEW REPUBLIC, 98 (1939), 199-200, and called it "one of the first critical studies of any solidity and scope by an American of his generation." In the 1940s reviewers dealt with both T's criticism and fiction and tended to admire each, although there was some confusion about determining his political and critical values--see Howard Mumford Jones's "E.M. Forster and the Liberal Imagination," SATURDAY RE-VIEW, 26 (August 28, 1943), 6-7. With the publication of THE LIBERAL IMAGINATION in 1950, which consisted of his best work in the past ten years, his reputation was secured. Charles J. Glicksberg historicized him by adding T at the end of his survey of distinguished critics of the first half-century (part 2, section A): "He has produced in THE LIBERAL IMAGINATION . . . a work which virtually puts him at the head of the critical brotherhood in this century."

In the 1950s T's lack of any critical theory became more obvious as the New Criticism seemed to retain its prestige. William Van O'Conner rose to T's defense by reminding readers that T was interested in what literature "does" rather than merely what it "is"--see O'Conner's "Lionel Trilling's Critical Realism," SEWANEE REVIEW, 58 (1950), 490-91. In his history (part 1, section B) O'Conner insists that T is not oblivious to formalist values. For example, in his essay "Manners, Morals and the Novel," T is concerned with the social aspects of literature, but "his examination of deficiencies in character drawing in the latter part of Helen Howe's novel [show] how social attitudes affect the very structure of a work."

T's displeasure with the "conditioned" quality of modern society earned him the enmity of liberals who felt he was a conservative in disguise. Joseph Frank's controversial essay, "Lionel Trilling and the Conservative Imagination," SEWANEE REVIEW, 64 (1956), 296-309, compares T to Babbitt and dismisses T's brooding as a substitution of "contemplation for an active grappling with social reality." Frank's essay is reprinted in his THE WIDENING GYRE: CRISIS AND MASTERY IN WORLD LITERATURE (New Brunswick, N.J.: Rutgers University Press, 1963).

But T is vindicated by Louis Fraiberg's PSYCHOANALYSIS AND AMERICAN LITERARY CRITICISM (see the introduction to this present guide) where T is praised as the critic who best used Freud's ideas. T's theory of the "mithridatic" function of tragedy is singled out as a particularly brilliant contribution. All through the 1950s and part of the 1960s, T and Jacques Barzun taught their seminar in "cultural criticism" at Columbia; Barzun describes T's approach in the Festschrift of 1977 (see above).

One of the first published essays on T of monograph length is the chapter on him by Nathan A. Scott, Jr., in his THREE AMERICAN MORALISTS: MAILER, BELLOW, TRILLING (South Bend, Ind.: Notre Dame University Press, 1973). Scott does a complete survey of T's intellectual history and concludes that throughout his work the view that man is both "angel and beast" establishes a balanced but "anxious humanism." Robert Boyer's monograph, the first separately published work on T, entitled LIONEL TRILLING: NEGATIVE CAPABILITY AND THE WISDOM OF AVOIDANCE (Columbia: University of Missouri Press, 1977), continues the exploration of T's polarity: T "was of two minds on almost everything." Boyer suggests that T's fascination with "negative capability," the quality he admired in Keats and James, explains his own strength as a critic. He balanced his empathy, says Boyer, with rational detachment.

Denis Donoghue in a recent essay, "Trilling, Mind, and Society," SEWANEE REVIEW, 86 (1978), 161-86, returns to the central issue in all of T's work since MATTHEW ARNOLD (1939)--the artist's connection with society. T never felt the artist "might dispense with society and find within himself a sufficient moral authority." Nevertheless, says Donoghue, T, unlike the structuralists, rejected deterministic ideas of language and society. Like the Romantic theorists he admired and taught, T thought mind should reduce "multiplicity to unity." Donoghue compares T to R.P. Blackmur: T felt society was the final truth; Blackmur, the imagination itself. "T's favorite virtue was patience, Blackmur's quirkiness."

David Kubal, who did a study of T's only novel for the BUCKNELL REVIEW, 14 (1966), 60-73, entitled "TRILLING'S MIDDLE OF THE JOURNEY: An American Dialectic," has published another essay, "Lionel Trilling: The Mind and Its Discontents," HUDSON REVIEW, 31 (1978), 279-95. Kubal alludes to a letter T sent him in 1966, "responding to a proposal that a literary meeting be set up around his ideas." T seems somewhat intrigued, but the meeting never came about. Kubal uses T's ambivalence over such a meeting as a departure for a survey of T's last writings in which Kubal feels T does come to grips with the polarities of his thought by reaffirming the power of the independent mind.

RESOURCES FOR FURTHER RESEARCH

Chace, William. "Lionel Trilling: The Contrariness of Culture." AMERICAN SCHOLAR, 48 (1978-79), 49-58.

Daiches, David. "The Mind of Lionel Trilling." COMMENTARY, 24 (1957), 66-69.

Green, Martin. "Lionel Trilling and the Two Cultures." ESSAYS IN CRITICISM, 13 (1963), 375-85.

Hirsh, David H. "Reality, Manners, and Mr. Trilling." SEWANEE REVIEW, 72 (1964), 420-32.

"Lionel Trilling." SALMAGUNDI, 41 (1978), 3-110. Special Issue.

> Mark Shechner contributes "Lionel Trilling: Psychoanalysis and Liberalism"; Joseph Frank's "Lionel Trilling and the Conservative Imagination" should be read in conjunction with his earlier essay (see above); Robert Langbaum, in "The Importance of the Liberal Imagination," maintains that T compared the Stalinists to the structuralists; Helen Vendler takes issue with T's interpretation of Wordsworth in "Lionel Trilling and the Immortality Ode"; and T, Irving Howe, Leslie H. Farber, and William Hamilton participate in "SINCERITY AND AUTHENTICITY: A Symposium."

Podhoretz, Norman. "The Arnoldian Function in American Criticism." SCRUTINY, 18 (1951), 59-65.

Raleigh, John H. MATTHEW ARNOLD AND AMERICAN CULTURE. Berkeley and Los Angeles: University of California Press, 1957.

Warshow, Robert. "The Legacy of the Thirties." In his THE IMMEDIATE EXPERIENCE. New York: Doubleday, 1962, pp. 33-48.

K. EDMUND WILSON (1895-1973)

The "Upstate" New York background of Edmund Wilson (hereafter W or EW) created in him a mix of respect for the common man and a sense of patrician responsibility for culture. Under the influence at Princeton of Christian Gauss, who taught him that literature reveals the secrets of social and cultural identity, W turned into a student of world literature on a grand scale. He began his career as a reporter on the NEW YORK EVENING SUN, and, after service at a French hospital base and in the Intelligence Corps during World War I, he found a job on the staff of VANITY FAIR. From 1926 to 1931 he was associate editor of the NEW REPUBLIC. AXEL'S CASTLE (1931) was a tour de force in mass literary education. Thousands of readers, among them hosts of college students and faculty, lost their fear of Proust, Joyce, and Eliot through W's brilliant exposition.

His clear analysis of the evolution from naturalism to symbolism suddenly gave modern writers a history and contributed to making these literary movements legitimate subjects for study at the university. Always W searched tirelessly for the cultural phenomenon, the political or social fact, the idea or person-ality, which would help him get at the heart of a literary text. His quests took him from Marxism to Freud, and after World War II through an even broader range of historical and intellectual realities: the American Civil War and the emerging nations and people of the day; the Dead Sea Scrolls and the newest editions of the American classics. His curiosity never flagged. Toward the end, if the objects of his interest seemed less significant than in earlier years, the reliability of his learning was never in doubt. He seemed to enjoy it all too much. Despite his occasional wrongheadedness and a tendency to paranoia, he was a critic to his bones. One has to go back to Hazlitt to find his equal.

BIBLIOGRAPHY

Arthur Mizener's checklist in the PRINCETON UNIVERSITY LIBRARY CHRONICLE, 5 (1944), 62-78, has been superseded by William J. Lewis' "Edmund Wilson: A Bibliography," inclusive through 1964 for W's books and articles, in the BULLETIN OF BIBLIOGRAPHY, 25 (1968), 145-51. A complete primary and

secondary bibliography has been compiled by Richard David Ramsay, EDMUND
WILSON: A BIBLIOGRAPHY (New York: Lewis, 1971), which is reliable
through 1969. Ramsey's thoroughly annotated section, "items about W," runs
for thirty-eight pages.

WORKS OF CRITICISM (AND RELATED PROSE)

I. CRITICISM: AXEL'S CASTLE: A STUDY IN THE IMAGINATIVE LITERA-
TURE OF 1870-1930 (1931), THE TRIPLE THINKERS: TEN ESSAYS ON LIT-
ERATURE (1938), THE WOUND AND THE BOW: SEVEN STUDIES IN LITERA-
TURE (1941), THE BOYS IN THE BACK ROOM: NOTES ON CALIFORNIA
NOVELISTS (1941), NOTEBOOKS OF NIGHT (1942), CLASSICS AND COM-
MERCIALS: A LITERARY CHRONICLE OF THE FORTIES (1950), THE SHORES
OF LIGHT: A LITERARY CHRONICLE OF THE TWENTIES AND THIRTIES (1952),
THE BIT BETWEEN BY TEETH: A LITERARY CHRONICLE OF 1950-1965 (1965),
and THE FRUITS OF THE MLA (1968).

II. HISTORICAL AND TRAVEL ESSAYS: THE AMERICAN JITTERS: A YEAR
OF THE SLUMP (1932), TRAVELS IN TWO DEMOCRACIES (1936), TO THE
FINLAND STATION (1940), EUROPE WITHOUT BAEDEKER (1947), THE SCROLLS
FROM THE DEAD SEA (1955), RED, BLACK, BLOND, and OLIVE: STUDIES
IN FOUR CIVILIZATIONS (1956), A PIECE OF MY MIND: REFLECTIONS AT
SIXTY (1956), THE AMERICAN EARTHQUAKE: A DOCUMENT OF THE JAZZ
AGE, THE GREAT DEPRESSION, AND THE NEW DEAL (1958), APOLOGIES
TO THE IROQUOIS (1960), PATRIOTIC GORE: STUDIES IN THE LITERATURE
OF THE AMERICAN CIVIL WAR (1962), THE COLD WAR AND THE INCOME
TAX: A PROTEST (1963), O CANADA: AN AMERICAN'S NOTES ON CA-
NADIAN CULTURE (1965), THE DEAD SEA SCROLLS: 1947-1969 (1969), UP-
STATE: RECORDS AND RECOLLECTIONS OF NORTHERN NEW YORK (1971).

III. AUTOBIOGRAPHY, DIARIES, AND LETTERS: A PRELUDE: LANDSCAPES,
CHARACTERS AND CONVERSATIONS FROM THE EARLIER YEARS OF MY LIFE
(1967), THE TWENTIES: FROM NOTEBOOKS AND DIARIES OF THE PERIOD
(Ed. Leon Edel, 1975), LETTERS ON LITERATURE AND POLITICS: 1912-1972
(Introd. Daniel Aaron; Foreword Leon Edel, 1977), and THE NABOKOV-WILSON
LETTERS (Ed. Simon Karlinsky, 1979).

REPRESENTATIVE SECONDARY SOURCES

Ramsey's secondary bibliography (see above) is not as inclusive as Vitelli's on
Van Wyck Brooks (part 3, section D), but it is more selective and therefore
perhaps more useful, even though its annotations are not so extended.

Adverse criticism of W always centers on his tendency to summarize or paraphrase the works he discusses. Stanley Edgar Hyman (part 1, section B) calls
W a "translator" of the great modern writers, a specialist in plot-synopsis and

not above plagiarism in his scholarship. This may be the most vituperative essay in Hyman's book; he removed it from the 1955 reprint of THE ARMED VISION. Walter E. Sutton (part 1, section B) sees the "translator" in W in a different light: W introduced "a new generation of American readers" to the modern tradition of symbolism (AXEL'S CASTLE), and through his "clarity of style" made difficult modern writers intelligible. Although interested in close analysis, W has always stressed the "social relevance of literature." Sutton also credits W with a keen awareness of Freud's equation between neurosis and art in W's essay on Henry James's THE TURN OF THE SCREW, in THE TRIPLE THINKERS, and the essays in THE WOUND AND THE BOW.

Whereas critics like Hyman turn W into a dishonest hack, many see him as a paragon of Puritan, even Roman virtue: "Incorruptibility and professionalism" mark all of W's literary heroes writes Sherman Paul, EDMUND WILSON: A STUDY OF LITERARY VOCATION IN OUR TIME (Urbana: University of Illinois Press, 1965). To maintain his own "integrity" W always remained something of an "outsider." Paul sums up W by discussing his union of "conservative impulse" and "radical idea." Paul's is the first book devoted exclusively to W; although mainly on account of W's intellectual development, it also serves as a biographical introduction. For an informative account of W's radical phase, consult Murray Kempton's "The Social Muse" in his PART OF OUR TIME: RUINS AND MONUMENTS OF THE THIRTIES (New York: Simon, 1955).

In his short but balanced study, Werner Berthoff, EDMUND WILSON (Minneapolis: University of Minnesota Press, 1968), praises W for his instinctive taste and his belief in literature as a humane activity and an index to civilization: "Free of any dogma or blinding ideology, he became a natural historian of the literary life." But the "lack of any controlling idea" appropriate to "the full dimension" of his subject gives even his best books, such as AXEL'S CASTLE and PATRIOTIC GORE, a descriptive rather than analytical power. He is, concludes Berthoff, the quintessential "literary journalist." Charles P. Frank, in a slightly longer book, EDMUND WILSON (New York: Twayne, 1970), also attempts to assess the core of W's achievement. He concludes that W's fiction, long neglected, actually illustrates his criticism and supplies the theoretical key to all of his work: The meaning of literature for W, Frank believes, constitutes the relation of a perceptive individual to his social environment. Admiration for W reaches its zenith in a book like Leonard Kriegel's EDMUND WILSON (Carbondale: University of Southern Illinois Press, 1971): W would be able to claim a preeminent position in our literature even if AXEL'S CASTLE and TO THE FINLAND STATION were his total output. Kriegel sees him as a twentieth-century Emerson.

W's descriptive gift for bringing alive a book, country, person, or historical moment has always tempted critics to deny him theoretical power. Charles P. Frank (see above) is an exception, and so is Delmore Schwartz. In an essay written a little less than forty years ago, "The Writing of Edmund Wilson," reprinted in Schwartz's SELECTED ESSAYS OF DELMORE SCHWARTZ, ed. Donald A. Dike and David H. Zucker (Chicago: University of Chicago Press, 1970), W's ability to give himself up to an experience is seen as part of an even subtler gift, the ability to confront various theories as well. When W moved from Marxist to Freudian approaches, he was being flexible for the sake of literature, not flippant in his politics or intellectual committments. Here is how Schwartz puts it: "Yet one of W's virtues as an author has always been to avoid giving himself to any systematic view of Life, to see how Life is more than any systematic views of it, but at the same time to see how systematic views are useful instruments."

Although W's critical and descriptive approaches are difficult for Americans to grasp, they are not uncongenial to European intellectuals. The English writer John Wain, in his ESSAYS ON LITERATURE AND IDEAS (London: Macmillan, 1963), puts it quite simply: "W has kept alive the older notion of the critic as the man who, first and foremost, KNOWS more than the reader. Whether or not one agrees with his judgments, an article by him is always informative." In other words W knew more than any one or two theories could explain--to himself or to his readers. John Wain has recently edited AN EDMUND WILSON CELEBRATION (Oxford: Phaidon, 1978), containing a dozen contributions divided into three "quasi groups": 1. EW--the man, 2. artist as critic, and 3. critic as artist. Alfred Kazin's "The Great Anachronism: A View from the Sixties" is the major contribution to "quasi group" 1, and John Updike's "Wilson's Fiction: A Personal Account" is a moving tribute in group 3.

RESOURCES FOR FURTHER RESEARCH

Adam, Robert M. "Masks and Delays: Edmund Wilson as Critic." SEWANEE REVIEW, 56 (1948), 272-86.

Botsford, Keith. "The American Plutarch, the Last Roman, or Plain Mr. Wilson." TEXAS QUARTERLY, 6 (1963), 129-40.

Brown, E.K. "The Method of Edmund Wilson." UNIVERSITY OF TORONTO QUARTERLY, 2 (1941), 105-11.

Douglas, George H. "Edmund Wilson: The Critic as Artist." TEXAS QUARTERLY, 17 (1974), 58-72.

Fraiberg, Louis. PSYCHOANALYSIS IN AMERICAN LITERARY CRITICISM. Detroit: Wayne State University Press, 1960.

Hicks, Granville. "The Intransigence of Edmund Wilson." ANTIOCH REVIEW, 6 (1946-47), 550-62.

Kazin, Alfred. "The Imagination of a Man of Letters." AMERICAN SCHOLAR, 34 (1964-65), 19-27.

Kermode, Frank. "Edmund Wilson's Achievement." ENCOUNTER, 26 (1966), 61-70.

Levin, Harry. "The Last American Man of Letters." TIMES LITERARY SUP-PLEMENT, 11 October 1974, pp. 1128-30.

Podhoretz, Norman. "Edmund Wilson: Then and Now." DOINGS AND UN-DOINGS. New York: Farrar Straus, 1964.

Struve, Gleb. "The Moralist and the Magician." TIMES LITERARY SUPPLE-MENT, 2 May 1980, pp. 509-10.

An extensive review of THE NABOKOV-WILSON LETTERS, above, which highlights the critical perspectives to be found in this important primary resource.

L. YVOR WINTERS (1900-1968)

The reputation of Yvor Winters (hereafter W or YW) as a loner or maverick is reflected in his beginnings. No Fugitives, Rhodes scholarship, Harvard, Princeton, Columbia, or New Masses coterie offered him the reflection of ideas in the conversation and thought of others, so vital to almost any original or strongly creative mind. He had attended only four quarters at the University of Chicago when tuberculosis sent him to New Mexico, where he worked as a school teacher in the coal camps south of Santa Fe. After getting his M.A. in Romance languages at the University of Colorado in 1925, he taught French and Spanish at the University of Idaho. In 1927 he enrolled as a graduate student at Stanford and was shortly appointed to an instructorship in English. Awarded his Ph.D. in 1934, Winters was kept at Stanford where he spent the rest of his teaching career writing poetry and criticism. He summed up his critical creed in THE FUNCTION OF CRITICISM (1957), a point of view from which he never wavered through twenty-five years of analytics and polemics: A poem is "a rational statement about a human experience. It is a method for perfecting the understanding and the moral discrimination." Although the morality of a poem's meaning is seen largely as an organistic balance of form and content or a classical equilibrium, never as merely a didactic message, W's moralism owes a great deal to the New Humanists whom he attacked in his youth but eventually recognized as his forbears. Armed with a textualist approach, W consistently challenged the contextualism of the New Critics. W was an angry man. There are some who feel his anger was prophetic, in the biblical sense; others think it merely dyspeptic.

BIBLIOGRAPHY

The standard bibliography of Winters' writings is by Kenneth A. Lohf and Eugene B. Sheehy, YVOR WINTERS: A BIBLIOGRAPHY (Denver: Swallow, 1959). It covers the period from 1921 to 1957 with some entries for 1958. There is also a four-page unannotated listing of books and articles about Winters. For the period of 1957 to 1968, consult the checklist at the back of Richard J. Sexton's THE COMPLEX OF YVOR WINTERS'S CRITICISM (The Hague: Mouton, 1973).

THE CRITICAL WORKS

NOTES ON THE MECHANICS OF THE POETIC IMAGE (1925), PURITANISM AND DECADENCE (1937), MAULE'S CURSE: SEVEN STUDIES IN THE HISTORY OF AMERICAN OBSCURANTISM (1938), THE ANATOMY OF NONSENSE (1943), EDWIN ARLINGTON ROBINSON (1946), IN DEFENSE OF REASON (1947), THE FUNCTION OF REASON (1957), FORMS OF DISCOVERY: CRITICAL AND HISTORICAL ESSAYS ON THE SHORT POEM IN ENGLISH (1967), and UNCOLLECTED ESSAYS AND REVIEWS (Ed. Francis Murphy, 1977).

REPRESENTATIVE SECONDARY SOURCES

John Crowe Ransom defined W as "The Logical Critic" in THE NEW CRITICISM (1941) and accused him of subordinating "the poetic interest to the moral." W retaliated by accusing Ransom of the inability to distinguish between didacticism and morality in art (ANATOMY OF NONSENSE), and W's critics have trod carefully ever since. Despite his eccentricities, dogmatism, and belligerence, W has been taken seriously. René Wellek calls him a "critic of stature" in CONCEPTS OF CRITICISM (part 1, section B) and S.E. Hyman (part 1, section B), as early as 1948 in THE ARMED VISION, a work not exactly noted for its impartiality, deals more-or-less evenly with W: W is important because he stresses evaluation, practically an "extinct critical function in our times." Unfortunately, his exaggerated Johnsonianism leads W to some curious evaluations. Edith Wharton's "precision" in moral matters is favored over Henry James's ambiguities. W's favorite pejorative terms are "obscurantism" and "romanticism." Finally, Hyman comes down hard on W's narrowness of knowledge, dogmatism, and impoliteness in professional discourse; nevertheless, says Hyman, his insistence on moral evaluation makes him a "bad critic of some importance."

Keith E. McKean, THE MORAL MEASURE OF LITERATURE (Denver: Swallow, 1961), objects to lumping W together with Babbitt and More. W is a moralist, but the "key concept in [his] criticism is not control but balance." W does not insist on any particular ethical principles; what does concern him is the balance between feeling and reason that the artist must achieve. This balance is at once an aesthetic and moral imperative. Walter E. Sutton (part 1, section B) notes that although W's insistence on the moral and rational qualities of literature put him at odds with the New Critics, he used their textualist approach for his own purposes. This is particularly true of MAULE'S CURSE, in which W resorts to close analysis of the text to trace the connections between "obscurantism" and "moral confusion" in some important American writers. Like Hyman, Sutton remarks on W's invective and his bad literary manners. But W is an important corrective, says Sutton, to the prevailing formalism of the New Critics.

He should not have the last word on W's capacity for controversy, but Charles I. Glicksberg (part 2, section A) writes that "A man who can compose such vitrolic diatribes is scarcely entitled to pose as a defender of reason."

Richard J. Sexton's THE COMPLEX OF YVOR WINTERS'S CRITICISM (see above) is a comprehensive historical survey, but strangely out of keeping with W's own critical values: Sexton describes his own book as "descriptive and expository rather than evaluative."

RESOURCES FOR FURTHER RESEARCH

Barrett, William. "Temptations of St. Yvor." KENYON REVIEW, 9 (1947), 829-31.

Blackmur, Richard P. "A Note on Yvor Winters." In his THE EXPENSE OF GREATNESS. New York: Arrow Editions, 1940.

Daniel, Robert. "The Discontent of Our Winters." SEWANEE REVIEW, 51 (1943), 502.

Foster, Richard. THE NEW ROMANTICS. Bloomington: University of Indiana Press, 1962.

Graff, Gerald. "Yvor Winters of Stanford." AMERICAN SCHOLAR, 44 (1975), 291-98.

Holloway, John. "The Critical Theory of Yvor Winters." CRITICAL QUAR-TERLY, 7 (1965), 54-68.

Kimbrough, Robert. "Discipline of Saving Grace: Winters's Critical Position." RENASCENCE, 15 (1963), 62-67.

Levin, Harry. CONTEXTS OF CRITICISM. Cambridge: Harvard University Press, 1958.

Mizener, Arthur. "Three Critics." SEWANEE REVIEW, 3 (1944), 597-604.

Schwartz, Delmore. "Primitivism and Decadence." SOUTHERN REVIEW, 3 (1938), 597-614.

      The "correspondence" between W and Schwartz following the ap-pearance of this article is in SOUTHERN REVIEW, 3 (1938), 829-31.

_____. "A Literary Provincial." PARTISAN REVIEW, 12 (1946), 138-42.

INDEXES

AUTHOR INDEX

This index includes all authors, editors, compilers, translators, and other contributors to secondary works cited in the text. References are to page numbers and alphabetization is letter by letter.

Author Index

Bohn, William E. 29
Booth, Wayne C. 121, 169
Borland, Hal 89, 103
Botsford, Keith 196
Bowden, Edwin T. 29
Boyd, Ernest 68
Boydston, JoAnn 74
Boyer, Robert 191
Bracker, Jon 41
Bradbrook, M.C. 173
Bradford, Robert W. 34
Bradlee, Frederick 16
Brennan, Bernard P. 57
Brinnin, John Malcolm 57
Brodbeck, Max 12
Brooks, Cleanth 15, 77, 117, 126, 134, 140, 159, 167, 187
Brooks, Van Wyck 68, 115
Broughton, George 94
Brown, Clarence Arthur 129, 139
Brown, E.K. 196
Brown, Merle E. 169
Brown, Tatnall, Jr. 41
Brown, William R. 57
Brownell, William Cracy 124
Bruccoli, Matthew 48
Boyer, Robert 191
Boynten, Percy 134
Bryer, Jackson R. 172
Burke, James Henry 13
Burke, Kenneth 169

C

Cairns, Huntington 66
Calverton, Victor Francis (George Goetz) 115, 135
Campbell, Joseph 120
Cargill, Oscar 12, 24
Carson, Rachel 89
Cater, H.E. 52
Chace, William 192
Chalker, John 174
Chapman, John Jay 57
Chase, Richard 94
Cheney, Frances 172
Cheslock, Louis 66
Chesterton, G.K. 117
Chesnick, Eugene 94

Chielens, Edward E. 16, 129, 136
Childs, K.W. 58
Childs, Marquis 62
Churchill, Allen 29
Clark, John Abbott 25
Coates, Robert M. 30
Cohen, Hennig 95
Colby, Frank M. 30
Colum, M.M. 165
Commager, Henry Steele 12
Conder, J.J. 53
Conrad, David R. 76
Cook, Martha 185
Cooke, Alistair 66, 67
Core, George 187
Coughlin, Phyllis F. 161
Cousins, Norman 17
Cowan, Louise 134, 183
Cowley, Malcolm 30, 125, 126, 127
Coyle, Lee 25
Crane, Ronald S. 146, 160
Crawford, Bartholow V. 51
Crews, Frederick 15
Crocker, Leslie G. 153
Culler, Jonathan 128
Cunningham, Adrian 174
Cuppy, Will 39
Curley, Dorothy Nyren 9
Curti, Merle 16

D

Daiches, David 192
Dakin, Arthur Hazard 177, 178
Dam, Hari 62
Daniel, Robert 201
Davies, Robert M. 177
Davis, Robert Gorham 126
Day, Donald 48
Day, Douglas 127
Day, Martin S. 12
Dell, Floyd 115, 126
Devlin, John C. 108
DeVries, Peter 30
Dickinson, T.H. 25
Dike, Donald A. 156, 195
Dobie, J. Frank 89
Dolmetsch, Carl 68

Author Index

Guth, Dorothy Lobrans 34

H

Hackett, Alice Payne 13
Hackett, Francis 31
Hagemann, E.R. 17
Hahn, Emily 84
Hamilton, William 192
Hamlin, William J. 169
Handy, William J. 126, 146
Harbert, Earl N. 53
Hardy, John Edward 161
Harlan, Louis R. 79
Hart, James D. 9, 13
Hartman, Geoffrey H. 123
Hawes, Elizabeth 28
Haycraft, H. 9
Headings, Philip R. 175
Heid, William 28
Heilman, Robert B. 126
Hemphill, George 186
Hendrick, George 11
Herzberg, Max J. 9
Hevens, W.W. 28
Hicks, Granville 103, 125, 136, 146, 196
Hinshaw, David 80
Hirsch, E.D. 123
Hirsh, David H. 192
Hobson, Fred C., Jr. 68
Hochfield, George 53
Hocks, Richard A. 58
Hoffman, Daniel 136
Hoffman, Frederick J. 58, 119, 135-36
Hohenberg, John 17
Holder, Alan 94
Holloway, John 201
Holmes, Charles S. 31
Honeycutt, Ann 28
Hook, Sidney 74
Hoopes, James 164
Horgan, Paul 89
Horton, Rod W. 12
Hough, Graham 182
Howard, Richard 187
Howe, Irving 147
Howe, T. Irving 192
Howells, William Dean 25

Hoyt, Edwin 43
Hull, Byron D. 58
Huneker, Josephine 124
Hyman, Stanley Edgar 131, 140, 156, 165, 168
Hynes, Samuel 95

I

Ibsen, Hendrick 66
Immler, Frances 185

J

Jacobs, Robert D. 161
James, Henry 56, 156, 195
Janssens, G.A.M. 136
Jarvis, F.P. 183
Johnson, Allen 9
Johnson, Carl E. 108
Johnson, Ellwood 58
Jones, Ernest 63, 119
Jones, Howard Mumford 13, 124, 165, 190
Jones, Roy E. 34
Jung, C.G. 120

K

Kaplan, Abraham 76
Karlinsky, Simon 194
Kazin, Alfred 69, 123, 124, 137, 156, 196
Keefer, Truman Frederick 80
Kelly, Fred C. 24, 39
Kemler, Edgar 67
Kempton, Murray 195
Kenner, Hugh 175
Kermode, Frank 197
Ketchum, Richard M. 48
Kimbrough, Robert 201
Kinney, Arthur F. 42
Kinney, James R. 28
Kinsman, Clare D. 159
Kirkwood, M.M. 77
Knight, Grant C. 137
Knox, George 169
Kohler, Dayton 165
Korge, James 185
Kramer, Dale 31

Author Index

Nolte, William 66, 69
Nordell, Roderick 35
Nordstrom, Ursula 35
Nugent, Elliot 28

O

O'Connor, William Van 131-32, 191
Ohlin, Peter H. 95
Olson, Elder 127
O'Neill, William L. 40, 147
Ong, Walter J., S.J. 161
Oppenheimer, George 42
Osborne, Scott 102
Oulahan, Richard 96

P

Pannick, Gerald J. 155
Parrington, Vernon Louis 137
Parsons, Thornton H. 153, 179
Partington, Paul 75
Pattee, Fred Lewis 26
Paul, Sherman 195
Pearce, T.S. 175
Pendleton, James D. 59
Perry, J. Douglas, Jr. 96
Perry, Ralph Barton 56
Peters, Mildred Brooks 181
Peterson, Theodore 17
Peyre, Henri 132
Phillips, Robert, Jr. 102
Phillips, William 116, 125
Phillipson, John S. 96
Pilkington, John 43
Podhoretz, Norman 14, 192, 197
Porter, John 174
Prescott, Frederick C. 118
Pritchard, John Paul 132, 153, 182
Pritchard, William H. 157
Pynchon, Thomas 51

R

Rahv, Philip 116
Raleigh, John H. 192
Rama, V.V.B. 107
Rampersad, Arnold 75
Ramsay, Richard David 194
Ramsey, Roger 96
Ransom, John Crowe 116, 117,
  127, 140, 156, 200

Ratner, Joseph 74
Reston, James 62
Rich, Everett 80
Riesman, David 78
Riggenbach, Jeff 69
Robinson, James Harvey 6
Roboek, A.A. 118
Rosenfeld, Paul 165
Rosenstone, Robert 103
Ross, Ralph 70
Roth, Robert J. 74
Royce, Josiah 59
Rubin, Louis D., Jr. 69, 126, 161,
  183
Rueckert, William H. 167, 168
Ruland, Richard 69, 134
Ruoff, Gene W. 96
Rupp, Richard H. 96
Russo, Dorothy Ritter 24

S

Sachs, Hans 118, 119
Salzman, Jack 140
Sampson, Edward 35
Samuels, Ernest 52
Samuels, Margaret 29
Sanders, Marion 109
San Juan, E. 59
Santayana, George 59, 114, 134
Sayre, Joel 29
Schapsmeier, Edward 63
Schapsmeier, Frederick 63
Schilpp, Paul 74
Schlamm, William S. 31
Schmalhausen, S.D. 116
Schneider, Isidor 146
Scholes, Robert 128
Schoon, Margaret 84
Schorer, Mark 15-16
Schott, Webster 35
Schwartz, Delmore 156, 195, 201
Scott, Nathan A., Jr. 191
Seib, Kenneth 96
Sexton, Richard J. 199, 201
Shafer, Robert 125, 178
Sheean, Vincent 109
Sheehy, Eugene B. 199
Shepard, Odell 152
Sherman, Stuart Pratt 125, 179
Simon, Myron 153, 179

Author Index

TITLE INDEX

This index includes all primary and secondary titles of books, reports, and proceedings cited in the text. In some cases titles have been shortened. References are to page numbers and alphabetization is letter by letter.

Title Index

Title Index

M

Title Index

Title Index

Title Index

SUBJECT INDEX

This index is alphabetized letter by letter and references are to page numbers. Major areas of emphasis have been underlined.

Subject Index

Barzun, Jacques 191
Beardsley, Monroe C. 145
Beebe, William 90, 101
Behaviorism, Richards' literary criticism
   and 118
Belloc, Hilaire 117
Bellow, Saed, compared to James
   (W.) 58
Benchley, Robert 29, 39
Bergson, Henri, theory of rigidity
   by 30
Berthoff, Werner, on Wilson 195
Beston, Henry 107
Bibliographies. See Literary bibliog-
   raphies
Biography
   Gamaliel's "psychograph" technique
     in writing 84
   Stone's development of the bio-
     graphical novel 85
   See also Literary biographies
Bishop, Ferman 186
Blackmur, B.R.P. 116, 125, 130,
   131, 142, 155-57
   on Tate 187
   Trilling compared to 191
Blacks
   DuBois on 75
   Washington on 78-79
Bliven, Bruce 107
Bodkin, Maud, myth criticism of 120
Bok, Curtis 83
Book-of-the-Month Club
   Gunther and 102
   Morley and 41
Book reviews, collections of and
   guides to 10, 11
Bowen, Catherine Drinker 84-84
Boyer, Robert, on Trilling 191
Bradbrook, M.C., on Eliot 172
Bradford, Gamaliel 84
Brooks, Cleanth 130, 142, 159-61,
   167
   compared to Blackmur 156
   on Eliot 174
   influence of Kant on 127
   influence on Tate 185
   on Ransom 161, 181
   the SOUTHERN REVIEW and 117

Sutton on 127
Tate compared to 186, 187
Brooks, Van Wyck 115, 116, 118,
   119, 131, 132, 142,
   163-66
   DeVoto's criticism of 73
   Dupee on 143
   Sullivan's parody of 42
Broun, Heywood 107
Brown, Merle E., on Burke 169
Brownell, William Crary 124-25,
   132, 139, 142
Bryant, William Cullen 141
Burgess, Gelett 47
Burgum, Edwin Berry, on Ransom 183
Burke, Kenneth 115, 118, 119,
   120-21, 125, 130, 131,
   141, 142-43, 167-69
   Blackmur compared to 156, 157
   More compared to 181

C

Calverton, V.F., as editor of the
   MODERN QUARTERLY 115
Calvinism, influence on Muir 102
Campbell, Joseph, myth criticism of
   120, 128
Canby, Henry Seidel, on Rourke 85
Capitalism
   attack on by the radical critics
     116
   Veblen on 78
   Wylie on 80
Carmer, Carl 84
Cather, Willa, Mencken's support of
   65
Chalker, John, on Eliot 174
Characters and characterization
   of Ade 25
   of Bowen 84
   in Brooks's (C.) criticism 159
   handbooks on 9
   of James (H.) 55, 59
   in Trilling's criticism 191
Chase, Richard 130, 143
Chesterton, G.K. 117
Chicago, University of, the Neo-
   Aristotelians at 117-18,
   132

Subject Index

Dialects, Dunne's use of 40
Dialogue, Agee's sense of 93. See
     also Language and linguistics
Diction 14
    Thurber's use of 27
Didion, Joan, influence of Agee on
    94
Dike, Donald A., on Wilson 195-96
Dobree, Bonamy, on Eliot 174
Documentaries
    by Agee 96
    by Stewart 103
Dostoyevsky, Feodor
    Blackmur on 155
    Rahv on 116
Drama, of Ade* 25. See also
    Theater critics
Dreams, literary implications of
    Freud's theory on 118, 119
Dreiser, Theodore
    Lewisohn on 118, 137
    Mencken's support of 65
    naturalism of 125
    radical literary criticism and 115
Dryden, John, Eliot on 172
DuBois, William Edward Burchardt 75
Dunne, Finley Peter 40
Dupee, F.W., on Brooks (V.W.)
    143, 164-65
Durant, Will 84

E

Eastman, Max 40, 126
    influence on Reed 103
    the MASSES and 115
    the MODERN QUARTERLY and
    116
Economics
    of Veblen 77
    of Washington 79
Education
    Adler on 83
    Dewey on 74
    Washington on 79
Ego psychology, literature and 118-
    19, 127-28
Eiseley, Loren 89
Eliot, T.S. 114, 121, 125, 130,
    131, 132, 137, 143, 144,
    153, 171-75

on Babbitt 152
    influence on Blackmur 157
      on Tate 185
      on the New Critics 116
    Mencken's criticism of 65
    More on 178
    the PARTISAN REVIEW and 116
    Ransom compared to 181, 182
    Schwartz on 144
    Tate compared to 186, 187
    Vivas on 145
    Wilson on 193
Ellton, William, as a New Critic
    117
Emerson, Ralph Waldo 135, 137,
    141
    Blackmur compared to 157
    Eliot compared to 174
    influence on Babbitt 152
      on Muir 102
      on Mumford 76
    James (W.) compared to 57
    Trilling compared to 189
    Wilson compared to 195
Environment, influence on aesthetic
    judgments 135
Epigrams, by Burgess 47
Epithets, Ade's use of 25
ESQUIRE, literary quality of 17
Ethics. See Morality; Work ethic
Existentialism, American introduc-
    tion to French 116
Expressionism. See Literary criticism,
    schools of

F

Fables
    by Ade 23, 24, 25
    by Thurber 27, 32
Fadiman, Clifton, on Morley 41
Fantasy, elements of in Thurber's
    fiction 31
Farrell, James T. 143
Fascism, the AMERICAN REVIEW
    and 117
Federal Writers' Project. American
    Guide Series 13
Ferber, Edna 39
Ferguson, Francis 143
    on Tate 187

Subject Index

Happiness, Marquis on 41
Hardy, Thomas, Schwartz on 144
HARPER'S
  De Voto and 73
  history of 16
Hartmann, Geoffrey, on Frye 128
Hawthorne, Nathaniel 137
  allegory in the work of 146
Heid, William 28
Heilman, Robert B., on Brooks (C.)
    160
Hemingway, Ernest
  Adams (H.) compared to 54
  style of 144
Hemphill, George 186
Heroes
  Adams' (H.) treatment of his-
      torical 54
  DeVoto's use of 74
Hevens, W.E. 28
Hicks, Granville 125, 143
Historians
  Adams (H.) as 53, 54
  Adams (J.T.) as 83
  Allen as 83
  Bowen as 84
  McWilliams as 108
  Robinson as 85
History, literary criticism and 141,
    145
  in Brooks's (C.) work 160, 161
  in Ransom's work 183
  See also Literary histories
Hoffman, Frederick J., Freudian
      interpretation of literature by
      119
Holbrook, Stewart 84
Holmes, Oliver Wendell, Jr., on
      Day, Jr. 40
Hook, Sidney, on Burke 168
Hoopes, James, on Brooks (V.W.)
Horgan, Paul 89
Hough, Graham, on Ransom 182
HOUND AND HORN (periodical)
  Blackmur and 155
  history of 136
Howard, Richard, on Tate 187
Howe, Helen, Trilling on 191
Howe, Irving 130
Howe, Mark Anthony de Wolfe 84

Howells, William Dean 132, 141
  sexual self-consciousness of 118,
      137
Hulme, T.E., compared to Tate
      186
Humanism
  of Lippmann 61
  of Trilling 191
  See also Literary criticism,
      schools of
Huneker, James Gibbons 113,
      114, 124, 139, 143
Hyman, Stanley Edgar 143
  on Blackmur 156
  on Brooks (V.W.) 165
  on Burke 168-69
  on Eliot 172
  on Wilson 194-95
  on Winters 200

I

Idealism
  of James (W.) 55, 57
  of Mumford 76
Idiom, Ade's use of 25
Imagery, in Brooks's (C.) criticism
      159
Imagination 160
  of Blackmur 191
  value of according to Santayana
      77
Impressionism. See Literary criticism,
      schools of
Individualism
  of Agee 94
  of Dell 126
  of the nineteenth-century
      Romantics 125
  of White (E.B.) 79
Industrialism. See Capitalism
Innocence, in Agee's fiction 96
Irony
  in Brooks's (C.) criticism 142,
      159, 160, 161, 167
  Cuppy's use of 47
  Veblen's use of 78
  White's (E.B.) use of 34

J

James, Henry 57, 58, 141, 171
  Blackmur on 155
  Brooks (V.W.) on 163
  characterizations by 55
  influence on Blackmur 157
    on Thurber's criticism 31
    on Trilling 191
  pragmatism of 59
  sexual self-consciousness of 118,
    137
  William on 59
  Wilson on 195
  Winters on 200
James, William 13, 55-59, 74
  influence on Robinson 85
Johns, Foster. See Seldes, Gilbert
    Vivian
Johnson, Samuel, Eliot compared to
    171
Jonson, Ben, Eliot on 172
Journalism, use of literary techniques
    in 14, 94
Journalists
  Agee as 93, 94, 95
  Lippmann as 63
  White (E.B.) as 79
  See also Foreign correspondents
Journalists, humorous
  Adams (F.P.) as 39
  Marquis as 40
  Rogers as 48
Journals. See Literary periodicals
Joyce, James
  Freud's influence on 119
  Mencken's criticism of 65
  Perelman compared to 47
  Thurber compared to 30
  Wilson on 125, 193
Jung, C.G. (Jungianism), in
    literary criticism 120, 128
Juvenile literature. See Children's
    literature

K

Kafka, Franz
  Freud's influence on 119
  Vivas on 145

Kant, Immanuel, influence on the
    New Critics 127
Kaufman, George 39
Kazin, Alfred 130, 144
  on Blackmur 156
  on Trilling 189
Keats, John
  influence on Trilling 189, 191
  symbolism of 143
KENYON REVIEW 117, 140
  Ransom and 181
Kieran, John 89
Kriegel, Leonard, on Wilson 195
Krieger, Murray 130
  on Brooks (C.) 160
  on Frye 128
  on the New Critics 117
Kris, Ernst, on literature and psy-
    chology 119
Krutch, Joseph Wood 118, 119,
    127, 144

L

Labor and laboring classes, Wylie's
    attack on 80
LADIES HOME JOURNAL, Bok and
    83
Language and linguistics 146
  Ade's use of 25
  Agee's use of 93
  Blackmur's use of 155, 156
  in Burke's criticism 167, 169
  Eliot's poetry and 173
  as gesture 142
  James' (W.) use of 57
  Mencken's use of 65
  the New Critics' concern with
    116, 118, 141, 155
  in the "new journalism" 94
  as paradox 142
  in structuralist criticism 121
  Sullivan's use of 42
  Thurber on 27
  Thurber's use of 30
  in Trilling's criticism 191
  White's use of 33
  See also Dialect; Dialogue; Style,
    literary
Lardner, Ring 39
  Mencken's support of 65

M

R

Subject Index

Radicalism (con't)
  of Wilson 195
  See also Literary criticism, schools
    of
Radio drama, Ade's stories adapted to
    23
Rahv, Philip 130, 144
  profile of and tribute to 126
  the PARTISAN REVIEW and 116
Raleigh, Walter, on Ade 23
Ransom, John Crowe 116, 117,
    130, 144, 181-84
  Blackmur compared to 156
  on Blackmur 156
  on Burke 168
  on Eliot 172, 174
  influence of Kant on 127
    of Richards on 187
  influence on Tate 185
  KENYON REVIEW and 117
  Tate compared to 186, 187
  on Winters 200
  Young on 161
Read, Herbert, on Tate 187
Realism in literature
  bibliography on 10
  James (W.) and 58
Reed, John 103
  Luhan and 84
Religion
  in James' (W.) philosophy 57
  More and 177, 179
  in myth criticism 120
  need for the New Humanism to be
    based upon 125
  and poetry 174
  relevancy of for Lippmann 63
  Wylie's attack on 80
  See also Calvinism; Puritanism
REVIEW OF REVIEWS, THE 16
Rhetoric. See Language and
    linguistics; Style, literary
Rice, Grantland 108
Richards, I.A. 137
  as a behaviorist 118
  on Eliot 174
  influence on the New Criticism
    116
  on Tate and Ransom 187
Robinson, Edwin Arlington,
    compared to James (W.) 59

Robinson, James Harvey 85
Rogers, Will 47-48
Romanticism 125
  Babbitt's opposition to Rousseau's
    152
  of Dell 126
  More and Germanic 179
  of the New Criticism 127, 134
  of Ransom 181
  rejection of by the New Human-
    ists 114
  Trilling and 191
Roosevelt, Franklin D.
  Steffens and 77
  White (W.A.) and 79
  See also Depression (1929); New
    Deal
Ross, Harold, as editor of the NEW
    YORKER 29, 30
Rourke, Constance 85
Rousseau, Jean Jacques
  Babbitt's opposition to 151, 152
  New Humanistic opposition to
    114

S

Sachs, Hans, on literature and psy-
    chology 118-19
Santayana, George 13, 76-77, 141,
    171
  attack on the New Humanists
    114
Satire
  by Ade 26
  by Mencken 68, 70
  by Parker 42
  by Thurber 27, 31, 32
  by Veblen 78
  by Wylie 80
SATURDAY REVIEW OF LITERATURE
  history of 16
  Morley and 41
Schmalhausen, S.D., as editor of
    the MODERN QUARTERLY
    116
Schorer, Mark 146
Schwartz, Delmore 144
  on Blackmur 156
  correspondence with Winters 201
  on Wilson 195, 196